MAKING LOCAL NEWS

MAKING LOCAL NEWS

Phyllis Kaniss

THE UNIVERSITY OF CHICAGO PRESS
Chicago and London

The University of Chicago Press, Chicago 60637
The University of Chicago Press, Ltd., London
© 1991 by The University of Chicago
All rights reserved. Published 1991
Paperback edition 1997
Printed in the United States of America
00 99 98 97   5 4 3 2
ISBN: 0–226–42347–6 (cloth)
ISBN: 0–226–42348–4 (paperback)

Library of Congress Cataloging-in-Publication Data

Kaniss, Phyllis C.
    Making local news / Phyllis C. Kaniss.
        p. cm.
    Includes bibliographical references and index.
    ISBN 0–226–42347–6 (alk. paper)
    1. Journalism—Social aspects—United States.   2. Local mass media—
United States.   3. Journalism—Political aspects—United States.   4. Local
government and the press—United States.   5. City planning and the press. I.
Title.
PN4749.K35 1991
302.23′0973—dc20   90–21587
                                                                          CIP

To Paul Wheeling

Contents

Acknowledgments   ix

Introduction   1

Chapter 1   The Historical Development of the Local News Media   13

Chapter 2   Commercial Pressures on Local News   46

Chapter 3   Professional Values of the Local Journalist   71

Chapter 4   Local Television News   101

Chapter 5   Alternative Voices in the Local Media   133

Chapter 6   Local Government Officials as News Sources   160

Chapter 7   Philadelphia's New Convention Center: A Case Study   188

Conclusions and a Look to the Future   220

Notes   235

Index   254

Acknowledgments

When I began the research for this book seven years ago, I knew relatively little about how the local news media worked. Trained in urban and regional analysis but always fascinated with the world of journalism, I became interested in looking at how journalists covered and influenced urban policy. In the years that followed, many people gave generously of their time to help me understand the relation of the local media to the affairs of cities and regions.

I am grateful first to the many journalists who took time from their busy schedules to speak thoughtfully and frankly about their profession. In particular, I would like to thank Gene Roberts and Gene Foreman of the *Philadelphia Inquirer* and Gil Spencer and Zachary Stalberg of the *Philadelphia Daily News*, for their interviews, as well as for allowing their editors and reporters to take time from work to speak to me and my students. I would also like to thank the editors of the *Seattle Times*, the *Detroit News*, the *Detroit Free Press*, and the *Houston Chronicle* for similarly welcoming my interviews of their reporters and editors. In addition, Randy Covington and Steve Eisman of KYW-TV graciously provided access to their logbooks and tapes for the research on local television coverage of the Philadelphia convention center.

While many journalists, local officials, and others contributed to my research, I would particularly like to thank Donald Drake, Tia O'Brien, Michael Scholnick, and Robert Douglas for the ongoing conversations which helped shape my understanding of the media and the city. Over the years, I also had the good fortune to have a legion of students who mined newspaper databases, taped local newscasts, and carried back to Philadelphia newspapers from all over the country, some of which I drew on for my research. In particular, I would like to acknowledge the excellent research provided by Kim Verbonitz for chapter 3's "Luring the Teams" case, Veronica Bradshaw on black radio stations for chapter 5, Diana Sabloff and Jennifer Cowan on television coverage of the convention center in chapter 7, and Kirk Marcolina on Videotex and Audiotex for the concluding chapter. Carol Longmore, Susan Orman, Michael Simon, Sara Pugach, Stacy Miller, Clayton Rose, Lisa Lazarus, Morgan Neville, Lourdes Segovia, Julia Pirkey, and Adrian Kendall also contributed research.

George Gerbner provided a supportive home for my research and teaching at the Annenberg School, during the time when I developed many of the ideas for the book. I am particularly grateful to Marsha Siefert for her encouragement and vision at a time when progress on the book had slowed. John Tryneski offered skillful advice that was very valuable to me in the revision of the manuscript, and I was fortunate to have Kathryn Kraynik's fine editing.

I would also like to thank John Massi for his tireless assistance in collecting tapes of local television news and the staff of the Annenberg School library for their continual help in finding information. Greg Slayden provided expertise and hours of work to generate the computer maps of newspaper markets in chapter 1, and Gene Gilroy contributed her skills as a graphic artist. The maps are based on data from American Newspaper Markets' *Circulation,* 1962 and 1988/89. I am also grateful to Lorraine Webber for her patience and diligence in the preparation of the manuscript.

Finally, I would like to thank my husband, Paul Wheeling, for his contributions to this book. A source of continual support and encouragement, he was always eager to listen to and challenge my ideas. He also provided invaluable assistance in the design and management of my databases, particularly for the content analysis of local television news in chapter 4. Perhaps most heroic, though, was his forbearance with much ranting about the news at times when he would have preferred to be left in peace to watch sports highlights. It is to him, with love and gratitude, that this book is dedicated.

Introduction

March 30, 1984, Philadelphia. A small article on the front page of the *Philadelphia Inquirer* announces that developer Willard Rouse has requested permission from the City Planning Commission to build two office towers, in the range of fifty-five stories high, in the heart of the city's downtown business district. The request was of interest, the article noted, because the towers would violate Philadelphia's long-standing "Gentleman's Agreement," which maintained that no building exceed the height of the statue of William Penn standing 548 feet from the ground atop City Hall.

In the weeks that followed this announcement, Philadelphia's newspapers were flooded with much longer articles—soon joined by columns, editorials, letters to the editor, and even cartoons—focusing on the question of whether tradition should give way for economic development. The local television stations sent cameramen into helicopters to photograph aerial views of William Penn's statue, while radio talk shows invited the developer and his chief foe, former City Planning Director Edmund Bacon, to debate the issue with a call-in audience. At the very height of the controversy, the city's tabloid *Daily News*, the self-proclaimed "People Paper," conducted its own "People's Poll" on the question, heralding the results on its front page the following day.

The city's political leaders and administrative officials were not to be left out. The Planning Commission staff prepared a lengthy study estimating the employment and tax revenues that would be generated by the office towers. Mayor Wilson Goode scheduled an unprecedented all-day televised public hearing on the subject. City council members called press conferences, some to oppose, others to support the towers, while community leaders proposed diverting tax revenues from the towers to neighborhood development projects. In the end, the controversy was settled with a compromise: a limited "skyscraper zone" was created within which buildings could exceed the 491-foot height limit, but in the rest of the city, the tradition would hold. And with this announcement, the flood of news stories trickled to an end.

Philadelphia's height limitation controversy is only one of many local policy issues across the country that have come to dominate metropolitan news coverage. In Philadelphia, it is the height of new skyscrapers or the proposal to build a new downtown convention center, in Houston, it is a referendum for a new rail system, in Miami, a plan for a new sports stadium, in Denver, a proposal to build a new airport. In each of these cases, the local news media have elevated a single issue to prominent regional concern and have played a key role in determining how that issue is cast before the local populace. In some of the cases, local news coverage has endowed a proposal with the credibility necessary to garner crucial public support, while in others, persistent controversy and criticism have halted new plans in their tracks.

This book looks at how such major local issues come to be recognized and covered by the metropolitan media. Why do certain policy questions come to receive intense coverage in the local media, while others are given only passing consideration or ignored? When a new plan or proposal is announced by local officials, what factors determine whether it will be covered with cheerleading fanfare or subjected to investigative scrutiny? In general, how do the economic interests of media owners, the professional values of local journalists, and the media strategies of local officials come together to influence what becomes local news?

Although long overshadowed by the national media, local news has always played an important role in the way a city and region understands its problems, its opportunities, and its sense of local identity. The primary concerns of local news are often quite different from those which dominate national news and tend to reflect issues that are closer to people's lives. The factors which influence the coverage of local issues are also quite distinct, resulting from the unique ties that bind the local media to their communities. Metropolitan newspapers, local television and radio stations, and the other local media are all intertwined with the economic, social, political, and even geographical conditions of their local areas in ways that have important implications for the news they cover.

First, the metropolitan media are local businesses that are linked to the fortunes of their local economies; they are dependent on other local businesses to provide advertising revenues and to generate the kind of economic growth that increases audience size. Metropolitan newspapers, in particular, have intimately felt the cycles of urban decline and growth. When the oil boom hit Houston in the 1960s, the city's newspapers and other media flourished with a major expansion in audiences and advertising revenues, but when the market collapsed two decades later, the local media felt the repercussions just as sharply.

2

Introduction

It is not simply regional growth or decline that affects the economic health of the local news firm, but also the demographic and political structure of metropolitan areas. Since cities began their first major expansion over space in the nineteenth century, the geographical pattern of residences, workplaces, and retail areas and the transportation networks that relate them have helped determine who advertises in and reads local newspapers. In addition, the political geography of the region has been crucial in influencing local news preferences. When most people lived and worked and voted in the same local political jurisdiction, big-city newspapers thrived, but the proliferation of many smaller, fragmented suburban governments has spurred interest in more localized news media.

It was the major transformation in urban form that occurred with postwar suburbanization that dealt a major blow to many metropolitan newspapers from which only now are some recovering. The decentralization of retail districts, the declining use of mass transit, the increasingly localized news interests of suburban residents, who have become the major targets of retail advertisers, have all contributed to the declining economic fortunes of many metropolitan newspapers. Even more important, however, has been the effect of the suburbanization and the decentralization of residential, economic, and political activity, on the splintering of local identity in metropolitan regions.

From the nineteenth century on, the economic fortunes of local newspapers in America have been dependent on their ability to link their audiences in a common bond of local identity. When the new department stores sought access to a mass audience, newspapers had to work to create a sense of citywide local identity that could overcome the wide differences in class, culture, and ethnicity among their readers. Urban boosterism as much as muckraking crusades served to create a new sense of attachment to the city and its institutions and thereby unified local news interests. In the late twentieth century, however, with fewer and fewer people living or working in central cities, voting in city elections, or sending their children to city schools, the attachment to the city has been powerfully weakened, and with it has come a loss of the sense of regionwide local identity.

Metropolitan newspapers have cast about in a number of directions for strategies to counteract or transcend the problem of splintered local identity: from "zoning" editorial content to expanding national news and consumer-oriented lifestyle features. But in their bread-and-butter coverage of the local environment they have continued to grapple with the geographical dilemma: how to define "local news" in an environment in which the majority of the audience is very interested in the events of their own townships or boroughs and fairly uninterested in events in neighboring areas. In their attempts to answer this question and to overcome the political fragmentation of the suburbanized metropolis, the metropolitan news media have been forced to define local news in a very particular way.

Although hardly recognized in the day-to-day rush of reporting, the major focus of local news coverage in media markets throughout the country has come to be placed on issues with the symbolic capital necessary to unite the fragmented suburban audience. In other words, in order to sell their product—a set of messages the hallmark of which is their uniquely local character—the metropolitan news media have had to produce local identity as much as they produce news and entertainment. In particular, they have been faced with the need to select and present local news so as to create the kind of local identity that captures the allegiance of an increasingly suburbanized audience.

From this perspective, the explosive news coverage of controversies like Philadelphia's height limitation debate is not surprising. Such issues are important because they carry the symbolic value capable of providing a common bond among the suburban audience. With every aerial view of William Penn's hat, with every headline chronicling the status of the "Gentleman's Agreement," the local media were reinforcing a sense of a common local identity among their readers. Importantly, it was a local identity that continued to be tied to the symbols and institutions of the city of Philadelphia. Even as metropolitan areas have become increasingly suburbanized and interactions between suburbs and city have weakened, the metropolitan news media have continued to stress the notion, if not the myth, that the city continues to control the fate of the entire region.

The need to focus on issues capable of binding together the suburban audience has not, however, led to an exclusive concentration on issues like height limitation, which are largely symbolic and aesthetic by definition. Rather, it extends to a focus on many more substantive central-city development projects which, although involving millions of dollars of public funds, often have limited repercussions beyond the borders of the downtown and the city itself. The extensive coverage of a downtown "People Mover" in Detroit, for example, where only a small fraction of the metropolitan population work downtown, much less use public transit, can only be understood if the project and the city itself are regarded as symbols of regional identity.

Introduction

The attraction of local news that reinforces symbolic links among the suburban audience influences not simply the selection of major issues but their presentation as well. Local news coverage often comes to accord elevated importance to the symbolic aspects of development issues, while de-emphasizing their economic, social, or environmental costs and benefits. The impact of a new project on the image of the city or on the city's ability to compete with other cities in a rivalry not unlike the clash between sports teams often takes precedence in news coverage over considerations of dollars and cents. When Denver residents were faced with the question of whether or not to build a new airport, for example, headlines heralded the importance of the new development in erasing the image of the city as a "cowtown" while devoting less prominent attention to the question of how bonds would be financed.

This search for symbolic issues and the casting of many substantive proposals in symbolic terms is also influenced by the personal and professional values of local journalists. A focus on the symbolic aspects of new proposals often masks the lack of technical expertise necessary to scrutinize estimates of economic costs and benefits so crucial to an informed evaluation of development projects. As one reporter noted tellingly, journalists choose their profession because of the strength of their verbal skills—writing and interviewing—not because of any quantitative expertise. Some journalists even admit to a "fear of numbers" in their profession that hampers coverage of major development projects and other local policies. In addition, a personal and professional bias toward city rather than suburban or regional news coverage—a "city myopia"— often leads the local journalist to distort the importance of downtown development projects to the metropolitan area as a whole.

The desire to gain prominent play for stories may also lead to a built-in bias in the consideration of many proposals for new development projects. In order to make their stories more appealing to audiences and therefore editors, reporters are more likely to emphasize the need for a glamorous new project than to focus on the reasons why the status quo is preferable. Similarly, emphasis on the symbolic aspects of a project—its impact on the image of the city or on the city's ability to compete in a "horse race" with other cities—carries more audience appeal than a focus on quantitative costs and benefits. Fragmented beat structures, lack of release time, and weak institutional memory also play a role in hampering the effective coverage of local development issues.

The creation of local issues and the public's understanding of those issues is also fundamentally affected by the news decisions of local television stations.

The importance of local television news grows with each passing year as new satellite technology has made local newscasts more competitive with national media for covering not simply local but national and international events for the local audience. Local television news is taking on an increasing importance in informing citizens about their worlds and is coming to play a major role in the outcome of many local issues. But the factors which determine the content of the local newscast are quite different from those which influence either local newspapers or network television news. The frequency of broadcasts—many local stations produce news at noon, five, six and ten or eleven—often puts a premium on the "latest" news rather than the most important. Coverage of a fire may displace news of a change in city policy if the blaze occurred at 8:00 P.M. and the Mayor's press conference was in the morning.

Moreover, the importance placed on video leads local broadcast journalists to give short shrift to many important but picture-less policy issues. Local issues like Philadelphia's height limitation debate are covered extensively because they offer attractive video prospects such as aerial shots of the statue of William Penn atop City Hall. However, other "video-poor" issues, such as the expenditure of one-half billion dollars for a new convention center, often receive limited consideration. The need for effective "sound bites" also affects the way policy is covered by local television: chanting marchers guarantee that protests and demonstrations, no matter how small, are given more prominent coverage than calm meetings, and emotion-filled pleas receive more play than dispassionate arguments.

The angle taken on local policy issues, whether by local television newscasts or metropolitan newspapers, is also strongly influenced by the actions of the local officials at their center. As with the national media, elected and administrative officials serve as key sources of information for the media and therefore affect the news coverage of policy issues. But in contrast to officials at the White House, State Department, or Congress, local leaders often have meager skills in dealing with the local media. The head of the transit authority or the commissioner of police are appointed to their positions because of their technical or managerial expertise, not necessarily because of their ability to deal with the press effectively.

Often these local officials have little or no understanding of how to gain positive coverage for their policy initiatives and as a result blunder into media strategies that prevent the public from learning the merits of their proposals.

Whether acting as "paranoid media avoiders," "naive professionals," or "dancing marionettes," these officials fail to deal with the media so as to get positive news coverage for what are often sound initiatives. In contrast, other local officials are more savvy in the realm of the twenty-second sound bite and the controlled release of information and understand how to present new initiatives from their most positive standpoint. Therefore, while some officials invite attacks from reporters on their every pronouncement, others are able to forestall any serious inquiry into ambitious and costly public plans.

As a result of these interrelated factors—the economic imperative of metropolitan news firms, the professional and personal values of individual reporters, and the uneven media skills of local officials—certain imbalances come to be incorporated into local news coverage of policy issues. In particular, many questionable proposals get treated with cheerleading boosterism, while some sound proposals and positions are hounded from the public arena. Major development plans involving millions of dollars in public funds often come to be examined more for their symbolic repercussions than for their economic costs and benefits, and far-reaching policy questions concerning alternative uses of public funds may be ignored.

The tendency for the local media to distort policy needs and the costs and benefits of alternative proposals is particularly disturbing in view of the fact that there are far fewer competing news sources at the local than at the national level. In all but the largest metropolitan areas, there is only one major metropolitan newspaper covering local issues of region-wide importance. Local television newscasts, while competitive, typically place greater emphasis on uncovering crimes than on presenting policy information, and when they do cover government, they often take their information almost exclusively from the press conferences that provide them with convenient video and sound bites.

There do exist alternative voices beyond the local mass media. But vehicles like suburban, community, or ethnic newspapers focus on issues of narrow interest to their particular communities, while city magazines and urban newsweeklies have been turning away from consideration of serious social and political issues to focus more on lifestyle than on government. Although they may play a limited role in policy questions and in influencing local elections, these alternative media fail to provide a consistent, competitive analysis of major regional issues. Therefore, while national policy is scrutinized by many commercial and public television programs, weekly news magazines, and the Washington bureaus of countless metropolitan newspapers, there are a relatively limited number of independent local sources to examine the wisdom of local policies and proposals.

There also tend to be more competing sources of policy information at the national than at the local level. Whereas many universities and nonprofit institutes undertake studies of national and international policies which are disseminated to the media, independent evaluations of local policy initiatives are rare. As a result, reporters dependent on sources for the analysis of new development projects are far more limited in scope at the local than at the national level. All of these factors make it particularly important to examine the kind of job the local news media perform in their coverage of local issues.

This study represents the first comprehensive examination of the local news-making process and the influence of local news on urban policy and regional development. In the past, the analysis of the news media in America has traditionally focused on the national media and their influence on presidential elections and domestic and foreign policy. In contrast, relatively little has been written about the local news media and the important role they play in the life of their cities and regions. In part, this neglect stems from the common misperception that local news is inconsequential, consisting of little more than homicides and fires, community squabbles over zoning changes, and features on ethnic folk festivals, all of which may be quickly dismissed.

But to local officials who know the damage that can be done by a negative headline in the morning newspaper or an unflattering pose on the six o'clock newscast, local news coverage is anything but inconsequential. Its messages are as capable of killing a multimillion dollar development project as helping it sail through a lengthy public approval process, as potent in winning a politician votes as in ousting an entire agency's management from their appointed positions. Local news plays a crucial role in the policy decisions of local officials to implement new initiatives or to eliminate and modify existing programs. It helps determine the allocation of what has become in many cases a dwindling state and local budget pie.

Local news can affect private decisions as well. It can send people packing to move out of homes in the city or suburbs and determine whether they send their children to public or private schools or let them play in the nearby park. The information that the local news media provide to their millions of readers, viewers, and listeners colors a multitude of public and private decisions, affecting everything from government decisions and local business investment to the more intangible molding of regional character and local identity.

The problem with trying to understand local news coverage, however, is that it is a far more difficult task than looking at the role of the national news media. Where many studies have conveniently selected a network television news program, or a weekly newsmagazine, or a national newspaper, such as the *Washington Post* or the *New York Times* in order to analyze the media's impact on national elections or policy, the local news media embrace thousands of newspapers, television and radio stations, city magazines, and other forms of localized media in markets throughout the country. As important as they are to the policies of their governments, the local news media have been neglected in part because they are so difficult to embrace and analyze on a general basis.

While this study does not claim to base its findings on all local media throughout the country, it is intended to provide insight into the general nature of the newsmaking process in areas that are geographically dispersed but subnational. The main focus is on the structure of the metropolitan news media, as opposed to rural or small-town journalism, and the chief concern is with news coverage of policy issues. It is based on a seven-year research effort that included analysis of data on local newspaper markets throughout the country as well as an examination of local news coverage of urban and regional development issues in a number of those markets. It is also based on over 100 interviews with journalists and local officials in Philadelphia, as well as in Houston, Detroit, and Seattle. While many of those journalists and officials are identified in the text, others requested anonymity and are referred to simply as "one reporter" or "one official."

The study begins with an examination of the historical development of the local news media in America and the social and political roles they have played in the life of urban areas. Specifically, chapter 1 will focus on the link between the growth and development of cities and the changing economic fortunes of the city newspaper, showing how the definition of local news has shifted over time with the changing demographic characteristics of the population. We will see how postwar suburbanization and the rise of television and suburban newspapers affected metropolitan newspapers and how an "umbrella" structure of competition has evolved between local television and newspapers in both the regionwide and more localized markets.

The economic structure of the local news media and the influence of commercial considerations on local news coverage will be the focus of chapter 2. What role do "sensationalism" and advertiser pressures play in shaping coverage and how valid is the argument that local news is biased by a pro-growth or "boosterism" mentality on the part of local media owners? We will see that other, more subtle commercial factors are often at work in influencing local news coverage. In particular, the need to capture the affluent, yet politically decentralized, suburban audience will be shown to shape the selection and presentation of local issues. In their attempts to create a sense of regionwide identity, the metropolitan media will at times exaggerate the relative importance of certain policy issues and distort the costs and benefits of plans and proposals.

We then turn to a consideration of the personal and professional values of the local journalist, from what makes a good story and warrants investigation to what reporters unconsciously believe is good for the city and region they call home. Chapter 3 focuses on the professional standards that influence local policy coverage, which may hamper the local journalist's ability to offer independent evaluation of new development initiatives. The focus on the downtown, the selling of the city's development, the tendency to accept without question the cost and benefit estimates of governmental sources, and a narrow definition of scandal will be explored.

From the city desk of the metropolitan newspaper, we move to the studios of the local television news operation in chapter 4, turning to look at the world of local broadcast journalism. Here we will see how the need for emotional sound bites and dramatic video, the limitations on time for local news stories, and the premium placed on timeliness, drama, and emotion affects local news coverage. Of particular interest will be the question of how local newscasts allot time to the coverage of government and policy issues in comparison with the more familiar fare of crimes, fires, and accidents. What kind of governmental issues receive the most attention from local television news and what kind of information is conveyed about alternative proposals in the local newscast as compared with the metropolitan newspaper?

The distinctive voices of the alternative local media will come under scrutiny in chapter 5. We will see how city magazines and urban newsweeklies have evolved from social and political commentators in the 1960s to the trendy consumer guides of the affluent lifestyle in the 1990s. On a very different front, the local specialized press, from black, Hispanic, and Jewish newspapers to the local gay press, will also be examined, pointing up the important political and social roles many of these newspapers play in their communities, from promoting group solidarity to evaluating the voting records of elected officials. The growing importance of weekly suburban and community newspapers will also be considered, along with a look at the news and information functions of local radio.

In chapter 6, the focus shifts from those who report the news to those who are covered by the news, examining the media strategies of local actors, ranging from the big-city mayor to the regional transit director and local police commissioner. We will see how both elected and appointed officials are affected by local news coverage and how, in turn, they try to influence the way their offices and policies are covered. Local officials come to adopt—or stumble onto—different strategies or styles through which they deal with the media. While some of these strategies succeed in getting positive coverage, at times even for ineffective officials and inefficient policies, other strategies will be shown to result in minimal or negative play for what may be sound initiatives.

A case study of how one particular development issue came to be covered by the metropolitan media and how news coverage helped shape policy is presented in chapter 7. Examining the case of a proposed Convention Center for Philadelphia, the reader will learn how the economic imperatives of the local media, the professional values of local reporters, and the media strategies of local officials can come together to influence local news coverage of a major new proposal. In particular, the case will point out how local news coverage of government policy is often weakest in those areas where the costs to the public may be in the millions of dollars.

The final chapter summarizes the major findings of how local news gets made and offers a look into the future, attempting to predict the impacts of a continually changing technology on both the local print and broadcast media. The opportunities and challenges offered by emerging technologies such as electronic publishing and cable television will also be examined with an eye on the question of how the traditional local media will respond to their new competitors. As a final consideration, we will look at what the future holds for the setting of a shared sense of local identity and whether we can expect to see a tightening or loosening of the ties which link city dweller and suburbanite alike in a common symbolic bond.

1

The Historical Development of the Local News Media

The link between newspapers and the growth and development of cities has often been ignored in the histories of American journalism, which have focused on the role of the press in the life of the nation.[1] The earliest American newspapers are remembered as the national political pamphlets, such as Tom Paine's "Common Sense," which concerned the country's struggle for independence. The "yellow journalism" of the 1880s is set in the context of the national movements of populism and progressivism and the importance of newspapers evidenced by their role in fueling the Spanish-American War. Similarly, the journalists identified as the early twentieth-century "muckrakers"— Lincoln Steffens, Ida Tarbell, Upton Sinclair—were not the editors and reporters of urban newspapers but writers for national magazines the aim of which was chiefly to change national policy.

And yet, in every era of American life, journalism has been tied not simply to the life of the republic but to the conditions of the individual cities which gave birth to newspapers. The first newspapers were founded in the first cities, and new newspapers spread only as urban centers spread and created new markets with their concentrations of population. When cities grew and prospered, so did their newspapers, and when in the second half of the twentieth century many urban areas began to decline, the effect on newspapers was devastating.

This chapter examines the link between the evolution of cities and of newspapers. We will see how the newspaper's form and content has changed as the city has evolved from mercantile to manufacturing to service economy, as the urban population has grown and gained in diversity, and as the physical form of cities has shifted from tightly clustered settlements along waterfronts to sprawling, decentralized metropolises tied together by highway ribbons. The challenge of new local media—namely, local television and radio and suburban newspapers—and the emergence of the new "umbrella structure" of competition between the regionwide and the more localized news media will also be discussed.

From the Commercial Newsletters to the "Penny Papers"

In the early days of the colonies, many of the country's news-papers were partisan newsletters financed by national political parties and candidates for office. However, in each of the towns along the Eastern seaboard of the United States, there were also newspapers that were uniquely local in nature. The commercial newsletters, as they were called, played an essential role in the economy of the early cities, which served as trading centers between an agricultural hinterland and European markets. The newsletters announced the arrival and departure of ships, listed the contents of cargoes, and served as a source of current price lists and other commercial data. They also carried local advertising related to the trade, providing space for importers' announcements, listings of auctions, cargo space availability, ship departures, and real estate sales. The audience of these commercial newsletters was limited to a small segment of the population—the mercantile elite—and they were sold by subscription only at the price of six cents.[2]

When general news was included in the newsletters, it tended to be news of Europe that had some bearing on trade and shipping.[3] Because the town's citizens could easily interact and communicate with each other as they passed in the streets or came together in taverns or meetinghouses, there was little need for social communication in the newsletters.[4] The earliest local newspapers, therefore, did not serve to entertain but rather to communicate information that was central to the functioning of the burgeoning mercantile economy. Indeed, the large growth in the number of newspapers in the late eighteenth and early nineteenth centuries has been tied to the growth of demand for commercial and trade information by an elite audience, rather than to any general need for information from the population at large.

When the first major transformation of American journalism occurred in the 1830s with the beginning of the so-called "Penny Papers," the change could be traced to the transition of American cities from mercantile to industrial economies. Although factories were small in scale in the early nineteenth century, the growing manufacturing sector came to require ever larger labor forces and larger markets for the goods produced. A dramatic growth took place in the population of cities: New York City grew from a population of 33,000 in 1790 to 215,000 in 1830. In the same period, Philadelphia grew from 44,000 to 161,000; Boston from 18,000 to 85,000; Baltimore from 13,000 to 63,000.[5]

Of even greater importance to the newspapers, cities were not simply growing in size, but were becoming the home of a growing urban middle class with considerable financial resources. This urban middle class represented a pool of potential newspaper readers who would also be potential consumers of the new set of goods being produced. Newspapers which could attract the urban middle class as readers could then sell that readership to advertisers. Therefore, it was the growth of cities as the locus of a concentrated consumer market that created the opportunity for the emergence of the Penny Press.

The newspaper editors of the day—James Gordon Bennett, Benjamin Day, Charles Dana, Horace Greeley—changed the price, the content, even the way the new papers were distributed as part of the strategy to garner larger circulations. The Penny Papers were sold, as their name implies, for a penny rather than the six-cent price of earlier papers, and instead of subscriptions, they were hawked in the city's streets by newsboys. Their content was also a dramatic departure from the earlier commercial newsletters or political treatises. News of abroad and of national government was replaced by local news that had little to do with the economy. As cities had grown in population and spread over space, the average urban dweller could no longer learn the town's happenings simply by strolling the streets and squares or patronizing his favorite tavern. The newspapers began to take on the function of telling stories about the town that had once flowed directly from person to person in the form of face-to-face communication.

The stories that the Penny Papers told about the city, although considered sensational for the day, set the stage for the kind of "news" we know today: descriptions of crimes and accidents taken from police records, detailed charges leveled during trials taken from court proceedings, gossip-filled tales of "human interest" about local aristocrats and the common man alike. As Schudson notes, "in the 1830s the newspapers began to reflect not the affairs of an elite in a small trading society but the activities of an increasingly varied, urban and middle class society of trade, transportation and manufacturing." Advertising, too, was democratized in the Penny Press, as public sales notices and legal notices were replaced by ads for patent medicines and the first want ads.[6]

In addition, the new papers, supported by revenues from readers and advertisers, differed from the earlier political newsletters which had survived on subsidies from political parties and therefore had to reflect the positions of those parties. The Penny Papers enjoyed a new freedom to reflect independent, nonpartisan editorial positions which were often colored by the strong and distinctive opinions of their flamboyant editors. In their efforts to secure larger circulations, flamboyance and sensationalism were the keys: stories were uncovered less for their importance to economic activities than for their ability to amuse, surprise, shock, even titillate the average urban dweller.

The newspaper's role in this era was, however, no less important than its earlier one. Newspapers became unique in their ability to communicate with an increasingly decentralized local population. In providing information to this local market about the newly manufactured products, newspapers played a key role in the early transition from an economy based on trade and cottage industries to a manufacturing-based market economy. They also served as an important instrument of intracity communication among a population growing not just in size and extent but in diversity as well. The newspaper, in seeking to communicate to a larger segment of the urban population, began to take on the role of intracity communicator that would become increasingly important as time went on.

Urbanization and the Mass-circulation Dailies of the Late Nineteenth Century

The forces for change in both cities and newspapers that began in the early nineteenth century were to mushroom a few decades later as manufacturing activity—fueled by improvements in industrial and transport technology—continued to attract increasing numbers of people to urban centers. Where in 1830 Philadelphia could count a population of approximately 160,000, by 1880, its numbers reached near 900,000. And in the course of the next forty years, the city's population was to double to reach close to 1,900,000 in 1920.

While many of the new arrivals to Philadelphia and other cities came from rural areas of the United States, still more came from foreign countries. The number of immigrants to the United States from 1830 to 1839 was one-half million; from 1880 to 1889, the newcomers totaled 5.2 million. Moreover, the last two decades of the nineteenth century began the shift in immigration from Northwestern to Southeastern Europe: from 1870 to 1879, 5.2 percent of the total immigrants came from Russia, Austria-Hungary, and Italy, from 1880 to 1889, the percentage increased to 14.6, and from 1890 to 1899, it had jumped to 66.2 percent of the total immigrants.[7] In 1890, 40 percent of New York's population was foreign-born, and many of them could not speak English. American cities were coming to be populated by people who were not simply different from native Americans in their culture, but often in their languages as well.

The city of the 1880s and 1890s was also dramatically different in its physical form as improvements in intracity transportation and in communication allowed more and more urban residents to move out of central locations into outlying areas. The city of the 1850s had been largely a walking city, with outlying areas less than three miles from the center. But starting in the late 1850s, horse-drawn streetcars became an important form of transportation within American cities; by the 1880s many of these streetcars had been electrified and supplemented by rapid-transit systems that allowed the urban population to spread to the new streetcar suburbs. With the new modes of transport, the city became vastly larger than a few decades before, with a typical radius of some ten miles from the city's center.

Another major change in the nature of the late nineteenth-century city that was to have major repercussions for the newspaper was the emergence of the central business district, anchored by big department stores. Before 1870, retailing activity had been dispersed throughout the city in small shops or pushcarts which moved through neighborhoods. The small-scale merchants competed with each other for customers from nearby blocks only, as buyers rarely ventured out of their immediate neighborhoods to purchase a product. The city was, in effect, divided into a multitude of tiny consumer markets. But after 1870, the growth in the purchasing power of urban residents and the expansion of the mass-produced manufactured goods presented opportunities for new economies of scale in retailing. At the same time, the development of the streetcar allowed city dwellers to travel over considerable distances to the city center to purchase such things as clothing, hardware products, and drugs. As a result of these factors, new centralized retail districts emerged, anchored by variety and department stores, like Stewart's in New York and Wanamaker's in Philadelphia.

The development of the department store and its need to draw on a citywide market had a major impact on the newspapers of the day. As Juergans has written, "Unlike the small shopkeepers of old, content to serve an area of several blocks, these princes of retailing looked to the entire city as their market and relied upon full-page displays in the newspaper to reach it . . . starting in the late 1870s Wanamaker took out entire pages in newspapers—within a year or two the display ad had become an accepted tool of merchandising."[8] Newspapers were unique in their ability to communicate information about products and stores to a concentrated but decentralized population. While in the 1830s there had been an incentive to expand newspaper circulation to the urban middle class to attract consumer advertising, in the 1880s, the incentive grew to reach the great mass of city dwellers who became the targets of advertising by both urban retailers and national manufacturers. More than ever before, the race was on to capture more and more urban residents as newspaper readers.

But the task of becoming a mass-circulation newspaper with appeal to all segments of the urban population was not a simple one in the city of the late nineteenth century. When Joseph Pulitzer took over as editor of the *New York World* in 1883, he confronted a city that posed both new opportunities and new challenges to newspapers. It was a city in which residents for the first time were riding, not walking, to work. It was a city with a population that was growing not simply in size but in diversity as well, including a sizable number of immigrants of different cultural backgrounds and often different languages, all trying to adapt to a new and very strange urban environment. And it was a city in which consumption had taken on a new importance, in which both English- and foreign-speaking populations were the targets of the advertising of manufacturers and retailers eager to stimulate sales.

But it was also a city of great social and political cleavages, where people rarely communicated with others who were located more than a few blocks away, where urban residents formed clubs and associations that were segregated along economic, ethnic, or racial lines that isolated one group from another.[9] It was just this kind of fragmentation and isolation that big-city newspapers needed to overcome in order to garner the citywide readerships demanded by retail advertisers. The urban newspaper needed readers and it needed a great many of them, not just from one or another ethnic group or class or from one or two neighborhoods in the city. In order to create a product that could capture this citywide market, Pulitzer and the editors who followed his lead transformed both the look and the content of the newspaper.[10]

The word-filled, grey monotonous front page of earlier newspapers was replaced with banner headlines, huge photographs, and exaggerated cartoons. For the city's immigrants struggling to learn English, the new visual quality was an essential element of attraction; if they couldn't understand all the words of the stories, they still could learn something about the environment from the pictures and from the simple words announcing the themes of the stories in their headlines. The new journalism was also uniquely designed to serve the new mobility patterns of the city. The same innovations that made the newspaper accessible to the immigrant and the poorly educated—the broad headlines, the illustrations, the short, livelier stories, the use of lead paragraphs to summarize stories—were appealing to the middle-class "suburban" commuter, capturing his attention at the station newsstand and holding his interest throughout the ride to work.[11] The suburbanization of the nineteenth century was therefore a boon to newspapers, as the commuting population became a new source of newspaper readers and helped boost circulation figures.

In an attempt to capture as large an audience as possible, Pulitzer also began the practice of sectionalizing the newspaper to appeal to different kinds of readers. Women, as organizers of the family's consumption, were wooed with their own sections featuring recipe suggestions and tips on the latest fashions, advice to the lovelorn, and tales of high society. The working man of the day was sought after with new sports sections that gave less emphasis to yachting and polo—the recreations of the aristocrat—and more play to those sports that interested the masses, like baseball, boxing, and horse races.[12]

Also important in the attempts to boost circulation was the shift in the tone and content of the paper as a whole. Where the Penny Papers had each tried to attract a narrow specialized segment of the newspaper market, the new journalism featured stories that would appeal to a wider and more heterogeneous urban population. In effect, the new newspaper broadened its messages so as to be acceptable to a wider range of urban residents. A new premium was placed on "objectivity" in the reporting of news, in part for the very practical reason that a story so labeled could be palatable to a diverse readership.[13]

But most important, the newspapers had to make changes that would help overcome the fragmentation and sense of social isolation of the urban population. It was the attachment to a multitude of different ethnic subcultures that threatened to stand in the way of mass circulations, keeping people tied to their own foreign-language or specialized newspapers instead of a citywide communication organ. One of the ways newspapers approached this task was by working to create an interest in and a concern for the welfare of "the city" as an organic entity, to encourage their readers to make a connection between the city's public interest and their own private interest.[14] To create this sense of identity with the city as a whole, newspapers relied on three major devices: boosterism, crusading, and the push for the construction of major public works.

While urban boosterism of the nineteenth century has been viewed as an instrument used by local chambers of commerce to stimulate economic development, it was also an important device employed by newspapers to create a common source of pride among a disparate urban readership. For example, newspapers actively worked to create a sense of interurban rivalry between nearby cities in an attempt to increase their circulation. As Nord describes it, when both St. Louis and Chicago were competing to host the World's Columbian Exposition in 1890, the *St. Louis Republic* called Chicago "a settling basin for the refuse of the world," while the *Chicago Tribune* claimed that St. Louis was "nothing more than a flag station on certain Chicago railroad lines."[15] The stimulation of a sense of competition and the general boostering of the home town, worked to foster a unified urban consciousness and, ultimately, to raise circulation.

The need to create a common citywide identity also encouraged newspapers to stand as the prime supporters of the construction of the new public works projects of the day. When the *New York World* launched a campaign to raise funds to build a granite pedestal for the Statue of Liberty in 1885, for example, it was embarking on a drive that was not simply interesting but which could also help to symbolically unite all its readers. The same was true of newspaper editorials for new subway systems, bridge spans, or public parks: such grand and massive projects all worked to create a sense of a citywide public interest and a set of citywide public needs.

Just as boosterism and the construction of new public projects worked to create a strong sense of local identity, so did the muckraking crusades that became a fundamental part of the urban journalism of the late nineteenth century.[16] Stories about local railroad barons or utility owners using their monopolies to charge exorbitant rates in return for poor service served to link the audience through a common sense of outrage just as boosterism united them in pride. When William Randolph Hearst's *San Francisco Examiner* took on the Southern Pacific railroad, "the . . . war . . . would go on for years with no immediate victory except in circulation."[17] Similarly, when E. W. Scripp's *Detroit News* championed Mayor Hazan Pingree's fight to force the private gas, electric, and telephone companies to reduce their charges, there was a resulting gain in readership.[18]

In their attempts to capture mass circulations, the newspapers came to play many important functions in the city of the nineteenth century. One of the key roles was in helping to acculturate the immigrants and other newcomers to America's cities to their new way of life. As Schudson describes it, the newspaper became a kind of "use-paper" not just for the new immigrants but for the urban poor and barely literate workingman as well, offering a "compendium of tips for urban survival." [19] Robert Park pronounced William Randolph Hearst a "great Americanizer," [20] but it would be more accurate to call him and the other editors the "great urbanizers," for their newspapers were instrumental in teaching the new arrivals from rural areas—whether of the United States or abroad—about how to cope in the city. As Hofstadter has written:

> [The newspapers] found themselves undertaking the . . . ambitious task of creating a mental world for the uprooted farmers and villagers who were coming to live in the city. The rural migrants found themselves in a new urban world, strange, anonymous, impersonal, cruel, often corrupt and vicious, but also full of variety and fascination. . . . The newspaper became not only the interpreter of this environment but a means of surmounting in some measure its vast human distances. . . .[21]

Newspaper crusades were also of major importance, not simply because they resulted in social reform or the construction of badly needed public works, but because they worked to strengthen city government itself. The mid-nineteenth-century local governments reflected the era's general mistrust of public intervention in the private market. City governments were loosely structured and highly decentralized, with responsibility for governing divvied up among a multitude of commissions and officials with overlapping authority. Coordinated decisions, whether to build new public works or to regulate the utilities, were almost impossible to achieve, except through the systems of graft that local machines set up. The elections for local office were viewed more as a time to consult the boss on how to vote than as an opportunity for spirited public involvement.[22]

But the newspapers' tales of the private interest run wild—irresponsible streetcar drivers killing pedestrians in the road, slum landlords subjecting their tenants to abhorrent living conditions—brought forth a public outcry for punitive action by city government. Stories of threats to public health by unsanitary sewers or of stymied economic growth through failure to build a new bridge helped create a new political climate that set the stage for local government to take on new more powerful functions. Ironically, by following their own economic interest—the pursuit of mass circulations that could be used to attract advertising—the urban newspapers of the late nineteenth and early twentieth centuries became a key force in pushing for the constraint of private interest by the actions of local government.

As a result, the newspapers were able to play a crucial role in the urban reform efforts of the day and helped tame the physical environment of the city, which had been transformed by rapid urbanization, industrialization, and technological breakthrough. The newspapers were instrumental in tempering the individualistic ethics of the urban populace so as to gain an empowered role for city government as the regulator of public utilities and as the provider of public goods and services essential to the future growth and development of the city.

Importantly, as city government became stronger, it became more and more important to the newspapers as both a source of local news coverage and a fount of symbols of local identity. Coverage of city government gradually took a place of preeminence over either the courts or the police as a source of local news, because it was city government more than street crime or trial summations that offered the kinds of symbols and images capable of creating a common local identity among the fragmented urban population. The primary bonds of ethnicity and class did not disappear, but a new type of bond began to emerge, tying immigrant and streetcar suburbanite alike to a common geographically based identity.

This local identity tied to city was essential because it allowed the newspapers to draw together their entire local market into a common set of interests and therefore allowed the newspaper to deliver to its advertisers the kind of mass citywide consumer market they needed. In effect, in order to become a true mass medium, urban newspapers needed to produce local identity as much as they produced local news. They became the chief constructors of citywide local identity and produced a more democratic newspaper because it was in their economic interest to do so.

And in city after city the strategy proved successful. Between 1880 and 1909, circulation of daily newspapers in the United States went from 3.6 million to 24.2 million. Individual newspaper circulation became very large, with the largest newspapers approaching one million circulation by 1900. In New York City, the combined daily circulation of all newspapers in 1830 was 16,000; by 1899, it was 2,700,000.[23] The city newspaper, with its massive and diverse readership, had assumed a role as an integral urban institution.

Suburbanization and the Fragmentation of Local News Markets

In the nineteenth century, urban growth, even outside the existing political boundaries of the city, had proved a boon to newspapers, expanding the pool of potential readers and generating increased demand by advertisers for access to the growing local consumer market. The decentralization accompanying that growth actually benefited newspapers, for as the city spread out in space, people began commuting to work by public transportation and using the newspaper as a companion for the trip.

Urban growth had also created new informational needs. Newcomers to the city looked to the newspaper for help in adjusting to a new way of life, while the middle and upper classes were attracted by stories of a city that was no longer "knowable" through a stroll in the square. And it was the massive urban growth that had set the stage for centralized, large-scale retailing in department stores that created the need for dramatic display advertising in citywide communication outlets. In short, the growth of the city and the expansion of the local population in the late nineteenth century had greatly benefited the mass-circulation newspapers of the day.

But the growth of suburban areas in the second half of the twentieth century had no such sanguine effect on metropolitan newspapers. Suburbanization radically transformed the structure of local retail markets and with it the demand by advertisers for target audiences. At the same time, the changing metropolitan structure altered the demand for local news by those audiences and made it increasingly difficult for the metropolitan newspapers, as well as the other local news media, to find news of interest to the entire local market.

At the center of these changes was the shifting relationship between the central city and the suburbs and the change from a centralized to a decentralized metropolis. When the early "bedroom communities" of the 1950s developed, their residents still commuted to work in the city, still shopped in downtown department stores, and continued to visit friends, relatives, and cultural attractions that remained in the city. But over time, as more and more jobs, stores, restaurants, and movie theaters followed people out to the suburbs, these ties to the central city were increasingly severed. Suburbs became increasingly independent entities, interacting more with one another than with the city at their geographical center.

The same demographic shift has occurred in metropolitan areas throughout the country: central cities have lost their dominance over suburban areas—in population, in employment, and in retail sales. Figures 1.1 and 1.2 show the pattern of loss of central city dominance as the center of population of major metropolitan areas. For example, in 1940, the city of Philadelphia contained 60 percent of its metropolitan area's population. By 1980, the city was home to

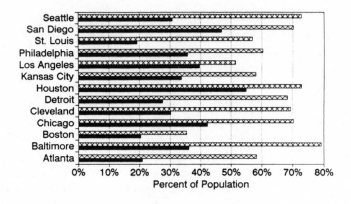

FIGURE 1.1   City Share of Metro Population. Source: *Statistical Abstract of the United States*, 1987, and *U.S. Census of the Population*, 1940.

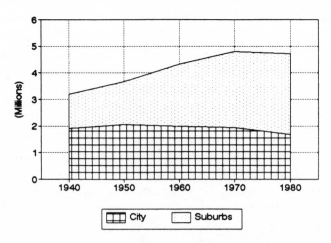

FIGURE 1.2   City Share of SMSA Population, Philadelphia. Source: *Statistical Abstract of the United States*, 1987, and *U.S. Census of the Population*, 1940.

only 36 percent of the metropolitan area's population. Baltimore went from having almost 80 percent of its region's population in 1940 to 36 percent in 1980. Similarly, Detroit, home to 68 percent of its metropolitan area's population in 1940, contained only 28 percent by 1980.

Importantly, the trend was present in the newer cities of the South and West, as well. In 1940, the city of Houston represented 73 percent of its metropolitan area's population, but by 1980—even with extensive annexation—the city's share of the regional population had fallen to 55 percent. Similarly, while the city of San Diego experienced significant growth between 1940 and 1980, its suburbs grew at a faster rate and began to gain dominance. The city of San Diego went from representing 70 percent of its metropolitan area's population to only 47 percent by 1980. In most metropolitan areas of the country, more people were coming to live in suburbs than in central cities.

Moreover, income disparities between city and suburb were increasing, with growing numbers of suburbanites having significantly higher incomes than those of central-city residents. In 1985, only 17 percent of households with incomes of more than $50,000 lived in the central cities of the nation's largest metropolitan areas.[24] In many metropolitan areas, the most affluent residences form a ring around the central city, in which the poorest of the region's families live. This demographic shift has meant that the largest- and most affluent segment of the metropolitan newspaper's market—the market of most interest to its advertisers—has come to reside in the suburbs.

As residential areas have suburbanized, so too have centers of employment. In older and newer cities alike, the percentage of all metropolitan-area jobs in central cities has been declining, and in most metropolitan areas of the country, the majority of the jobs are in the suburbs. For example, while in 1960, 57 percent of the metropolitan workforce in Detroit worked in the central city, by 1980, the figure had fallen to 27 percent. Similarly, the number of metropolitan workers working in the city of Chicago fell from 69 percent in 1960 to 44 percent in 1980. Even in such metropolitan areas as Houston, where the city has been able to annex many growing outer areas, the city's concentration of employment has been steadily dropping, from 84 percent in 1960 to 72 percent in 1980 (see table 1.1).

At the same time, city retail districts have been losing out to suburban malls. In Detroit for example, in 1982, only 15 percent of the metropolitan area's retail sales were in the city. Similarly, in Atlanta, the city had only 21 percent of the region's retail sales, while the city of Chicago had 31 percent of its region's

TABLE 1.1   Workplace Changes in Selected SMSAs, 1960–80

	% of SMSA Workforce Working in Central City	
SMSA	1960	1980
Atlanta	70	36
Baltimore	66	45
Boston	44	32
Chicago	69	44
Cleveland	72	43
Dallas/Ft. Worth	76	45
Detroit	57	27
Houston	84	72
Los Angeles	52	44
Philadelphia	57	39
St. Louis	57	33

SOURCE: U.S. Bureau of the Census, *Census of Population: 1980; Journey to Work: Characteristics of Workers in Metropolitan Areas* (Washington, D.C., July 1984), and *Census of Population: 1960; Characteristics of the Population* (Washington, D.C., 1963).

TABLE 1.2   Central-city Share of SMSA Retail Sales for Selected Cities: 1963–1972–1982

	Central-city Share of SMSA Retail Sales		
City	1963	1972	1982
Atlanta	62.0%	43.7%	21.7%
Boston	55.0	38.5	26.7
Chicago	54.0	41.1	31.2
Cincinnati	48.6	34.6	27.5
Cleveland	46.8	31.1	21.9
Dallas	69.0	61.1	34.8
Detroit	42.6	27.2	15.1
Los Angeles	46.6	44.5	38.7
Milwaukee	61.5	46.1	38.4
Minneapolis	60.4	39.8	15.6
Philadelphia	42.7	33.3	25.8
St. Louis	37.5	23.3	15.6

SOURCE: U.S. Bureau of the Census, *Census of Retail Trade*, 1963, 1972, 1982.

TABLE 1.3   Use of Public Transit for Worktrips in Selected Metropolitan
Areas, 1980

Metropolitan Area	Percentage of Metropolitan-area Residents Using Public Transit for Worktrips
Atlanta	7.3
Baltimore	10.2
Boston	12.6
Chicago	20.4
Dallas	4.3
Denver	4.3
Detroit	3.6
Houston	3.2
Los Angeles	7.0
New York	49.3
Philadelphia	14.0
St. Louis	5.7
San Francisco	22.1
Seattle	9.6
Washington, D.C.	14.8

SOURCE: U.S. Bureau of the Census, *State and Metropolitan Area Data Book*, 1986 (Washington, D.C. 1986).

retail sales (see table 1.2). The pattern in the late nineteenth and early twentieth centuries of centralized downtown retail centers drawing customers from throughout the city and beyond has been broken. In its place is a new pattern of decentralized retail markets focused around suburban malls, where many advertisers seek access not to the entire regional market but only to a particular submarket surrounding their store.

With fewer people living, working, and shopping in central cities than in suburbs, there has also been a dramatic abandonment of public transit in favor of the private automobile. In Detroit, for example, 26 percent of Detroit's metropolitan-area population used public transit for worktrips in 1953. Twelve years later, in 1965, the proportion had fallen to 8.2 percent, and by 1980 it was only 3.6 percent. Similarly, in Dallas 17 percent of the population used public transportation for worktrips in 1950, but by 1980, it was only 4.3 percent[25] (see table 1.3). Picking up a newspaper at the newsstand to read on the commute to and from work has ceased to be a habit for the majority of metropolitan residents.

The political geography of the metropolis has changed as well. With suburbanization came the proliferation of new political jurisdictions outside the central city, as many suburban areas incorporated themselves as municipalities and created new school districts and other local governing units. Unlike a century before, when cities had gobbled up outlying towns into their jurisdictions, these new townships and boroughs were remaining resolutely independent—not just of the city but of each other, since one of the attractions of suburban life was the ability to exercise a strong say in small-scale governments.[26] The result has been a pattern of political geography in which one large, although declining, centralized jurisdiction is surrounded by many smaller decentralized jurisdictions. So while the central city's government remains the biggest fish in the metropolitan sea, the majority of metropolitan residents are represented by a multitude of small area governments.

The increasing independence of the suburbs and the weakening of their ties to the city have had major repercussions for the metropolitan newspaper. With the changing structure has come a change in the local news interests of the newspaper's major market. Instead of reports of city council meetings, suburbanites want to hear about the decisions of local zoning boards that might effect their own property values or change the nature of their homogeneous communities. Stories about a troubled city school system have become less compelling than the listing of school lunch menus at the local high school where they send their own children.

For the same reasons that increasing numbers of people have turned their backs on urban living, so have they come to reject newspapers which continue to take their names from those cities and which give the city primary local news emphasis. And, at the same time as they have lost interest in news of the city, suburbanites have come to demand news of their own small communities. The dilemma facing the metropolitan newspaper has been how to cover "local" news in a politically fragmented metropolis where suburbanites are very interested in news of their own locality but relatively uninterested in the affairs of other small jurisdictions.

This question has become vital to the economic survival of metropolitan newspapers because increasingly it is the suburban audience that is in demand by the newspaper's advertisers, both because of their sheer numbers and their affluence. Unfortunately, at the very time that the metropolitan newspaper was losing its hold on this suburban market, new local media were emerging that would thrive, at least in part, because they were better suited to the new urban form. The first source of competition came from the local broadcast media, the second came from suburban newspapers and shoppers.

The Challenge of Local Radio and Television

The first source of competition to metropolitan newspapers for both audiences and advertisers came from radio. While in 1935, newspapers received 45 percent of all advertising to radio's less than 7 percent, ten years later in 1945, newspapers accounted for only 32 percent of ad revenues, with radio having risen to almost 15 percent.[27] Although radio was dealt an immediate blow by the emergence of television in the 1950s, it has regained a position of importance on the local media scene, in part because it has proven to be well suited to the physical form of the city in the age of the metropolis.

With the advent of automobile use for the journey to work, radio has become the ideal "drive-time" companion for the car-bound commuter. Its band reaches out easily over the breadth of the region, therefore it faces none of the newspapers' distribution problems or time delays in disseminating information. Radio has also proven to be particularly attractive to advertisers concerned with reaching specific demographic groups within the major regional market. The large number of specialized radio stations in big cities has resulted in a significant degree of audience segmentation. In choosing a radio station, an advertiser can pinpoint a particular submarket of the population for his message.[28]

If radio was to prove a strong competitor for newspapers in the age of the metropolis, television's advent caused even larger reverberations. Like radio, television was suited technologically to simple transmission of its messages across a dispersed regional environment. In its early days, television was hardly competitive with newspapers in the delivery of news—until the 1970s most local news programs lasted little more than fifteen minutes—but it was very competitive in terms of providing leisure-time entertainment to a regionwide audience. Importantly, unlike newspapers, television's appeal to the regional market was not based on its geographic identifications with either city or suburb. Indeed, with most programming originating from the national networks, television served to reinforce a homogenized national identity and to effectively loosen local ties.

Because of its unique technological ability to combine visual images with sound, television enjoyed a natural advantage with those advertisers eager to project an image for their product to a regionwide audience. By the 1960s, television had begun to take on the major share of national advertising, particularly the manufacturer-to-consumer advertising that newspapers had held since the nineteenth century.[29] Whereas in 1950, 25 percent of newspaper advertising revenues (nationwide) came from national advertising, by 1978 national advertising accounted for only 14 percent of newspaper ad revenues.[30] Some categories of national advertising have stayed with newspapers, most notably cigarettes and tobacco, which are prevented by law from advertising on television. Other large national advertisers remaining with newspapers include: automobiles, food, airlines, televisions, appliances, wine, beer and liquor, soap and cleaners.[31] Although television has gained in its share of local advertising, newspapers continue to represent the primary medium for advertising by general merchandisers (department stores), financial institutions, clothing, food and drug stores, housing agents, and local entertainment.

The onset of television has, however, had several major impacts on metropolitan newspapers. First, by taking away the lion's share of national advertising, television has made newspapers more dependent than ever on local advertising and indirectly on the health of the local economy. When the local economy is strong, plentiful job opportunities and high residential mobility generate large volumes of classified ads, and healthy retail sales stimulate retail advertising. But each local recession will bring these revenues down again, causing a direct negative impact on the metropolitan newspaper.

Second, television has created a form of entertainment that competes with the newspaper for the leisure time of audiences. As television-viewing has increased, newspaper-reading has decreased, and the habit of reading more than one newspaper a day has become rare. And as television news at both the national and local level has been strengthened, it has presented a greater challenge to the newspaper's major news delivery mission. To the extent that television news fulfills people's need to be informed about the world, it decreases their demand for information from newspapers. In particular, television has been especially powerful in drawing the blue-collar working-class audience away from newspapers.[32]

Third, television has presented a subtle challenge to newspapers in its use of the visual image and in the brevity and succinctness of its presentation of information. Just as newspapers in the 1880s appealed to the masses with new visual effects in the form of cartoons, photographs, and banner headlines and with time-saving devices like lead paragraphs to summarize news stories, so television has come up with the visual qualities that make it increasingly accessible and appealing to the mass audiences of the twentieth century. Newspapers now have to contend with the need to appeal to a population that responds more to visual stimuli than did an earlier generation.

The Growth of Suburban Newspapers

While metropolitan newspapers have been losing their national advertising base to television and radio, another perhaps more threatening form of competition has moved in on the local advertising base. The very decentralized, fragmented regional structure that posed problems for the metropolitan newspaper has created opportunities for a new, more localized form of communications outlet—the suburban daily newspaper. Often growing out of weekly papers or from the papers of nearby secondary urban centers or formerly rural areas, the suburban dailies have molded their content to a new suburban way of life. In particular, they cater to the increased involvement of suburban residents in the affairs of their smaller-scale local governments and to their need for increased information about those affairs. These suburban weeklies and dailies expanded their circulation dramatically throughout the 1960s and 1970s, and by the 1980s, many had put out their own Sunday editions.

An indicator of the change that has taken place can be found in comparing the growth of circulation in metropolitan newspapers to the growth in circulation of suburban newspapers within an individual metropolitan area. Using Philadelphia as an example, the circulation of metropolitan newspapers went from 1,344,000 in 1940 to 763,000 in 1988. In the same period, suburban newspaper circulation increased from 147,000 to 461,000.[33] Whereas suburban newspapers represented less than 10 percent of all daily newspapers sold throughout the Philadelphia region in 1960, by 1988, they accounted for 38 percent of the dailies sold in the region.

Not only were suburban newspapers able to meet the local news needs of suburbanites better than metropolitan newspapers could, but they were able to offer important advantages to advertisers, as well. Many suburban retailers wanted to reach only a submarket of the regional market: consumers living within a certain radius of their store. Therefore, they were not concerned with a newspaper's total circulation but rather with its "penetration" (percentage of households reached) within the target market. In many areas, a suburban newspaper was able to offer higher penetration of that market than the metropolitan newspaper and to charge lower rates, as well.

31

The growing competition between metropolitan and suburban newspapers for the suburban market can be illustrated with data from the Philadelphia region. Table 1.4 examines metropolitan versus suburban newspaper penetration of the counties in the Philadelphia metropolitan area.[34] In 1962, during the early phase of suburbanization, the two major metropolitan newspapers in the Philadelphia region, the *Inquirer* and the *Bulletin,* each reached approximately one-third of the households in the seven suburban counties surrounding the city of Philadelphia. By 1988, however, the *Bulletin* had closed, and the *Inquirer* alone could capture less than 20 percent of the households in five of the seven suburban counties. At the same time, many suburban newspapers, like the *Courier Post* or the *Gloucester County Times,* were enjoying penetrations of suburban counties as high as 37 and 36 percent, respectively.

As the penetration of suburban areas by metropolitan newspapers has decreased, suburban newspapers have become an increasingly attractive buy to smaller suburban retailers. For example, a store located in a mall in suburban Bucks County, Pennsylvania, could reach 34 percent of the county's households by advertising in the *Bucks County Courier Times,* as opposed to 17 percent by advertising in the *Inquirer.*[35] While major regional advertisers (multistore chains) or national chains continue to seek access to a regionwide market, increasingly they have come to advertise in only the metropolitan newspaper with the best suburban penetration. Where suburban newspaper groups exist, as with the Westchester-Rockland group in the New York City region, advertisers may make a single media buy to reach a wide range of suburban readers in a market.

Another threat to the advertising base of the metropolitan newspaper has come from the free weekly "shoppers," or advertising supplements with no editorial content produced for local retail outlets. Shoppers pinpoint a demographic group or localized market and saturate it by mailing or delivering ads to every household, thus offering "total market penetration." While the per capita cost of delivering shoppers is often high, the total cost may be lower than if the retailer used the metropolitan press. As Bogart has found, shoppers have increased in number from 1,012 in 1977 to 1,445 in 1988 and have grown in circulation in that period from eleven to twenty-one million, posing strong competition for both daily newspapers and paid community weeklies.[36] As a result, by the last decades of the twentieth century, the metropolitan newspaper faced new competition not simply from television, but from suburban newspapers and "shoppers" as well.

TABLE 1.4   Penetration* of Counties in Philadelphia SMSA by Metro and
Suburban Papers, 1962 and 1988

County	1962	1988
BURLINGTON, NJ		
Metro Papers		
Bulletin	32	—
Inquirer	32	18
Daily News	5	2
Suburban Papers		
Camden Courier Post	16	12
Burlington County Times	28	31
CAMDEN, NJ		
Metro Papers		
Bulletin	29	—
Inquirer	34	19
Daily News	14	4
Suburban Papers		
Camden Courier Post	62	37
GLOUCESTER, NJ		
Metro Papers		
Bulletin	36	—
Inquirer	28	16
Daily News	6	3
Suburban Papers		
Camden Courier Post	17	17
Woodbury/Gloucester	37	37
Vineland Times Journal	3	2
BUCKS, PA		
Metro Papers		
Bulletin	37	—
Inquirer	25	17
Daily News	4	3
Suburban Papers		
Levittown/Bucks	44	34
Allentown Call	3	3
Doylestown Intelligencer	15	14

TABLE 1.4   *Continued*

County	1962	1988
CHESTER, PA		
Metro Papers		
Bulletin	30	—
Inquirer	32	20
Daily News	9	4
Suburban Papers		
West Chester Local	28	30
Coatesville Record	18	5
Phoenixville Phoenix	9	5
Pottstown Mercury	7	5
DELAWARE, PA		
Metro Papers		
Bulletin	55	—
Inquirer	38	30
Daily News	10	8
Suburban Papers		
Chester/Del County Times	28	28
MONTGOMERY, PA		
Metro Papers		
Bulletin	48	—
Inquirer	39	31
Daily News	9	6
Suburban Papers		
Lansdale Reporter	6	7
Norristown Times Herald	18	12
Pottstown Mercury	10	7
PHILADELPHIA, PA		
Metro Papers		
Bulletin	69	—
Inquirer	52	29
Daily News	37	29

*The term "penetration" is used to indicate the percentage of households reached.

SOURCE: Based on data from American Newspaper Market's *Circulation*, 1962 and 1988–89, Malibu, California.

34

The New "Umbrella" Structure of Local Media Competition

The changing urban development pattern and the emergence of new communications outlets have changed the nature of the competitive structure of the local news media. While from the turn of the century onward, there has been a steady decrease in the number of newspapers within any one city, suburbanization and competition from local broadcast media has accelerated the process, producing a striking trend toward one-newspaper cities. Whereas in 1923, almost 40 percent of American cities had two or more newspapers, by 1978, only 2.3 percent of cities (thirty-five in total) had more than one newspaper.[37] By 1989, only nineteen cities had commercially competitive metropolitan newspapers. Even in the large multinewspaper cities, there has been a decline in the number of metropolitanwide newspapers. For example, in the period between 1940 and 1989, New York City went from having eight to three major metropolitan papers, Los Angeles from eight to one, Boston from nine to two, Philadelphia from five to two, Boston from six to two, and Detroit, Kansas City, Dallas, Cleveland, and St. Louis from three to two.[38]

Many of the metropolitan newspapers that have closed were afternoon papers. While some of these papers were the circulation losers in their cities (for example, the *Detroit Times,* the *Chicago Herald Tribune,* and the *Houston Press*), in other cases, newspapers that went out of business had larger circulations than their competitors, which survived. For instance, the circulation of the *Philadelphia Bulletin,* which closed in 1982, had long exceeded the circulation of either the *Inquirer* or the *Daily News,* its two chief competitors. The *Bulletin* and other similar afternoon newspapers died not because their circulation was not high enough, but because they were unable to attract the kind of readers—the suburban audience—demanded by their retail advertisers. Because they are distributed during the day and thus contend with heavy transport congestion, big-city afternoon newspapers have always tended to have more limited market areas than morning newspapers. In particular, afternoon newspapers have relied more heavily on street sales than on home-delivery as have morning newspapers.[39]

As a result, afternoon newspapers were harder hit by the loss of dominance of the city's central business district, as well as by decreased mass transit use, and fewer central-city commuters. In addition, because afternoon newspapers have traditionally had a larger blue-collar and lower-middle-class readership, they have faced stronger competition for their audiences from television. Those afternoon metropolitan newspapers that have attempted to follow their blue-collar audiences to the suburbs have continued to face difficulties getting a timely product to outlying areas. As a result, the readerships of these newspapers have come to be concentrated more in city than suburb and have become less attractive to advertisers.

While the number of metropolitanwide newspapers within any one city has decreased, the surviving big-city newspapers have had to contend with an increasing number of smaller daily newspapers published in suburbs and smaller cities in the outer rings of metropolitan areas. From 1955 to 1975, cities with populations between 100,000 and 500,000 witnessed an 18 percent increase in numbers of newspapers, while in cities with populations between 50,000 and 100,000, the number of newspapers increased by 31 percent.[40] In addition, many metropolitan newspapers face strong competition from suburban weekly papers as well.

As a result of competition from both the broadcast media and suburban newspapers, the circulation of the surviving metropolitan newspapers has not kept pace with regional population growth. As Bogart points out, while the total population of the nation's metropolitan areas grew by 29 percent between 1960 and 1987, the aggregate circulation of morning newspapers published in the top fifty central cities grew by only 2 percent in the same period.[41] Table 1.5 shows the relation between regional population and circulation of all metropolitan newspapers for selected metropolitan areas, revealing a declining metropolitan newspaper circulation per regional population. For example, where in San Francisco in 1940, 3,291 metropolitan newspapers were sold per 10,000 regional population, by 1980, that figure had fallen to 2,037. The trend is similar in Houston, where 4,889 metropolitan newspapers were sold per 10,000 population in 1940, as compared to 2,523 in 1980. Increasingly, audiences were turning away from metropolitan newspapers toward television, suburban and smaller-city newspapers, and other forms of leisure-time activity.

With the growth of newspapers in smaller cities outside of metropolitan areas—places which had traditionally taken their news from the closest big city—the market for the metropolitan newspaper has changed considerably in the postwar era. When Robert Park described the nature of newspaper markets in the first half of the twentieth century, he found that metropolitan newspapers were able to carve up the nation into a set of exhaustive markets. Where the New York City newspaper market ended, for example, the Boston market be-

TABLE 1.5   Relation of Total Circulation of Metropolitan Newspapers to
Metropolitan Population, Selected Cities, 1940–80

	TMC per 10,000 population	
Area	1940	1980
Atlanta	4,012	2,151
Baltimore	4,625	2,300
Boston	6,844	2,701
Detroit	3,844	2,840
Houston	4,889	2,523
Kansas City	10,139	4,506
Los Angeles	2,963	1,757
Miami	3,682	2,962
New York	4,310	3,376
Philadelphia	4,202	2,245
St. Louis	4,218	2,210
San Diego	2,103	1,790
Seattle	5,322	2,803

SOURCE: *Editor and Publisher Yearbook*, 1940, 1980; U.S. Bureau of the Census, *Census of Population and Housing*, 1940; and *Statistical Abstract of the United States*, 107th ed., 1987.

gan.[42] Just as residents of rural and small-town hinterlands traveled considerable distances to shop in city department stores in that era, so did they take their news of the world from big-city newspapers.

Even as late as 1962, many metropolitan newspapers enjoyed extensive market areas, as maps 1.1–1.10 on the following pages illustrate. For example, in 1962 the *New York Daily News* reached more than 20 percent of the households in 23 counties of New York, New Jersey, and Connecticut. By 1988, however, the picture was quite different: the *News* enjoyed those kind of penetration levels only in New York City and in Nassau and Westchester counties. Similarly, as the maps show, the markets for the *Chicago Tribune*, the *Philadelphia Inquirer*, the *Denver Post*, and the *Houston Chronicle* have also diminished in extent from 1962 to 1988. In most areas of the country, the market for metropolitan newspapers has fallen largely to the contours of the metropolitan area itself. And within that market, the most crucial audiences lay in the rings of suburbia and, increasingly, "exurbia" that are outside of the central cities which give these newspapers their names.

By 1990, the metropolitan newspaper has come to confront a dramatically

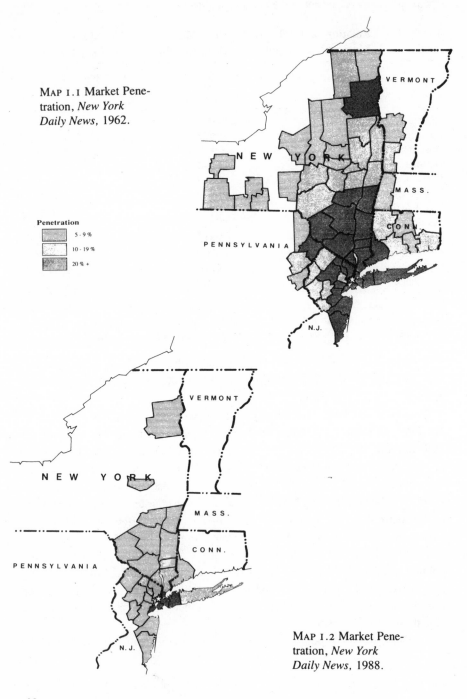

MAP 1.1 Market Penetration, *New York Daily News*, 1962.

Penetration

5 - 9 %

10 - 19 %

20 % +

MAP 1.2 Market Penetration, *New York Daily News*, 1988.

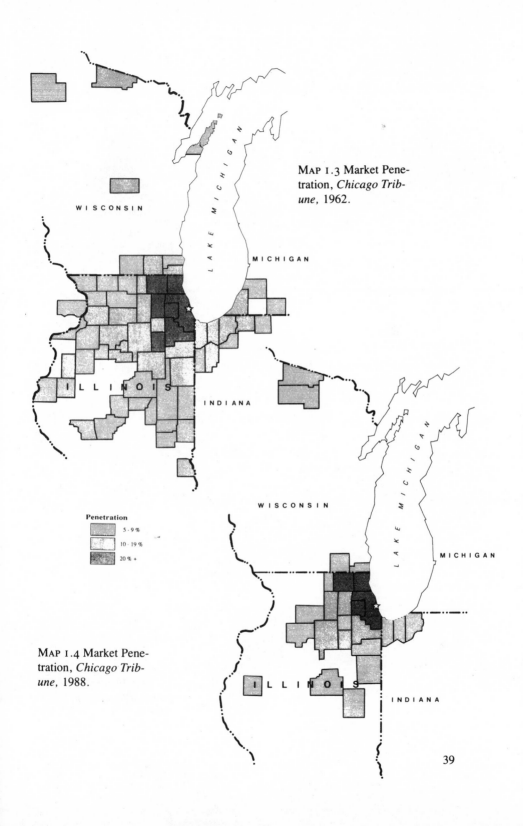

MAP 1.3 Market Penetration, *Chicago Tribune*, 1962.

MICHIGAN

LAKE MICHIGAN

WISCONSIN

ILLINOIS

INDIANA

Penetration

5 - 9 %

10 - 19 %

20 % +

MAP 1.4 Market Penetration, *Chicago Tribune*, 1988.

WISCONSIN

MICHIGAN

LAKE MICHIGAN

ILLINOIS

INDIANA

39

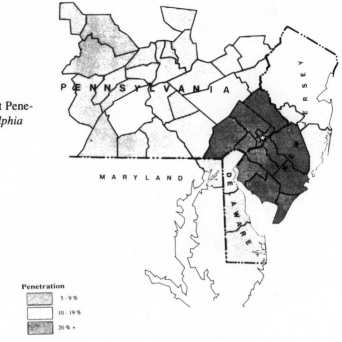

MAP 1.5 Market Pene-
tration, *Philadelphia
Inquirer*, 1962.

Penetration
- 5 - 9 %
- 10 - 19 %
- 20 % +

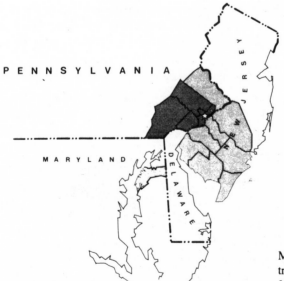

MAP 1.6 Market Pene-
tration, *Philadelphia
Inquirer*, 1988.

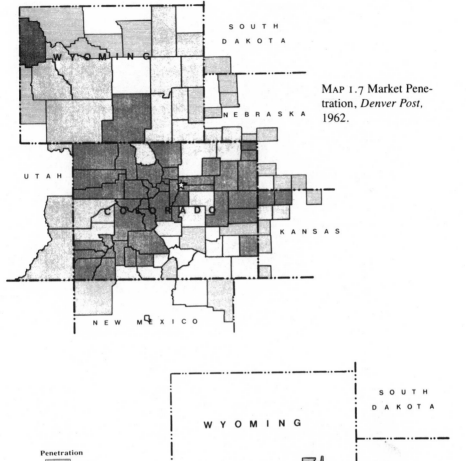

MAP 1.7 Market Pene-
tration, *Denver Post*,
1962.

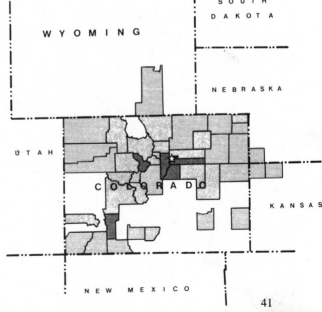

Penetration

	5 - 9 %
	10 - 19 %
	20 % +

MAP 1.8 Market Pene-
tration, *Denver Post*,
1988.

41

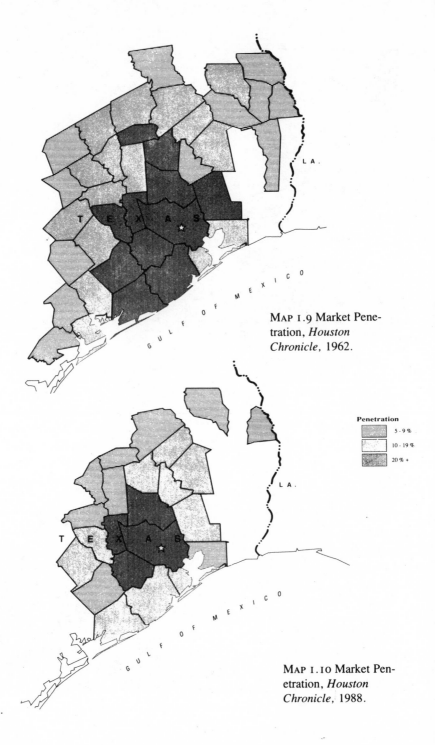

MAP 1.9 Market Pene-
tration, *Houston
Chronicle*, 1962.

Penetration
5 - 9 %
10 - 19 %
20 % +

MAP 1.10 Market Pen-
etration, *Houston
Chronicle*, 1988.

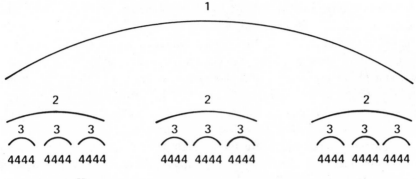

KEY:
LEVEL ONE: NEWSPAPER IN LARGE METROPOLITAN CENTER
LEVEL TWO: NEWSPAPERS IN SATELLITE CITIES
LEVEL THREE: LOCAL DAILIES
LEVEL FOUR: WEEKLIES AND OTHER SPECIALIZED MEDIA

FIGURE 1.3   Rosse's "Umbrella" Model of Newspaper Competition. Reprinted from James N. Rosse, "The Evolution of One-Newspaper Cities," a discussion paper for the FTC Symposium on Media Concentration, pp. 50–52.

new structure of competition. While the number of metropolitanwide newspapers within any one city has decreased, the survivors have had to contend with increased competition for audiences and advertisers from other media, including television, radio, suburban daily and weekly newspapers, and free shoppers. This new competition is above all a geographic and demographic competition, the intensity of which varies within the metropolitan area. James Rosse has described the form of this competition as an "umbrella" structure, composed of hierarchical levels of competition (see fig. 1.3).[43] Level one in the hierarchy or "umbrella" consists of one or more metropolitan newspapers, which compete with television, radio, and city magazines for a regional audience and for the national and local advertisers that want to reach that audience. The metropolitan newspaper in turn competes with many smaller newspapers within the umbrella for smaller segments of the local market.

In particular, level two consists of newspapers in satellite cities, which do not compete with each other, but which do compete for readers and advertisers within segments of the metropolitan newspaper's market. For example, in the New York region, the *Newark Star Ledger* and *Long Island Newsday* both compete with the metropolitan newspapers based in New York City, like the *New*

York Times and the *New York Daily News*. Level three consists of smaller suburban newspapers that also compete with metropolitan newspapers, like the *Middletown Times Herald* in New Jersey, which competes with both the *Star Ledger* and the New York City newspapers. Level four represents the weekly, twice/thrice weekly newspapers, shoppers, and other specialized media that serve a portion of the metropolitan area. In New York, the *Village Voice*, a weekly political and cultural newspaper, and the *Amsterdam News*, a weekly black newspaper, would be examples of Level-four newspapers.

In summary, the umbrella structure is characterized by competition between levels of the hierarchy, where there is typically little competition between media on the other levels. In some markets, however, there is competition between newspapers on the same level of the hierarchy in areas where their markets overlap. For example, in Anne Arundel County and Howard County in Maryland, two metropolitan newspapers, the *Baltimore Sun* and the *Washington Post* compete directly for audiences. The *Sun* also competes, however, with newspapers at lower levels of its umbrella. For example, in Anne Arundel County, the *Sun* competes with a daily paper originating in Annapolis, the *Capital*, and a weekly paper in Howard County. At the same time, it competes with television, radio, city magazines, business weeklies, and free weeklies for audiences and advertisers in other parts of its market.

The existence of such an umbrella structure of competition suggests that even in cities with one metropolitan newspaper, or with two metropolitan newspapers under joint ownership, alternative editorial voices exist with the potential to provide different slants on local affairs. For example, the managing editor of the *Baltimore Sun*, when asked if the two *Sun* newspapers (the *Sun* and the *Evening Sun*) which are co-owned, might not cover news unfavorable to the papers, replied, "We'd be afraid not to," noting that readers would hear alternative viewpoints on talk-radio, in the city magazine, and in the free weeklies in Baltimore.[44]

Therefore, while competition has declined among major metropolitan newspapers in many cities, there still exists substantial competition for audiences and advertisers between those newspapers and local television and radio, and new smaller-scale suburban newspapers.[45] Importantly, however, whether the medium is newspaper, television, radio, or magazine, the economic imperative that has emerged is the same. All local news media must attract some or all of the suburban audience, sought by national advertisers because of their mass and by many local advertisers because of their demographics. In other words, for all of the local news media the battleground of competition increasingly lies in the suburbs.

The question that follows is how this new structure of competition has influenced the nature of local news coverage. In particular, has the umbrella structure of competition between the local media produced the kind of examination of local issues necessary to inform citizens about local policy needs? The next chapter will examine the kinds of commercial pressures that exert influence on the local news media's coverage of policy issues.

2 Commercial Pressures on Local News

The local news media, whether metropolitan newspapers, local television and radio stations, or city magazines, are commercial enterprises that must make a profit in order to survive. While journalists have traditionally insisted that editorial decisions remain independent of business decisions—maintaining that there is a kind of "separation of church and state" between news and business departments—many critics have argued that commercial considerations play a central role in determining the form and content of news. Moreover, the increasing financial pressures on media organizations from corporate owners have led to a more explicit connection between commercial considerations and editorial content.[1]

But those who argue that the profit motive underlies news decisions do not agree on how that influence works. The general public views the so-called "sensationalism" of the news as the result of reporters and editors "just trying to sell newspapers" or boost their ratings. More sophisticated media critics have offered different explanations. Some argue that profit considerations lead to the censorship of news, so as to protect advertiser interests or the products of the large conglomerates that own many media firms. Looking specifically at the local news media, others have claimed it is the news firm's interest in the growth of the locality or links to the downtown business community that bias local news coverage.

This chapter will examine these differing explanations of how economic interests influence the selection and presentation of news content.[2] While these commercial considerations play an important role in local news decisions, there is an even more crucial commercial imperative facing any local news firm: to produce news that meets the interests of its specific target audience. Increasingly, it has become the need to capture suburban readers and create a common regional identity that influences how the metropolitan news media cover local policy issues.

The Role of Sensationalism

The most common explanation of how economic considerations affect news coverage is that news is selected and presented not so much for its importance as for its ability to entertain. In their attempt to sell newspapers or raise ratings, the news media are said to give greater prominence to stories that elicit emotion than to those that inform. For example, while little media attention is given to the fact that each year thousands of children die or are injured in automobile accidents because they are not strapped into car seats, the plight of 18-month-old Jessica McClure trapped in a well in 1987 received tremendous media attention, seemingly because it made a more dramatic and entertaining story.[3] By making these kind of news decisions, the media have left themselves open to accusations of distorting reality and exaggerating certain rare menaces while downplaying other more pervasive threats.[4]

In addition to magnifying the importance of atypical occurrences, the attempt to produce a marketable commodity is also said to lead the media to focus on the trivial, although entertaining, aspects of important events and issues. Herbert Gans has called this process "highlighting," explaining that reporters, in order to "sell" their stories to their editors and news directors, often "select the highlights about an actor or activity, deleting the routine or expected, whatever is not sufficiently important, novel, dramatic, or distinctive." The result, according to Gans, is a "highlighted reality which is . . . an exaggerated summary of the observed events."[5]

The need to sell the news is also used to explain national election coverage that focuses less on issues and positions than on symbols and rhetoric and on where each candidate stands in the "horse race." When George Bush ran for president in 1988, for example, more attention was said to be paid to his call for a mandatory pledge of allegiance at a local flag factory than to his stand on the environment. At the same time, the national media have been accused of sensationalizing when examining the private lives of candidates. For instance, many critics claimed it was the media's objective to titillate their audience that led to their coverage of the alleged "womanizing" of presidential candidate Gary Hart, not the desire to inform the electorate of his qualifications for office. Similar objections were raised in 1987 after Judge Douglas Ginsberg was nominated to the Supreme Court and the media gave greater attention to the judge's apparent marijuana-smoking in the previous decade than to his judicial experience.

The local news media has similarly been attacked for giving prominent attention to trivial, but entertaining, stories about local events and the activities of local officials. In what was to be his last column for the *New York Times*, reporter Sidney Schanberg bemoaned the way his own newspaper gave front-page coverage to a story about a Cajun restaurant being closed down for health violations while virtually ignoring important developments in the protracted proposal to build an underground highway on the West Side of Manhattan. "Too often in this town, the media's idea of big news is the Mayflower Madam's little black book or the fall-off in rentals in the Hamptons . . . ," he wrote in his weekly column, claiming that such "trivia" dwarfed continued consideration of questions concerning the multibillion dollar Westway project.[6]

In addition, the local news media, far more than the national media, are frequently accused of sensationalism for their often graphic coverage of crimes, fires, accidents, and other local disasters. Detailed descriptions of the bodily damage inflicted on assault victims, interviews with survivors recalling tragedies and describing feelings of loss, photographs of mangled automobile parts after highway crashes, or tearful relatives marching beside coffins at funerals are all pointed to as attempts by the local media to capitalize on a public fascination with gore and pathos.

The charge of sensationalism and the claim that the need to sell leads to news that entertains rather than informs is, however, actively disputed by many journalists. Some claim that emotional stories filled with descriptive detail provide crucial information and keep audiences from dismissing the implications of tragedies. For example, a reporter who covered a story about a child who had died after a fall from a housing project window, defended her inclusion of heart-wrenching details like how the boy "used to pound on neighbors' doors and cheerfully toddle into their apartments . . . tugging around his blue-and-yellow maintenance wagon, a cart with a mop and broom that he used while playing clean-up."[7] The reporter noted that "detail is one of the most important things of all, to vividly describe that a little child died. It is important for a reporter to make it a clear image, to show that this was a life."[8]

Similarly, news coverage that may appear gory and sensational to some is often intended by journalists to convey important information to their readers. For example, *Philadelphia Inquirer* editor Eugene L. Roberts, Jr. discussed the rationale for his newspaper's coverage of the public suicide of Pennsylvania State Treasurer Budd Dwyer, in which a photograph of Dwyer placing a gun in his mouth was run on the front page: "I generally stay away from bloody pictures but I did decide to run this graphic photograph, " Roberts said. "It was a high state official who called a press conference and, in front of TV cameras and reporters and photographers, committed suicide. We shouldn't duck that. It was an inherently horrible, disturbing event but one of the things that newspapers have to do is cover horrible, disturbing events. I don't feel comfortable shielding readers from things . . . I don't think we ever progress in society by averting our eyes from things that may be painful."[9]

Aside from being strongly refuted by many journalists, the simple sensationalism argument leaves certain questions unanswered. First, if only the need to sell motivated news decisions, how does one explain the wide variation among local news media in the way they select and present news? Despite the fact that all local news firms need to attract audiences, they each make very different decisions as to how much emotional or graphic content to include in their definition of local news. In particular, local television newscasts, more so than newspapers, tend to place a high premium on selecting and presenting news so as to appeal to emotions.[10]

In addition, local newspapers themselves will vary in their decisions on how much play to give stories of human tragedy, scandal, and crime. Newspapers whose audiences are better educated and more affluent use more dispassionate language in their headlines and stories and give greater prominence to government versus crime stories than do newspapers that appeal to a middle- or working-class audience. Moreover, journalists at the less upscale newspapers claim that their dramatic headlines and colorful, often lurid language are simply tools used to attract the interest of their audience, in part to better inform them.

For example, Zachary Stalberg, the editor of the *Philadelphia Daily News,* a tabloid newspaper sold on the newsstand, noted that page-one headlines were crucial in getting people to pick up the newspaper on impulse. He described a controversial case where the *Daily News* played the story of Nelson Mandela's release from prison with less prominence than a large front-page photograph of boxer Mike Tyson being knocked out in a weekend fight.[11] "No newspaper is a teaching tool," said Stalberg. "A newspaper is not what's important from an historical sense, but what we think is important to readers." He added that because the *Daily News* is sold almost entirely on the newsstand, "We don't have the freedom that other papers do. If you're 75 to 80 percent home-delivery you can afford to run an all-Mandela front page. But our job is to reach as many readers as possible. The more readers we get to read the newspaper, the more likely they are to read the serious coverage of the city, the editorial that pushes them in the right direction. The game is to get them into the tent."[12]

Once "in the tent," both newspaper readers and even local television viewers find much in the local news concerning government and policy that is dispassionate and unemotional, the presence of which belies the simple sensationalism argument. The lurid details of the gangland slaying or the shot of fire fighters dousing flames in the perennial five-alarm fire may be viewed as appealing to the audience's taste for sensation, but the other drier accounts of the election campaign for a suburban commissioner or the proposal of a new sewage disposal system do not. While the local media clearly must be concerned with audiences and advertisers, the answer is not necessarily sex and scandal, crime and tragedy—particularly when it comes to coverage of local policy issues.

The Role of Advertisers: Censoring News to Protect Products

While the general public often believe that news is distorted in order to pander to the baser instincts of audiences, another theory holds that the true threat to the free flow of information arises from the media's need to please their advertisers. Benjamin Bagdikian argues that from the nineteenth century to the present, advertisers have effectively muzzled news coverage in order to protect the image of their products.[13] In the nineteenth century, it was editorial validation of the powers of the patent medicines (major newspaper advertisers at the time), which were later shown to be nothing more than sugared water.[14] In the twentieth century, Bagdikian claims that the most shameful case of editorial protection of advertiser products came with news coverage—or lack thereof—of the first links between cigarette smoking and disease as a result of the fact that tobacco companies were major newspaper advertisers.[15]

Bagdikian has also considered the link between local advertisers and local news coverage, arguing that the editorial content of many of the special sections in newspapers, which have historically served largely as vehicles for specialized types of advertisements, has been compromised by the need to please advertisers. As an example he points to the weekly food sections, supported largely by supermarket advertising, which he claims would be unlikely to run an article showing how the cost of coupons raises the price of food.[16] Similarly, he argues that automobile advertising has restrained reviews of new automobile safety standards or evaluations of individual models and views the content of local real estate sections in the recent past as little more than reprinted press releases from local developers singing the praises of their new developments.

Many journalists, however, deny such censorship of news by advertisers. For example, *Philadelphia Inquirer* editor Gene Roberts said his newspaper would not bow to advertiser pressures, adding that "It's been a long time since anyone seriously tried." He told of a case from the early 1970s when one of the news-paper's large advertisers did try to get a story cancelled. "We said we were certainly going to run it. He said, 'I don't think I've made myself clear. If you run that story, I'll cancel $700,000 of advertising.' I said, 'I'm in charge of news, I have nothing to do with advertising. If you want to talk to the person in charge of advertising, I'll see if I can find you his number.' So we ran the story and he cancelled the $700,000 of advertising." [17]

The refusal to give in to advertiser pressures at major metropolitan news-papers like the *Inquirer,* while based on a strong sense of professional ethics, may be grounded in solid economic reasons as well. Newspapers may be willing to alienate an individual advertiser to produce news coverage that impresses their audience enough to ultimately raise circulation. In other words, the short-run loss of a single advertiser may be warranted by the long-run increase in audience size that results from maintaining the quality and credibility of the editorial product.

It may also be that in the current structure of competition among the local news media, there are many cases in which an advertiser needs the local news firm more than the firm needs the advertiser. A woman's magazine might suffer a devastating economic blow if an article on lung cancer and smoking sent all their cigarette advertisers to a competitor. [18] But a metropolitan newspaper is unlikely to lose its cigarette advertising by printing similar articles since the tobacco companies, prohibited from advertising on television, have few alter-natives to reach the regional market. In addition, in large media markets where newspapers have a broad and diversified advertising base, threats by any one individual advertiser may have a limited impact. As one editor noted, "The bigger you are, the easier it is to ward off advertiser pressure." On the other hand, in smaller newspaper markets, individual advertisers may have far greater power to censor editorial content.

The philosophy of the owner is also said to play a role in determining whether advertisers influence editorial content. While many journalists noted that the Knight-Ridder corporation, which owns the *Inquirer* and *Daily News,* was known for respecting the separation of editorial and advertising decisions, other chains do not have the same reputation. In addition, some journalists noted that a local owner who is close to the local advertising community can be more easily swayed than a non-local corporate owner, who can "better isolate from that influence," as one editor put it. In general, while the need to please advertisers might lead to some censorship of local news, particularly in smaller markets, it does not seem to be a major factor in explaining what does and does not become local news.

The Local News Firm's Interest in
Regional Economic Growth

A different theory of how economic interests influence news coverage focuses on the interests of the local news firm in the economic growth of the locality. Since the news firm's profits are dependent on audience size and advertising revenues, the greater the total population of the locality and the healthier the economy, the more potential readers or viewers and advertisers the news firm can hope to attract. Such growth is particularly important to the metropolitan newspaper, which faces great economies of scale within its regional market. While the fixed costs of producing its first copy are high, the costs of producing additional copies are relatively small, in comparison with the advertising revenues generated by additional circulation.[19]

Therefore, as Molotch has noted, the metropolitan newspaper can be viewed as "the most important example of a business which has its interests anchored in the aggregate growth of the locality . . . a paper's financial status (and that of other media to a lesser extent) tends to be wed to the size of the locality)."[20] As a result of this interest in growth, it is argued, the local news media often take on the role of a booster, much like an arm of the local chamber of commerce, actively promoting the kinds of policies and projects that would generate economic growth of the area. According to this theory, publishers or media owners at times muzzle their reporters' critical coverage of certain sacred cow public development projects that may promote growth at the expense of environmental quality or the sacrifice of other socially valuable uses of public funds.

For example, Jones analyzed the *San Jose Mercury*'s editorial and news coverage of a proposed new downtown airport and found that the newspaper had a decided bias in favor of airport construction despite the environmental consequences.[21] He traced the bias to a general motive for regional economic growth as well as the newspaper's particular interest in increasing air travel, which would in turn increase airline advertising. Jones claims that a newspaper like the *Mercury* also has an interest in promoting the kind of regional development that attracts upper-income people to the area—often at the expense of the interests of the poor—because more affluent readers attract greater revenues from national advertisers. He writes,

> It is probably unreasonable to expect a newspaper or broadcast station to remain neutral in this process of expansion, simply reporting objectively the growth of the community. Too much is at stake financially. Often, we can expect media owners to boost their own communities and, in the process, assume the characteristics of the local chamber of commerce members. Once a community reaches the take-off point in its development, and if the local media become involved, can news coverage of such 'progress' remain balanced and objective?[22]

Similar ideas were expressed by Banfield and Wilson, who noted that the newspaper's interest in economic growth "inclines it toward boosterism, and inclines it also, on occasion to 'play down' or even suppress news that would put the city in a bad light." While they note that this boosterism instinct is often in conflict with the newspaper's traditional crusading function, the "conflict is managed by crusading intermittently and by choosing targets circumspectly. In the usual case, a steady low paean of praise to the city is interrupted briefly by cries of alarm when the time comes once more to remind citizens of their civic duties or to go to the aid of the beleaguered tax payer."[23]

In some cases, a local media firm's interest in regional growth has been traced to specific links between the firm—or the conglomerates that, increasingly, control such firms—and other local companies. For instance, in Jacksonville, Florida, Devereux examined the news coverage of a proposed Westinghouse plant that would produce floating nuclear plants. News coverage was particularly important to the future of the plant, since the project required local and state permits and pollution control approvals, in addition to important tax breaks from the state government. Devereux argued that the proposed plant received very favorable coverage in the *Jacksonville Times-Union* because the company that owned the newspaper also owned the local railroads that would transport materials to the new plant. In this case, the newspaper's interest in local growth, when combined with its ties to a company that would benefit from the project, was said to lead to biased coverage.[24]

The Downtown Bias

Many of the proponents of the local-newspaper-as-booster theory contend that the newspaper is indifferent as to the kind of growth that takes place in the region. For example, Molotch states,

> The local newspaper tends to occupy a rather unique position; like many other local businesses, it has an interest in growth, but unlike most, the critical interest is not in the specific geographical pattern of that growth. That is, the crucial matter to a newspaper is not whether the additional population comes to reside on the north side or south side, or whether the money is made through a new convention center or a new olive factory. The newspaper has no axe to grind, except the one which holds the community elite together: growth.[25]

In contrast, others have claimed that the metropolitan newspaper does indeed have an interest in a particular pattern of economic growth: the dominance of the central city over the suburbs. In the past, this argument was based on the metropolitan newspaper's advertising revenues being directly dependent on the strength of the downtown business district and, in particular, the downtown department stores. For example, Banfield and Wilson wrote in 1963, "The metropolitan daily's orientation to the city—and above all, to its central business district—is to be explained, perhaps, by the fact that three-fourths of its advertising come from local sources, especially department stores."[26]

In addition, the circulation of many newspapers was once tied to the level of downtown commuting, since many papers were sold on the newsstand in central cities and their sales depended on their readers' use of public transit systems, which were usually focused on the downtown. Therefore, it has been argued, local news coverage has been biased in favor of support for policies and projects that strengthen the downtown. For example, Banfield showed how the *Chicago Tribune* actively supported a new downtown convention center. When an editor of the *Tribune* was asked why the newspaper crusaded so insistently for the center, he answered, in part,

> Why did we put so much time into this? Because it's good for the city. But partly from selfish motives too. We want to build a bigger Chicago and a bigger *Tribune*. We want more circulation and more advertising. We want to keep growing, and we want the city to keep growing so that we can keep growing.[27]

Similarly, Banfield showed how all four of Chicago's politically diverse newspapers were in favor of subsidizing improvements in the Chicago Transit Authority in 1956. Banfield claims they all supported the measure because it would encourage travel into the central business district and patronage of the downtown retail outlets, which were the papers' major advertisers. "Their interest was like that of the other big businesses in the central district; it coincided especially with that of the department stores, upon whose advertising they principally depended. The *Sun-Times'* tie to the group was particularly close; its editor and publisher was Marshall Field, Jr." [28]

Evidence for the metropolitan newspaper's support for the strengthening of downtowns also can be found in accounts of the Urban Renewal program of the 1950s and 1960s and the urban redevelopment programs of the 1970s and 1980s, in which public funding was used to reconstruct central cities. For example, Wolt and Gottlieb describe how the *Los Angeles Times* backed a downtown redevelopment plan that had been criticized as a " 'tax rip-off' to subsidize downtown interests at the expense of the overall region" by saying in an editorial, "Any city—and especially a city as spread out as Los Angeles—is as healthy as the sum of its parts." [29] They also describe a case in which the newspaper's architectural critic was fired because, they claim, he criticized a downtown development project the paper's owners supported. [30]

Similarly, in Newark, the *Newark News* supported slum clearance, with the result, as Kaplan pointed out, that "critics of the Newark Housing Authority [the agency directing Newark's urban renewal program] generally receive[d] short shrift in the editorials in the *News*." [31] In Norfolk, Virginia, Abbott writes that "the editors of the *Pilot* and *Ledger* joined in supporting every step of the [urban renewal] program and proudly analyzed the 'benevolent contagion of redevelopment and its renewal in Tidewater.' "[32] Abbott includes the newspapers when he writes that "renewal advocates wrapped themselves in the flag of civic progress, defining their concern as 'the city as a whole' . . . [they] claimed . . . the real beneficiaries of urban renewal were not merely downtown department stores and newspapers but rather the entire metropolitan population, since the central business district was the one 'neighborhood' that was common to everyone." [33]

For some analysts, this downtown bias has also been tied to the fact that many newspapers have downtown real estate holdings, the value of which would be influenced by public projects. For example, Hartman argued that in San Francisco, the *Chronicle* and the *Examiner* were strongly in favor of the

Yerba Buena development project, the site of which adjoined their own downtown property holdings.

> San Francisco's dailies, like virtually all major newspapers, have numerous threads binding them to the area's corporate, financial, and political leadership. However, in the case of the Yerba Buena Center [a downtown redevelopment project] the *Chronicle's* and the *Examiner's* stakes are more direct. Headquarters for both papers directly adjoin the project area, and in addition the *Examiner* owns two large and valuable lots adjoining the Central Blocks. As large landowners, both newspapers stand to gain financially from the substantial increase in land values the YBC project will trigger in the . . . area."[34]

In more recent times, some urban analysts have noted how metropolitan newspapers, although adopting a regional perspective, are often clearly more oriented to the central city than the suburbs. For instance, Danielson and Doig, in discussing the *New York Times'* coverage of regional development projects note, "the *Times'* regionalism, however, is heavily oriented toward the primacy of New York City and the Manhattan business district. As the city goes, so goes the region . . . From the *Times'* Manhattan vantage point, regionalism often means that the parasitic suburbs must come to the aid of the life-giving city. . ."[35]

The Publisher's Ties to the Local Business Community

A related argument traces downtown boosterism to the publisher's ties to the downtown business structure and his desire to use his newspaper to protect his business interests and those of his associates. The Chandlers in Los Angeles,[36] Joseph Knowland in Oakland,[37] Walter Annenberg in Philadelphia,[38] Colonel McCormick and Marshall Field in Chicago[39] have all been portrayed as powerful figures whose membership in city power elites has led to a particular slant in the news reporting of their newspapers. The image has been of the publisher's conversations with other business leaders at lunch or society balls leading to censorship of what their reporters and editors might otherwise print as local news.

For example, Hebert describes the publisher of the Atlanta newspapers as "a key occupant of the inner sanctum of power in the city" and claims that he reportedly warned that reporters on the two newspapers he owned "steer clear of the power structure's 'big boys.' "[40] Local television station managers are similarly viewed as having extensive ties to the local power structure that may lead to censorship of news coverage. For example, Altheide's case studies revealed a station manager who "regularly lunched and socialized with local officials. His editorials, as well as many of the news stories he generated, reflected his friends' interests."[41] Similarly, when in 1985, Sidney Schanberg was relieved of his column in the *New York Times* after criticizing the *Times'* coverage of the Westway development project in Manhattan, some observers suggested it was on the orders of the publisher who was said to strongly support the project.

The fact that many newspapers and television stations are owned by conglomerates and share interlocking directorates with other companies has led to the charge that censorship also takes place to protect those companies' interests. For example, Bagdikian claims that the *Los Angeles Times* downplayed a story about a state utilities commission ordering Pacific Telephone to make rebates to customers because the newspaper's parent firm, Times-Mirror, printed telephone directories throughout the West.[42] Similarly, he claims the *Baltimore Sun* killed a story about labor negotiations at Johns Hopkins Hospital because a director of the newspaper was also a director of the hospital.[43]

Whether such censorship actually took place is open to question, since editors at some of the newspapers have disagreed with Bagdikian's claims and argue that his evidence for such charges is lacking. Some journalists claim that while such censorship is frequent in small cities, there is relatively little direct interference by publishers of newspapers and owners of television stations in the larger media markets. Others note, however, that even in those larger markets, there may be a subtle reading of the publisher's (or corporate owner's) preferences. As one reporter admitted, "Any reporter wants to please his editor who wants to please the publisher," suggesting that reporters tend to internalize the preferences of their bosses without any explicit orders needing to be given.

The Local Media as Booster?

In summary, many critics have argued that local news coverage is biased by the economic self-interest of the local media firm in the growth of the region and particularly in the prosperity of the central city and its downtown area. In addition, some claim that these interests extend to the editorial protection of other local businesses to which the publisher or corporate owner may have economic or social ties. For a variety of reasons, then, the local media are often said to serve as shameless boosters for growth-oriented projects and for central-city development.

This portrayal of the local media as booster is not without some validity and the claim that local news organizations exhibit a city or downtown bias is often warranted. The boosterism argument has its weaknesses, however, particularly when it comes to explaining the steady stream of negative stories that appear in newspapers and on television, often concerning the ills of the central city. These stories of crime, racial disturbances, and governmental corruption, which often get picked up by the national media, are hardly the kind of public relations fodder that one expects of boosters, as is confirmed by the frequent outcries from city fathers trying to attract economic activity. For example, in 1984, Mayor Coleman Young attacked the Detroit news media for "overplaying" bad news about the city, citing in particular a *Detroit Free Press* front-page story headlined, "Detroit murder rate led the nation in '83."[44] If the local news media's news decisions were governed largely by an interest in local growth and maintaining the dominance of the city over suburbs, why would such damaging coverage have been undertaken?

Moreover, the rationales that are used to explain the boosterism and the downtown or city bias that does occur in the media are also flawed. While an interest in protecting downtown advertisers and landholdings may have once been responsible for metropolitan newspapers' central-city focus, it cannot explain the kind of coverage that has continued into the 1980s, when many of the major retail advertisers of newspapers are suburban chains and newspapers' property values represent a small element in their profit considerations. Indeed, some newspapers, like the *Houston Post*, have relocated from the downtown to outlying areas, and more and more newspapers, like the *Baltimore Sun*, have planned to build printing plants in outlying suburbs.

The image of the idiosyncratic local publisher as a long-time member of the old-city power elite has become outdated as local ownership of metropolitan newspapers has become a thing of the past. With the increasing ownership by chains and conglomerates, the publisher is now an organizational figure who must be more concerned with the bottom line, as produced by readership and advertising, than with not offending business associates. While publishers are generally integrated into local business associations, their primary concern must be with meeting the economic objectives of the parent corporation, not with furthering their own friendships and social ties. As the managing editor of the *Baltimore Sun* said, "The most valuable asset a paper has is its credibility. If people think we don't cover stories because they involve us, people will start wondering what else we don't cover."[45]

The contradictions in all of these theories suggest that if the local news is influenced by economic interests, then those interests are not quite as simple as they have been made out to be. While the local media must be concerned with the size of audiences and the economic interests of advertisers, sex and scandal and a progrowth form of local boosterism are not the answer. Rather, the primary concern of any local news medium—whether metropolitan newspaper, local television station, or city magazine—must be to win the allegiance of the local audience that is the target of its advertisers. The local news firm must match its messages to its particular local market, and, even more important, it must draw that market of dispersed and diverse readers together into a common local identity. It is not enough to produce sensational news; what is required is to produce news with the kind of sensation—or interest or entertainment—that carries with it the symbolic value capable of binding together the local audience.

The Economic Challenge of the 1990s: Attracting the Suburban Audience

The last chapter pointed up the importance of the suburban audience to the local news media, both because the great mass of the metropolitan population has come to reside in suburban and exurban areas and also because the most affluent people are to be found outside of central cities. Advertisers, whether national or local, have become increasingly attracted to those local media that can deliver some or all of the suburban market. As a result, the economic imperative confronting the local news media in the last decades of the twentieth century has been to capture suburban audiences in order to attract advertising. But how have the local news media, and particularly metropolitan newspapers, confronted the difficult question of how to cover the suburbanized metropolis in order to attract the suburban audience?

Throughout the 1950s and 1960s, despite the exodus of people and jobs from central cities, metropolitan newspapers continued to focus local news coverage almost exclusively on the activities of city governments and city institutions. By the 1970s, however, it became painfully obvious to the top management at many newspapers that suburban penetration levels were dropping and that changes were necessary to win back the suburban reader. While the need for greater coverage of the suburbs was clear, this was no simple task since each region was composed of a multitude of political jurisdictions, each with its own form of government, school district, and local zoning disputes. The solution many newspapers found to deal with the political fragmentation was to fragment the newspaper itself—a process that has become known as "zoning."

Zoning has involved changing the editorial and/or advertising content of local news sections—or adding entirely new news supplements as inserts—for different parts of the local market. In some cases, newspapers "zone" their local news sections, putting in different local news articles for different sections of the region. In other cases, they have added entirely new supplements as inserts that go to different geographic areas. In still other cases, only advertising content has changed between sections. Some newspapers zone segments once or twice a week, while others, like the *Chicago Tribune,* the *Hartford Courant,* the *Los Angeles Times,* and the *Atlanta Constitution,* have aggressively begun to zone local news every day.

The advantages of this kind of zoning of editorial and advertising content are twofold: first, they enable the newspaper to provide more localized coverage of the kinds of events and issues that hold only limited interest to the entire regional audience; second, zoning enables the metropolitan newspaper to offer smaller suburban advertisers lower advertising rates for space in a section of the newspaper that reaches only a subsection of the entire regional market. But zoning is not without its costs, both in terms of hiring new reporters to cover suburban events and printing and distributing separate sections of the newspaper that go to only certain subsections of the region. Such costs have placed constraints on the amount of zoning that can be done and, in particular, often limit the number of zones that can be created. Since it has been impossible to produce a separate news supplement for each small suburban jurisdiction, newspapers have been forced to make tough decisions about how to carve up and aggregate sections of their markets and how to decide which areas will receive zoned coverage.

The typical newspaper's incentive is to create zones only in those suburban areas which are the most desirable to advertisers, most often areas surrounding suburban malls and characterized by concentrated disposable income. Therefore, many metropolitan newspapers like the *Chicago Tribune,* the pioneer of zoners, created new local news supplements not for each subsection of their markets, but only for the more affluent suburban areas. In these areas, the "Suburban Tribs" as they were called, provided a level of detailed local news coverage that less-affluent areas—including city neighborhoods—did not receive.[46]

Metropolitan newspapers have tended not to produce editorial supplements in suburban areas where there is not enough local advertising to support the cost of producing the supplement, in part to prevent them from being accused of violating antitrust legislation by using their vast resources to crush suburban competition. This need for most local news supplements to be self-supporting in terms of local advertising revenues has reinforced the tendency for metropolitan newspapers to produce detailed local news coverage for only those geographic areas that are of interest to advertisers. With very little fanfare—zoned supplements for obvious reasons are promoted only within the zones—many metropolitan newspapers began to produce better-quality news for only those readers most desirable to advertisers.

Newspapers have also been quite selective in the way they have drawn their zones, seeking a socioeconomic homogeneity that facilitates the job of supplying news for these areas and selling circulation to advertisers. The *Chicago Tribune*'s zones, for example, were originally drawn to separate blue-collar and upper-middle-class households for just such reasons.[47] Although newspapers like the *Tribune* have not changed the slant of individual news stories or the content of editorials across their zones, they have taken advantage of homogeneous zones to provide stories that match the tastes of their audiences. Instead of trying to achieve a common consciousness on the part of their readers as newspapers in the late nineteenth century did, these zoned sections have actively set out to appeal to differentiated values and interests.

Despite the resources that have been devoted to zoning, the process has not turned out to be the solution it was hoped to be. While aggressive zoning has helped many newspapers maintain respectable suburban penetrations, the supplements of other metropolitan newspapers cannot compete in suburban areas where there is already a successful daily or even weekly newspaper that had earlier secured suburban loyalties. For example, the zoned supplements of newspapers like the *Chicago Tribune* have been viewed as most successful in areas like affluent Du Page County, where the paper filled a vacuum because no significant daily local paper had come into existence. But in other counties, the suburban Tribs were said to have a harder time competing with entrenched suburban weeklies that catered to small jurisdictions within the county. In some markets, metropolitan newspapers have started zoned supplements specifically in areas of their markets where a small daily or weekly might be poised to grow into a stronger threat; however, in many metropolitan newspaper markets, editors have begun to admit that "we are never going to be their local newspaper."

In addition, over time, many editors have realized that zoning carries with it the danger of detracting from the metropolitan newspaper's image by making it seem provincial. For example, the *Detroit News,* also one of the early experimenters with zoning, found itself going "to ridiculous extremes" according to one of its editors. "On the front page one day we'd have a combination of stories like 'Russia invades China' and 'Masonic Dinner held in Franklin.'" After an initial enthusiasm with extensive zoning, the *News* therefore pulled back to a more conservative strategy, admitting that they were "terrible at the Chicken Dinner business."[48]

Less fortunate than the *Detroit News,* which survived its mistakes, was the *Philadelphia Bulletin,* which began zoning in the late 1970s in an attempt to halt the erosion of its suburban circulation. In the suburban communities of southern New Jersey, across the Delaware River from Philadelphia, it went so far as to change the name of the newspaper to the *New Jersey Bulletin.* In explaining that kind of major image shift, the editor at the time was quoted as saying: "Most of our readers today live in areas which dissociate themselves from Philadelphia so that Philadelphia connotation becomes a liability." By changing its name, the *Bulletin* hoped to avoid that association and prevent the suburbs from "becoming 'hooked' on locally spawned newspapers conveying a greater sense of local identity."[49]

And yet, when the *Bulletin* died in 1982, many claimed it was in part because it undertook this kind of misguided zoning, which detracted from its image as a metropolitan newspaper. For example, the *Jersey Bulletin* reported Philadelphia Mayor Frank Rizzo's reelection in 1976 as an "area news brief" on an inside page, ignoring the obvious interest of the story to the regional audience. The *Bulletin* failed to recognize how this kind of zoning would encourage the tendency of outlying readers to further dissociate themselves from the city and reduce their reasons for reading a metropolitan newspaper.

In those markets where zoning is being undertaken for the first time, with a whole range of different supplements for different geographic areas and with new suburban reporters and editors having been hired and given new resources, there is often an admission that suburban reporting is something apart from the primary mission of the newspaper—a "marketing concept," as one editor put it, rather than a real attempt to provide comprehensive suburban news. As one

Detroit editor commented, "I doubt seriously whether any of our suburban readers are reading us because of our zoned supplements. If we dropped the zones tomorrow, I doubt anyone would notice."

Metropolitan newspapers, therefore, have had to look beyond zoning in their attempts to attract the suburban reader and have had to make other changes that circumvent the dilemma of how to cover the politically fragmented metropolis. On one front, they have begun to give greater prominence to international, national, and even state news, since all suburbanites have these units of government in common and, it is hoped, will turn to their metropolitan newspaper for news that is less provincial than what they get from their suburban newspaper. Metropolitan newspapers have also expanded coverage of lifestyle and arts and entertainment in magazine-type sections that hold particular appeal to upper-income readers regardless of where in the region they reside. Like the *New York Times*' daily sections on Sports, Science, Food, Home, and Weekend Entertainment, these sections draw on the kind of interests that most affluent suburbanites have in common.

Nonetheless, all of these strategies—zoning, expanding international and national news coverage, adding nongeographic lifestyle features—have not solved the fundamental problem of the metropolitan newspaper: how to provide the suburbanite with a compelling reason to read it. As increasing numbers of media outlets, both at the national and local level, compete to provide information for the suburbanite's limited leisure time and attention, the metropolitan newspaper is faced with the threat of becoming superfluous. The typical suburban dweller could easily get his national news from network television and *Time* magazine, his local news from the suburban newspaper, his lifestyle information from specialized magazines and feel no strong need to purchase a metropolitan newspaper originating from the nearby city. This threat is particularly strong in the outer rings of metropolitan areas where residents have the least ties to the central city, many of whom come from other metropolitan areas of the country.

The challenge facing metropolitan newspapers, therefore, is how to convince suburban readers that metropolitan newspapers can offer them information they need and want and that neither the national or highly localized media can offer. But even more important, metropolitan newspapers need to convince suburban residents that they all share common news interests only the metropolitan newspaper can report. In effect, a newspaper like the *New York Daily News* is competing with *Long Island Newsday* and the *White Plains Reporter Dispatch*—as much as with NBC Nightly News—not to win the suburbanites' interest but, more significantly, to capture their sense of identity. In order to keep their suburban readers, the *News* has to keep them feeling like "New Yorkers" rather than simply Americans or residents of quiet communities in Nassau and Westchester Counties.

Just as in the nineteenth century, newspapers needed to overcome ethnic and cultural fragmentation to capture citywide audiences, so have the metropolitan newspapers of the late twentieth century had to overcome the fragmentation of parochial suburban loyalties in order to maintain a regionwide audience. They have had to come up with a set of institutions, problems, controversies, and issues relevant to the entire market. But even more important, they have had to create a regionwide sense of identity that draws their audience together in a psychological if not a real form of interdependence.

The City as Symbolic Bond for the Suburbanized Audience

The task of finding local news of interest to all suburbanites, much less creating a new sense of regional identity, has not been a simple one. While nineteenth-century newspapers turned most conveniently to the city and to city government, the metropolitan news media of the twentieth century have had no such parallel institutions. Metropolitanwide government, had it formed, would have established an easily accessible source of local news events—meetings, decisions, proposals, controversies, governmental improprieties, all the stuff of traditional news coverage—and would have projected an image of something that all residents of the newspaper's market had in common. But suburbanites have actively opposed such regional governments, fearing the loss of their independence from the taxing and zoning powers of city governments. Even with the metropolitan newspaper's considerable power of influence, it could not hope to override the very real entrenched interests that fought against regional government.

In the absence of regional government, metropolitan newspapers and other regionwide news media have turned to those institutions or resources inherently regional in nature, as well as to those institutions that carry with them a regionwide symbolic character. The increasing prominence of front-page stories about football teams threatening to relocate, or major regional employers announcing job cutbacks, or even an impending hurricane can be explained by the need to find news capable of cutting across suburban jurisdictions and claiming the interest of the entire market. Similarly, metropolitan newspapers have assigned new beats covering such regional institutions as colleges and universities, hospitals, art museums and orchestras, which receive prominent local news coverage.

In some areas of the country, the news media have turned elsewhere to mold a sense of a unique regional character. The *Seattle Times,* for example, set out to create a sense of awareness in its readers of being part of the "Pacific Northwest" and focused much of their news coverage and investigative reporting on the natural resources of the region that were of passionate interest to the area's more affluent residents. As one editor explained it, "The rationale is that people are less located in place than they used to be . . . they are less Issaquah-oriented than Northwest-oriented. They don't care about every nickel-and-dime story in Podunk, so much as they're interested in how the logging industry is affecting the forests they hike in."

At times, the need to attract a regional audience leads to the importance of certain regional institutions getting blown out of proportion. The Metropolitan Transit Agency in Houston, for example, was covered extensively in the two major metropolitan newspapers, despite the fact that only about four percent of the region use public transit for work. Although the vast majority of people in Houston commute by automobile, there are only a limited number of stories that can be written about traffic jams. A metropolitan agency, in contrast, can be covered day in and day out, even though its activities may not have much actual bearing on the majority of the audience.

Although metropolitan transit agencies, regional natural resources, sports teams and weather emergencies have all proved useful for interesting the suburban audience, none has been capable of serving as the major source of local news coverage and symbolic regional identity. Rather, the most important continuous source of local news and regional identity for the suburbanized metropolis has turned out to be, ironically, the central city. Despite the fact that the majority of the audiences do not live or work in the city or vote in city elections or send their children to city schools, it is news of the city government and city institutions that takes premiere position over policy issues facing suburban communities.

For example, on one Sunday in January,[50] the *Los Angeles Time*'s two front-page local stories focused on a new downtown development plan and political maneuvering in the city's police department, the *Boston Globe* focused on the murder of a pregnant suburban woman in downtown Boston, the *New York Times*' local story covered victims of random violence in city neighborhoods, and the *Philadelphia Inquirer* considered the city's expenditure of funds from Benjamin Franklin's will and analyzed racial concerns in the city's Democratic party. While in other cities, local coverage focused on regional issues—the aftermath of the earthquake in San Francisco, the Browns' chances in the upcoming football championship game in Cleveland, a new oil recovery technique in Houston—coverage of suburban issues was noticeably lacking.

When questioned about why their newspapers continue to give such prominence to news of the city when most of their audience are suburban residents, editors and reporters give a variety of answers. The editor of the *Seattle Times* responded, "We have to cover [the suburbanites] some way . . . so we cover what is in their cultural hub."[51] In cities like Detroit, where almost three-fourths of the population live outside the city, the editor of the *Detroit News* was quite frank in explaining why they continue to cover Detroit. "Tradition," he said, "ease," and a sense that the suburban readership would far sooner read about controversial Mayor Coleman Young than about any lesser-known and less flamboyant suburban commissioner.[52] Similarly, the editor of the *Philadelphia Inquirer* commented, "We probably cover the city more reliably than the suburbs because it's easy. There are less bases you have to touch," referring particularly to the highly fragmented nature of suburban local governments in the Philadelphia region.[53]

However, many of the reporters and editors interviewed explained the continued focus on coverage of the city in the suburbanized metropolis by citing the importance of the city to suburban readers. They argued that the city continues to control the fates of the metropolis and that the suburbs could not survive without the city, statements which fly in the face of growing evidence that the city no longer plays a dominant role in most regions and that, increasingly, centers of population, employment, and retail activity are developing with relatively few interactions with nearby central cities.[54]

The continued focus on the central city and on the city's perspective on many regional issues can be explained by the city's overriding symbolic value and the role it plays in helping to create a unified regional identity. The city is covered so prominently not to protect advertisers or landholdings or to please publishers, as earlier theories have argued, and not because it holds much actual relevance to the lives of suburbanites, as many reporters would claim. Rather, the continued focus on the city has been maintained because the city is the only source of symbolism capable of drawing together the fragmented suburban market. However ironic, the city that many suburbanites rarely venture into is often the only thing they all have in common.

That downtown-oriented regionalism serves to create suburban unity explains why so much that is written and broadcast about the city is negative. Stories about corruption in city government, murders and rapes on city streets, and potential bankruptcy in city coffers cannot be viewed as examples of local boosterism. Nor can they be said to have much direct impact on the suburban reader, as many journalists would argue. Rather, such stories continue to dominate the front page because they strike a common chord in the suburban audience: a sense of relief in being safely tucked away in communities that are protected from such evils. As one newspaper editor in Detroit wryly noted to explain continued emphasis on the city: "Our readers like to sit out there in Grosse Pointe and read about all the terrible things happening in the city that they've managed to escape."

But, increasingly, newspapers are struggling with the question of how much negative news about the city to carry without driving their audiences away. While hoping to point out the fact that the city's problems are society's problems and that urban ills like drug abuse and homelessness may spread to the suburbs, there is an increasing sense that such "downbeat" stories are less than appealing to the target audience. Of concern are attitudes like those expressed in a survey carried out for the American Society of Newspaper Editors in 1985, which found that 65 percent of respondents felt that the news media in general emphasize bad news too much.[55]

If city news coverage were limited to such "bad news," to tales of crime and corruption, teenage mothers, and multiple murders, it would no doubt drive away many suburban readers. But, in fact, stories of urban pathology have come to be balanced with another more positive theme about the city that is capable of creating a strong symbolic bond among the whole suburban market: the redevelopment of the city. It is the stories of the rebirth of a glamorous, culturally vibrant, and historically rich central city and the redevelopment of the city as the economic center of the region and the new service-sector economy that have come to provide the true common bond for the disparate suburban population.

At the center of this positive city news are those downtown development projects that are aimed at changing the urban landscape. While suburban economic development in industrial parks and greenbelted office campuses continues to flourish with relatively little news coverage, it is the new waterfront condominiums, or the remodeled train-station-turned-mall, or the erection of the city's tallest skyscraper that attracts major local news coverage. These projects are given a place of prominence in the local news media not because of their importance to the regional audience, but because of their symbolic capital. They represent some of the limited number of upbeat stories that are capable of creating a symbolic focus on the city and of reinforcing the sense that the suburbs are tied to the city for their economic survival. Other development projects that are not downtown-oriented—a proposal for a new regional airport or sports stadium, for example—receive similar treatment because they also hold the capacity to psychologically bind the regionwide audience.

Because such large, glamorous projects carry with them important symbolic value—be it renewing historic sites or helping the region to improve its image and better compete with other areas—and because they carry with them the potential for political intrigue, their coverage is often magnified in such a way as to exaggerate their importance to the region as a whole. Such exaggeration may have an effect quite unintended by those journalists who unwittingly practice it: encouraging the approval of proposals with more symbolic than economic and social value. At other times, the need for stories with regional symbolism may lead the local news media to distort the criticisms of a proposed project, since a critical stance can be just as powerful a symbolic glue as a praiseworthy plan in pulling the regional audience together.

The need to find local news coverage with symbolic interest to the entire regional audience is not limited to the metropolitan newspaper. A similar economic imperative faces the other local news media as well. Local television and radio and city magazines all need to find local news that can interest the fragmented suburban audience and create a unified local identity. Television news has enjoyed some immunity, however, since their advertisers tend to be national manufacturers who care more about volume of customers than demographics. Therefore, the competition in local television news has always been more for total ratings and audience share than for a certain demographic group.

Television news has also remained relatively unscathed by suburbanization because two of its key features—sports and weather—are inherently regional in nature. In addition, many people watch television news not so much to find out what is happening in their locality as to enjoy the company of the local news anchors, who become local friends no matter what they are talking about.[56] In effect, local television news reporters and anchors are part of a small coterie of people who become known by the region as a whole and who find themselves, not surprisingly, the subject of gossip columns and profiles in the other local media.

But despite these built-in protectors, local television news has also been faced with the question of how to cover local news and how much emphasis to give to suburban coverage. In response, many television stations use suburban locales for their news stories—covering the traffic jams on suburban roads, the disputes over development and environmental threats, even covering snow-storms from suburban locales. But in one important way they have continued to follow the newspapers' lead in their news coverage: just as is the case with the metropolitan newspapers, they continue to give their most prominent and con-tinuous coverage to city government and to the activities of the city's mayor. And as with the newspapers, it is not because they are eager to court their city viewers but rather because city government and the city's most visible person-alities provide local television news with the kind of unified local identity they too need in maintaining their audience.

The local all-news radio stations are in a similar position. Since their most lucrative advertising periods are during morning and evening "drive-time," their listeners tend to be automobile commuters who are more likely to live in the suburbs than in the city. These radio stations, however, tend to make the same decision as to how to cover the news of the local area as do the newspapers and television: to give as much play as possible to regional topics—the transporta-tion network is a key one for radio—to sprinkle the news with suburban high-lights, but primarily to focus on the news of the central city, the news that all of their listeners can be expected to find interesting.

City magazines have been little different. These local news outlets often have the highest demographics of all the local media, and therefore their readers tend to be particularly concentrated in the suburbs. Yet the traditional focus of the "city" magazine, as their name implies, has been the city itself and that focus has not changed very much in the past two decades. While they have added new features, such as fast growth in the suburban industrial park or wife-beating in the suburbs, and while their restaurant reviews now include suburban as well as city reviews, their major political reporting continues to focus on city rather than suburban government. And they too, like the other local news outlets, are just as dependent on capturing and creating a sense of "localness" in order to maintain a uniquely local personality and remain distinct from national maga-zines.

In summary, then, the fundamental economic imperative facing all local news media of metropolitan areas in the 1990s is to select and present local news capable of attracting a regionwide audience and drawing that audience together in a unified regional identity. In searching for a consistent source of local news and local identity, the media have continued to focus on the affairs of the central city in such a way as to effectively exaggerate its importance to the region as a whole. In addition, an emphasis on the symbolic importance of regional projects rather than on the economic costs and benefits often leads to a distortion of local policy needs. The next chapter shows how the professional and personal values of individual reporters play into this economic imperative and further influence local news coverage.

3 Professional Values of the Local Journalist

The commercial pressures confronting the local news firm, particularly the metropolitan newspaper, set the agenda for the business of gathering news about city and region. There is a clear need to select and present news capable of interesting a diverse and dispersed suburban audience, so as to maintain a strong advertising base. This economic imperative encourages the creation of the city as a symbol of regional identity and at times may lead to the exaggeration of the importance of central-city policy needs and other regional development projects. In addition, the examination of the economic costs and benefits of proposed policies and projects may get shunted aside in favor of heralding the more symbolic effects of new initiatives.

But anyone familiar with the bustling activity of the modern newsroom or the fierce independence of individual journalists would doubt that the creation of symbols or the distortion of the costs and benefits of public plans comes about through any direct order from top management. Rather, the decisions of individual reporters play a key role in the selection and presentation of stories. This chapter sets forth an explanation of how local news comes to look the way it does through a combination of the constraints and incentives set by newspaper management and the internalized professional and personal values of local reporters. Both the newsroom hierarchy within which local reporters work and the professional and personal values which guide reporting influence the selection and presentation of local news.

The Newspaper Hierarchy and the Routinized Search for News

In most large, complex organizations, the major tasks of the organization are carried out through a combination of centralized policy-setting and relatively independent staff activities. Top management delegates decision making to staff members on different levels of the organization, each with their own set of tasks and objectives. At the highest level of a business organization, the objective is profit making, which management pursues by making policy decisions and resource allocations that constrain the activities of subordinates. Within those constraints, however, lower-level staff are free to carry out their

71

day-to-day tasks with relative independence, using their own standard operating procedures and professional objectives to guide their work. The higher-level constraints ensure that the goal of the organization is met, while the freedom of the lower levels allows for division of labor and efficiency of performance.[1]

In the metropolitan newspaper's hierarchy, the publisher and executive editors have profit making as their chief objective and make budgetary decisions and guide the overall direction of the newspaper so as to meet that objective. In an earlier era of family-run local newspapers publishers may have used their properties to help friends and hurt personal enemies, but in the 1990s most American newspapers are owned by groups and large conglomerates.[2] Publishers and top editors who are accountable to corporate directors must now be more concerned with the bottom line in their news decisions than with any personal vendettas. And that bottom line, as the last chapter showed, is increasingly tied to the ability to compete with small outlying newspapers for the suburban audience.

The need to attract and maintain the suburban audience has led to many changes in the metropolitan newspaper brought about through major policy decisions and budgetary reallocations set by top management. The decision to create new lifestyle sections or upscale features, to begin zoned editions or opt for new graphic design packages, to hire new sports writers or cut down on the city hall staff have all been made at the highest level of the newsroom hierarchy with an eye toward attracting the suburban audience and maintaining a strong advertising base. Similarly, while top editors rarely get involved in day-to-day news decisions, they do establish guidelines for their staff concerning what kinds of stories should appear on page one and what kinds of long-term investigative or analytical projects should be pursued, again, keeping in mind their important target audience.

These higher-level decisions create an environment of incentives and constraints within which individual reporters carry out their jobs. A large budget for a newly created section of the newspaper may prove attractive to reporters and editors working on other sections of the newspaper, thereby altering their focus of reporting interest. Similarly, a recognition of what kinds of stories get played on the front page or accepted as the topics of series and projects will tend to guide reporters in their selection of story ideas and their approach to the presentation of those stories. While reporters rarely cite the economic interests of the newspaper as their objective in finding and writing stories, they do acknowledge the need to please editors and the desire to get prominent play for their stories as a strong motivating factor. As one reporter said in an interview,

> I don't give one hoot about the economics of a story. Reporters could not care less about selling newspapers. Sure, we have professional pride—we want to write the most important story of the day, and have it given the greatest prominence, but we never think about whether it will sell newspapers. We want our paper to sell so that we get our paychecks every week, but it doesn't affect our thinking about stories. We get satisfaction when our stories are played well.

Within these incentives and constraints set from above, individual reporters enjoy a high degree of autonomy and operate according to their own professional standards and values concerning what makes a good story and what angle to take in covering that story. Like all professionals, journalists have a set of routinized "Standard Operating Procedures" that guide them in their day-to-day tasks. That is, they do not begin each day wondering where to look for news and how to define news. Rather, in the process of becoming a reporter, they learn to internalize certain professional values that guide them in their search for news and in the way they package what they find. These standard operating procedures both assure that the journalist will be able to fill the newshole each day and that he or she will fill it efficiently.

A number of sociologists have analyzed the work routines of professional journalists and how they function to meet organizational needs. Tuchman and others have argued that news is not the result of the personal idiosyncrasies of individual reporters or any rules of conduct written in stone, but rather "the product of specific ways of organizing newswork."[3] In particular, she has shown how the organization of newswork determines what events become defined as news or what is caught in the "news net" and how the trustworthiness of source information is established. Professional values and the practices of journalists are viewed as creating "frames" for occurrences that "both produce and limit meaning."[4]

Gans's study of network news and the national news magazines further examined the routinized selection and presentation of news and developed two major criteria that influence national journalists: "availability" and "suitability" considerations.[5] Deadline pressure and limited time available to gather news each day force journalists to limit their search for news to reliable and easily

73

accessible sources. Government press conferences and news releases, along with police checks and trial proceedings, provide a steady stream of daily stories and therefore become the chief sources of the news. Moreover, such stories are not only easy to find, but are also "suitable" in the sense of appealing to audiences. While news of the President's daily schedule or a mountain forest fire may not be the most important phenomena in the country, they are the easiest stories with audience appeal to find each day.

Gans's study also showed how government officials could manipulate news coverage by providing reporters with "suitable information," that is, information that could be easily transformed into news stories with audience appeal. For example, "media events" that provide "photo opportunities" make a reporter's job simpler and therefore are likely to be reported from a perspective favorable to the officials who orchestrate them. Because reporters are more likely to accept information from sources they consider trustworthy and authoritative, they tend to become overreliant on these official sources of information.[6]

The need for standard operating procedures functions at the local level as well and, along with the constraints and incentives set by top newspaper management, influences the way local journalists will approach coverage of the city and region. When combined with other professional and personal values about the city, they lead the local journalist to a particular definition of "local news" and to a distinct angle in the coverage of that news.

Local Journalists and the "City Myopia"

On August 20, 1987, the *Philadelphia Inquirer* ran a story on its front page headlined, "For city, the stakes in keeping Cigna are high." The article began,

> Philadelphia is in one of its most important economic development fights of the 1980's, one that could have a significant financial effect on the city's budget and on its vision of itself.
>
> In trying to keep Cigna Corp. from moving up to 4,400 workers out of Center City to the suburbs, the city aims to hold on to $7 million a year in wage taxes, a tenant for more than one million square feet of offices in a market hungry for tenants, and its upbeat image as a location for financial-services firms.[7]

The approach taken to the story of Cigna's impending move is interesting because it is written exclusively from the perspective of the city of Philadelphia. Alternatively, the move could have been considered from the corporation's perspective, as a change that would improve the company's profitability, employment potential, and service to customers. Still another approach might have considered the move as a boon to suburban communities, with the focus of the article on how the move would help suburban tax bases and employment and how it reflected the general momentum of development in the suburbs. But instead, the article and those that followed in subsequent days focused on the impacts of the move for the city—on its tax base, employment problems, and even on its "vision of itself." The actors quoted in the stories, in addition to the executives of the Cigna Corp., included the city's director of commerce, the city's mayor, and city business executives.

In the last chapter, we saw how such an exaggerated focus on the importance of the city may actually work to attract the suburban audience, since it creates a unifying symbol of local identity. It is unlikely, however, that the reporter who wrote this particular story had any such abstract motivation in mind. Nor is it to be expected that any centralized command came from publisher or editor to the reporter to adopt the city's perspective. Rather, articles such as the one described above are written from the city's perspective because of the individual reporter's own internalized professional values. In particular, the typical local journalist may be viewed as suffering from a kind of "city myopia," a distorted view of the local environment in which the central city continues to occupy the most important political, economic, and social position in the region.

This city myopia stems from a number of factors, some professional, some personal. From a professional perspective, the emphasis on city news and the adoption of a city-based perspective on regional events reflects the journalist's routinized search for news. The need for easily accessible information and the tendency to rely on official government sources who produce "suitable information" leads reporters to develop regular sources predominantly in city government. In contrast to the small-scale, decentralized suburban jurisdictions, large city government offices are better suited to producing the kind of press releases and media events that reporters track for their daily news coverage. In addition, many metropolitan journalists develop ongoing relationships with city government officials and tend to gain many of their ideas for stories from informal, regular conversations with them.

There is also a certain efficiency in the use of city government officials for news sources, since city offices produce information about a much larger number of people than do suburban government offices. To find out the latest test scores on city school children, a reporter need only go to the press office of the

75

city Board of Education. But to find out how suburban school children are being educated, reporters would be forced to go to hundreds of school district offices throughout the region. Similarly, to report on suburban economic development, the reporter would have to seek out scores of individual developers or county planners, while most city governments have large-scale economic development offices whose directors keep abreast of developments throughout the city and therefore make efficient news sources.

Geographical proximity also plays a role in the local journalist's search for news. The majority of metropolitan newspapers still have their main editorial offices in the heart of central city downtowns. City officials are therefore geographically closer to newspaper offices than are suburban government officials, and thus easier to reach for a story. Moreover, reporters on their daily rounds tend to see the city more than they do the suburbs. The construction of a new skyscraper therefore seems to be more newsworthy than the burgeoning industrial and office parks springing up throughout the region. Even the typical "beautiful day photo" will more often be shot in a city park than a suburban locale, simply because the photographer doesn't have to travel as far to get to the former as to the latter. As Sigal has noted, "Social location restricts reporters' sampling of news sources. Reporters are not free-floating atoms in a mass of humanity. They occupy fixed places, geographically and socially, that bound their search for sources of news."[8]

The city produces not only more accessible information, but also more of the traditional kind of news that journalists are used to reporting. City government is more apt to generate the kind of political corruption that leads to easily covered lengthy trials, and deteriorated, poverty-ridden neighborhoods are more often the sites of the crimes and fires that can be uncovered by daily checks with police and fire departments. The ethnic and racial diversity of the city, similarly, produces more protests and other visible forms of conflict than do the smoothly running, socially homogeneous suburban governments. Thus, professional values that place a premium on accessibility and the traditional definition of·news "suitability" play important roles in local journalists' continued focus on the news of the city in the suburbanized metropolis.

But city myopia also reflects the typical journalist's own personal view that the city is more important than the suburbs—and more interesting. While metropolitan life has become progressively more suburbanized, reporters for metropolitan newspapers still tend to discount the phenomenon of suburbanization and to believe quite sincerely that the city dominates the fates of suburbanites.

Despite growing research that suburban life has become increasingly independent from the city, interviews with local news reporters brought forth the same kinds of statements about why they continue to focus on news of the city. "Even if most people live in the suburbs now, they still tend to work in the city, so they care about what's happening with city government," or "What happens in the city affects the entire regional economy," or "Without the city, the suburbs could not survive" were some of the comments that were offered.

The professional and personal reasons for the local journalist's bias of city over suburb sometimes blur, as a personal belief in the supremacy of the central city—and even a decision to live in the city—allows for the rationalization of a professional preference for covering city news. To most metropolitan journalists, real news happens in cities, not suburbs. Coverage of an upcoming mayoral campaign is considered a plum that cannot hold a candle to contests for suburban commissioners. While assignments to the suburbs for the newspaper's zoned editions are accepted, in the past they have tended to be looked upon as a training ground for new reporters—or in some cases, a dumping ground for reporters who have failed at other beats, a kind of journalistic Siberia. In many markets, the coverage of the suburbs is still farmed out to "stringers," rather than to full-time reporters.

The economic interests of the newspaper have necessitated some constraints on the journalist's natural instinct to focus exclusively on the city rather than the suburb. Increasing numbers of reporters have come to be assigned to suburban beats and even general assignment and city-based reporters have been advised to include more suburban angles to their stories and to adopt a more regional perspective in their stories. For example, the city editor of the *Seattle Times* admonished her staff's use of the word "here" when referring to the city of Seattle. "This paper circulates lots of other places [than the city of Seattle]," she wrote in a memo, "and the people who live there probably think they're 'here' too." [9]

But while suburban news coverage is strengthened and regional news issues eagerly sought by top editors, the individual journalist's professional and personal central-city bias is allowed to continue because it works to set the city up as the symbol of regional identity. To the extent that the metropolitan newspaper (along with the other regional news media) are able to convince the suburbanite that he is still tied to the city and to use the colorful or gruesome stories emanating from that city to entertain him, a central-city focus works to the newspaper's economic advantage. Editors continue to give front-page play to stories dealing with the city far more often than those concerning the suburbs and to articles emphasizing the city's perspective in many regional events, and reporters competing to make the front page recognize those values. Therefore, the decision of newspaper management to continue to give greater prominence to city news coverage reinforces the natural city myopia of the individual journalist.

Within this city myopia, much of what is covered by local journalists is the kind of accessible news obtained by the routine search for information from sources in city government as well as the police and the courts. The bulk of news that emerges from these sources might be considered "downbeat" or "bad news": reports of gory city crimes, aching poverty, child abuse, drug and health problems, as well as the negative name-calling that often accompanies news of the conflicts between city government officials, their unions, and organized citizen lobbies. However, alongside these negative stories about urban pathology, there also appear other stories with a far more upbeat tone: stories concerning plans for the city's redevelopment.

The Selling of the City's Development

A similar blending of professional and personal values characterizes the local journalist's coverage of central-city redevelopment efforts. The renewal and redevelopment of American cities began in the postwar years with the passage of the federal Housing Act of 1949. Originally intended to provide low-income housing for the urban poor, the act actually provided funding of the Urban Renewal Program, which in the 1950s and 1960s helped many cities transform their downtowns from declining manufacturing centers to the more modern centers for the emerging service economy. Metropolitan newspapers were often in the vanguard of promoting such urban renewal plans, helping gain support for what could have been the highly controversial use of the power of eminent domain to clear the way for the new skyscrapers and plazas. As Gans noted in his study of the destruction of a neighborhood culture by the redevelopment of Boston's West End, newspapers were among the most enthusiastic supporters of a project they viewed as wiping out "a vice-ridden set of hovels in which respectable human beings could not be expected to live." [10]

Although newspapers did eventually report some of the downsides of the Urban Renewal Program and the citizen opposition to development proposals in the 1970s and 1980s, there has been a continued tendency for the local news media to present announcements for new "visionary" city development projects from their most positive perspective. Plans to construct new convention centers or sports stadiums, proposals to create new in-town malls or marketplaces in historic landmarks like old train stations, or projects proposing new land-use on the city's waterfront all tend to be unveiled by newspapers with great verbal fanfare and to be given far more prominent coverage than the massive private development of the suburbs.

While the last chapter explored the kind of economic interests that lie behind the newspaper's prominent and positive coverage of city redevelopment projects with symbolic value for the suburban audience, the professional and personal values of the individual journalist also play a major role. As with the local journalist's general city myopia, information-accessibility and the eagerness of sources explain in part the positive coverage of city development projects and the greater focus on the city's public redevelopment efforts than on the more widespread private development that has flourished in the suburbs.

Private suburban developers generally have little need for public attention in the metropolitan media for their projects and therefore spend little time scheduling the kind of media events that would help journalists find out about their activities. But city officials seeking many levels of governmental approval for public redevelopment projects are highly dependent on public opinion and therefore spend more time on media relations. The press conference called to announce a new project creates both accessible and suitable information for local journalists to ensure major coverage of the project. As a result, even though suburban development has far outstripped city redevelopment efforts in terms of investment dollars or square miles of land-use change, it is the city revitalization project, not the suburban industrial park, that has gotten major coverage. As Eugene L. Roberts, Jr., editor of the *Philadelphia Inquirer* has been quoted as saying, journalists missed the entire phenomenon of suburbanization in their news coverage—because nobody called a press conference to announce it.[11]

Information-accessibility also plays a role in how proposals for new projects are initially reported. The announcement of the proposal at a formal press conference ensures that the initial coverage of the new proposed project will come solely from the perspective of city officials. Deadline pressures encourage journalists to base their stories almost solely on the information from the press conference or accompanied press release and to accept the city officials' justifications for the need for the project, their estimates of the costs and benefits of the project, and their assessment of the competition by other cities for similar facilities. Rarely do journalists have the time following such a press conference to seek out independent sources of information that might have contradictory estimates of need, costs and benefits, or competitive factors. Instead, initial stories announcing proposals for new projects are often single-source stories.

In addition, local journalists' personal values often contribute to their willingness to believe the promises made by officials and to ignore questions of the relocation of existing residents and businesses or considerations of alternative uses of public funds for other neighborhoods outside of downtown or in the suburbs. As middle-class professionals who often live as well as work in the heart of city downtowns, reporters are often eager to see the city made more glamorous and cosmopolitan. Their own personal sense of pride in working for a newspaper in a particular city leads them to pick up on city officials' claims that one or another economic development project will help their city compete with others and gain recognition as a world-class center. They are also inclined to accept official claims that development projects will "wipe out slums" and tend to assume that people living in poverty will not mind being relocated from their run-down neighborhoods.

Therefore, the personal and professional bias in favor of downtown development projects, when combined with the newspaper's need for effective regional symbols, leads to a tendency for initial coverage of new downtown projects to be positive. As a result, the news coverage that sets the stage for the project's consideration and that provides the initial public perception of the project is marked by a decided central-city—and downtown—bias and is often reported solely on the basis of information supplied by the city officials who have a direct interest in seeing the project approved.

Local Journalists and the Fear of Numbers

Local news coverage of a major new development project often begins with a press conference called by top city officials to announce the new project to local print and broadcast journalists. At such sessions, officials present reporters not simply with qualitative arguments in favor of the project, but with quantitative estimates of its projected costs, along with estimates of the project's benefits, including the number of jobs that will be produced and the level of tax revenues that will be generated.

These estimates of costs and benefits are rarely questioned by journalists, despite the fact that they are dependent on a number of underlying assumptions that are subject to a wide range of interpretation. The cost of a project will vary dramatically according to different assumptions on such factors as the cost of acquiring the land for the project, the costs of relocation benefits that must be paid, or inflation in labor and other construction costs from the time the project is announced until it is finally approved and ground is broken. While city officials always present a dollar figure for the cost of a new project they are proposing, these estimates often prove to be millions of dollars below the actual cost of the project realized years later.

Moreover, the complexity of funding formulas for quasi-public, quasi-private development projects often prevents journalists from making clear exactly how much the local public contribution will be and from what other areas that funding will be pulled. While stories about police salary negotiations may make clear how increased wages or benefits could lead to cutbacks in other city services, development projects funded largely by bond issues are often viewed in news coverage as free goods, with debt service rarely portrayed as an expense that may cut into the city's budget.

In general, the costs of projects tend to be considered somewhat irrelevant in view of the huge benefits city officials always claim are to be derived from the investment in the city's capital needs. These estimates of benefits are also sensitive to underlying assumptions, in particular when determining how much direct and indirect employment and the level of tax revenues that will be generated by a project. An assumption must first be made about how many construction and operating jobs will be directly produced by a project; then a "multiplier" is selected to estimate how many indirect jobs will be created in the city and the region, as the project requires inputs and as the project's workers spend their income on other goods and services.[12]

While the concept of multipliers is essential to estimating the full range of benefits that will accrue from a public investment, the choice of a specific multiplier varies from case to case and strongly influences the results of any impact study. For example, the choice of a multiplier of 3.5—suggesting that for every one direct job created by the project, three and one-half indirect jobs will also be generated—may indicate a surplus of benefits over costs of a new project, where the selection of a multiplier of 1.5 would not. By employing a high multiplier when estimating the impacts of a new project, a city official or city-paid consultant could therefore increase the estimated benefits of the project. Similarly, by varying the assumption concerning the inflation rate, the future stream of benefits from a project may be increased or decreased.

While these assumptions are crucial to the evaluation of a major project, reporters are not trained to question estimates of multipliers or inflation rates the way they are trained to probe into official acceptance of favors. For example, in covering urban renewal and redevelopment, reporters have been described as "baffled by the technical questions involved,"[13] and they are, therefore, forced to rely on local officials to explain new proposals. In general, as a profession, journalists tend to be characterized by a fear of numbers that prevents them from delving into official estimates of costs and benefits. As one editor commented, "Reporters are not stupid, but sometimes they can't figure out how to dig in, they don't know how, especially when it comes to complex financial problems. It comes back to reporters and numbers. These are people who were hired for their verbal skills, writing stories, asking questions, not their math skills. They tend not to like numbers or not to have those skills."[14]

Because of this lack of understanding of quantitative information, it is accepted procedure for reporters to simply reproduce without question the estimates of the costs and benefits of proposed initiatives supplied to them by the officials who are proposing such initiatives. Fishman, in describing such routine procedures, has noted the pervasiveness of trust in "bureaucratic accounts." He has described the guiding principle of most journalists in establishing facts as "something is so because somebody says it," noting that "for reporters, the most credible information or the hardest data are accounts which come from the 'most competent' news sources, who, in turn, are bureaucrats and officials recognized as having jurisdiction over the events in question."[15] This routine reliance on bureaucratic accounts is particularly strong when it comes to the release of quantitative information by governmental officials or agencies.

For example, Caro's noted study of New York redevelopment czar Robert Moses, *The Power Broker,* documented many cases in which reporters accepted distorted statistics on costs and benefits from Moses. For example, press releases on Moses' Westside Improvement Project, undertaken in the midst of the Depression, stated that the cost of the project was $24 million, when the actual cost was somewhere between $180 and $218 million. "But New York's press did not attempt to analyze the cost, accepting instead Moses' $24,000,000 figure . . . Out of thirteen daily newspapers, not one had the slightest doubt that the Westside Improvement Project was anything but an 'improvement,' an unalloyed improvement, an absolutely unmitigated blessing to New York City," Caro writes.[16]

The only check on quantitative estimates of costs and benefits comes if an alternative—and equally reliable and trustworthy source—volunteers a critique of the official estimates and supplies a different one. An example from the Seattle newspapers illustrates the journalist's practice of unquestioningly accepting quantitative estimates produced by public officials and the way in which only another eager source will supply contradictory figures. In 1984, local officials in Seattle were seeking support for a proposal for the city to offer financial incentives to attract a fifteen-ship Naval Task Force to Puget Sound. While Seattle's Mayor Charles Royer was hesitant to offer perks like free port space to the Navy, Washington's governor and members of the state's congressional delegation strongly backed the proposal.

To support his position, Governor John Spellman commissioned a study to estimate the impacts of the Task Force on jobs and tax revenues. The results of the study were reported in a front-page story in the *Seattle Times* in January of 1984. Under the banner headline "Navy fleet could provide 15,000 jobs," the story noted that the battle group "could create as many as 15,000 permanent jobs in Washington, providing work for the state's unemployed, says a new state study." [17] The story went on to say:

> Location of the Navy battle group on Puget Sound also is expected to generate state and local revenues through sales taxes, as well as business and occupation taxes. State coffers stand to gain $216.4 million between 1987 and 1991. Annual collections would range from a low of $21 million in 1987 and a high of $51.9 million in 1989 and 1990.
>
> If the battle group is located in Seattle, the state estimated it would generate a total of $51.8 million in local revenues between 1987 and 1990.

In providing these estimates, the reporter did not mention until the eleventh paragraph that, of the 9,970 direct jobs generated by the project, 8,270 would be filled by the military—a fact which contradicted the state's claim (reported in the lead paragraph) that the jobs generated by the Task Force would be filled by the locally unemployed. Moreover, there was no questioning of the state's multiplier, which predicted an additional indirect employment of 4,985 jobs, or consideration of the employment "opportunity costs," that is, how many jobs might be lost by turning commercial port space over to the Navy for the task force.

While no source stepped forward to challenge these employment impacts, analysts employed by the city did come to question the tax impacts. Two weeks later their claims were reported, albeit in a story with a significantly smaller headline, "State overestimated local tax gains from proposed Navy base." [18] In this story, it is reported that the state overestimated local tax gains by roughly four times: the city analyst predicted local tax revenues could increase by $2.6 million as opposed to the state's estimate of $11.1 million. But without the city's study, the journalist and the local news media would never have caught the $8.5 million discrepancy.

A similar example of the journalist's fear of numbers came a few weeks later. In a story headlined "Poll shows support for Navy Fleet here" [19] the *Times* noted in its lead paragraph, "Most Seattle residents support location of a new Navy battle group on their city's shoreline, according to a poll conducted for the Seattle Chamber of Commerce." However, in the tenth paragraph of the article, it is noted that the actual percentage of respondents favoring selection of Seattle as the site of the battle group was only 56 percent. Moreover, when asked if they would also support allocation of state and local funds to help win the Task Force—the key issue of the public debate—only about 32 percent were affirmative. Thus, the story could have more accurately begun with the statement that most Seattle residents rejected the proposal of offering incentives to woo the Navy to Seattle.

This example points out a common tendency in local journalists to accept quantitative estimates without questioning how they were derived and to present them in news coverage much as they are packaged by the source who produces them, no matter how evident the source's self-interest in the estimate. In this case, although the reporter had the raw numbers at her disposal, she was reluctant to dispute the chamber's interpretation of them. While here the source of data was the Chamber of Commerce, in other cases the source is a consultant, hired and paid by city officials to assess a project.

Although the assumption among reporters is that such "independent" consultants would not risk their reputation by falsifying numbers, it is not unusual for a consulting firm to slant results toward the interests of their clients. As one consultant with a major national consulting firm noted in describing contracts from city governments to evaluate new projects, "The pressure is immense to say what they want you to say—to give the go-ahead for the project." On the other hand, consultants from other competing firms are reluctant to publicly criticize a study, since it might hurt their own future ability to attract clients. While many consulting firms are eager for the publicity they win by being quoted in newspapers, they are careful in deciding what kind of information to release to the media. "The trick is to say something they will print, but not controversial enough to upset present or future clients," noted the consultant.

In private interviews such consultants—and the city officials who hire them—respond to questions about the accuracy of their estimates of project costs and benefits by saying, "You can make the numbers dance when you want to" or "Numbers can say anything you want them to say." The implication is that "the numbers" can never be accurate and that proponents and opponents of a project will simply pick different numbers to support their cases, with neither being right or wrong. But while economic impact studies remain estimates based on assumptions and available data, some studies and estimates are better than others, being based on more realistic assumptions.

Most journalists, however, are unqualified to sort out the best estimates from the bogus estimates. Considering consultants authoritative sources and unskilled themselves in quantitative analysis, journalists fail to report the varying degrees of reliability of these estimates or to reflect in their reporting that the consultants hired to carry out such studies might be biased by the city officials who hired them. Even if the journalist wanted to check the numbers, it would be impossible to do so simply by calling another consultant or expert, since estimates are not like opinions that can be given off the top of the source's head—they require time, expertise, and resources.

Likewise, rarely would a reporter analyze the questions of a poll for bias or scrutinize the qualifications of the telephone service contracted to conduct a poll. Often, as in the case above, they will not question the interpretation of the results, even when presented with the raw numbers to examine themselves. Reporters defend this practice by noting that they always attribute such estimates to a source; the public knows that the poll was undertaken by the Chamber of Commerce or the City Commerce Director. But without analysis of the numbers, the audience of such articles tends to accept the findings as facts.

The Sexiness Quotient

In carrying out their jobs, local journalists are also motivated by other professional standards less related to their sources and technical expertise than to audience considerations. As described earlier in the chapter, individual reporters do not consciously consider their audience in finding and writing stories. But their concern with gaining prominence for their stories—in what is sometimes described as a "cutthroat competition to reach page one"—leads them to write stories to please editors who are concerned with audiences. So, while reporters may not write stories to sell newspapers, they do write in such a way as to sell their stories to the editors, who will accept or reject them and decide where they should be played in the paper.[20]

Beyond the objective of pleasing editors, reporters are also motivated by their own internalized professional standards of what makes a good story, which do in fact reflect a concern with audience appeal. The journalist's fundamental job is to create interest—for himself, for his editors, and ultimately for his audience. This need to create interest leads to the measurement of stories according to what might be called their "sexiness quotient." The concept of "sexiness," of course, depends on the specific audience for the newspaper; what is appealing to a working-class audience may be quite different from what appeals to a suburban professional audience. However, reporters learn quickly what kind of "sexy" story their own editors—keyed to the newspaper's particular audience—value highly and play prominently.

The sexiness quotient is important both in leading reporters to story ideas and in determining what angle they will take on a particular story and strongly influences the kind of coverage that will be given to city development projects. The proposal for a new downtown development project is an inherently "sexy" topic that reporters know their editors will be likely to play big, but it will be even sexier if the reporter stresses the need for the new project and its importance to the city—and region—in his or her coverage. A more balanced approach to the announcement of a new proposal—examining both sides of the issue dispassionately, considering alternative uses of funds, or the opportunity costs of the proposal—simply would not have the same appeal to editors and ultimately audiences.

The sexiness quotient therefore leads to a built-in bias in the coverage of new development projects. Because of the professional desire to gain prominent play for a story, a reporter is more likely to emphasize the need for a new project than to focus on the reasons why the status quo is preferable. If five people were in favor of the new project and five against, the supporters would always tend to get played most prominently, simply because the need for something new makes a sexier story. A reporter may be biased in favor of a new project—as opposed to using public funds to simply upgrade existing facilities—because the former rather than the latter policy produces more interesting news stories.

Audience appeal also affects the kinds of themes reporters use when they cover new development plans. Fishman has pointed out how journalists select some aspects of what they are reporting as important, while passing over others as "non-events."[21] In particular, he discusses how reporters decide what are "events" and "non-events" through the use of "news themes" that help decide newsworthiness. In the case of local development coverage, the use of certain "news themes"—and the exclusion of others—is evident. The news themes most often observed in development coverage include: (1) the "horse race" theme, which stresses the competition between cities for economic activity and, perhaps more importantly, prestige and suggests how the new development will help the city and region compete with other areas; (2) the "political play-by-play" theme, which focuses on who is fighting whom for approval of the project and who is likely to win; and (3) the "haste versus delay" theme, which emphasizes how slowly or quickly the project is moving toward completion.

It is not surprising that all three of these themes rely on sports analogies, since the theme of the "race" serves to enliven otherwise dry material and raise its sexiness quotient. For the same reason, the one theme that is consistently ignored is the "cost-benefit" theme: the examination of whether the public expenditure of funds necessary to "win" the "horserace" is warranted by the benefits or how much the demands made by different groups—whether from minorities seeking set-asides for contracts or suburban or state legislators seeking deals in favor of support—cost the public. In effect, the combination of the reporter's technical limitations and the need to raise the sexiness quotient leads to news coverage that stresses symbolic arguments more than hard costs and benefits.

The flip side of the sexiness quotient is the boredom factor, which leads reporters to lose interest in development projects as the months lead to the years necessary to gain approval and implementation. Often, it is not until months after a project is proposed that opposition forms to challenge the city's original estimates of need. But by that time, reporters are often bored with the issue and assume that their audience is also and will tend not to follow up on sources who challenge city claims. This boredom factor was cited by Meyerson and Banfield in their study of public housing in Chicago to explain how the *Sun-Times,* at one time a forceful supporter of public housing, eventually withdrew from active coverage of the issue. They noted,

> the struggle had become so protracted and complicated as to be
> tiresome to editors and readers alike. To keep track of its vicissi-

tudes—to know which sites were now under consideration and why they were or were not acceptable—was a full-time occupation. The technical staff of [the housing authority] managed to keep abreast of all developments, but people who had other interests—even the commissioners—found it almost impossible to know what was going on. The newspaper editors, probably themselves bored with the interminable twists and turns of the housing story, may have felt sure that their readers were bored with it too, as indeed they very likely must have been. Not only had the housing struggle become tiresome, but the issue. . . was no longer simple enough to be explained in headlines and a few leading paragraphs. To make sense of it required more time and effort than either the editors or readers were willing to spend.[22]

Thus, while the sexiness quotient works to create a positive thrust to the initial news coverage of proposals for new development projects, the boredom factor tends to discourage investigations later on in the project's approval process and implementation, when the plan has lost the interest of the "new."

Investigative Journalism and the Pulitzer Prize Mode

Investigatory journalism, the uncovering of threats to the public interest, has been prized by reporters from the days of Lincoln Steffens and the original muckrakers up to the time of Woodward and Bernstein's revelations about Watergate. Investigative journalism is valued at metropolitan newspapers both because of professional respect for uncovering wrongdoing as well as economic interests that recognize the value of impressing audiences with successful crusading. Indeed, the Pulitzer Prize, the most coveted award in journalism, is prized not simply by individual journalists, but by editors and publishers who often use such awards to market their newspapers. As Carlin Romano has pointed out, "Journalistic prizes win cachet for one's paper from people who may not read it but know that it has received prizes."[23]

While most newspapers carry on a continuous series of investigations of local and often national or international issues, these investigations are limited in their scope. In particular, local journalistic investigations tend to be focused on the illegal, unethical, or personally extravagant activities of public officials or the harmful actions of private individuals or business firms acting against the public interest. Though there is often great value to these investigations in keeping both public officials and private interests from plundering the commonweal, they too infrequently address questions like the efficacy or wisdom of public proposals and plans.

In part, the narrow definition of investigative journalism stems from the journalist's sense of what kinds of stories are considered interesting enough to make the front page or important enough to win prizes. Romano notes that "stories that provoke government reaction, or policy changes, permitting papers to cover the reaction and include it with their applications, win prizes. Stories that provoke little response do not. While the introduction of a Pulitzer prize for 'explanatory journalism' may change things, it has been true that investigative stories about government corruption, no matter how routine the scenario, win prizes, and explanatory stories about culture don't, no matter how fresh or difficult the reporting." [24] The search for scandal rather than policy evaluation is also tied to the journalist's technical limitations: evaluating an agency or official or project is difficult for reporters as compared to discovering a diversion of public funds for personal purposes.

For example, in 1985 the *Philadelphia Daily News* spent several days covering a story about the director of the Parking Authority who was alleged to be making personal telephone calls from his car phone, totaling a few hundred dollars. [25] But, the newspaper failed to devote comparable space to a consideration of the agency's recently implemented on-street parking program, which had brought in millions of dollars in additional revenues to the city. The stories about the car phone calls were both easier to find—originating most likely from a leak from within the agency—and more appealing to public emotion than the more important question of the director's effectiveness in his job. Similarly, during a 1988 controversy that pitted the chairman of the board of the Southeastern Pennsylvania Transit Authority (SEPTA) against the new general manager, both print and broadcast media played prominently a story about the high travel expenses incurred by the chairman of the board in trips abroad, while paying relatively little attention to the question of how well the transit agency itself was run.

When it comes to the coverage of urban development, investigations rarely are undertaken on the need for a new project being proposed by local government officials. For the reasons noted in the previous section, initial coverage of the project—undertaken at the time when the public at large is forming their impressions of the need for a project—is often biased in favor of a new glamorous undertaking. As the project progresses through the approval process, newspaper investigations will only be undertaken if evidence is presented to reporters that a public or private figure is benefiting unduly from the project—for example, from land speculation around the project or through the awarding of contracts as favors.

These investigations into private benefits from public development projects divert attention from the consideration of the actual need for the project. As one long-time development official noted, "You don't build a major development project with boy scouts latching thatches together. Somebody is always going to make a little profit off a public project, but if the city as a whole benefits, that shouldn't be a major concern." But the reporter's definition of scandal is centered on private greed rather than official misguidedness. While the Pulitzer Prize may be awarded for uncovering official bribes or kickback schemes, it is not likely to go to a reporter who discovers an inflated multiplier or an unrealistic discount rate. Yet, while the bribes may involve the misuse of hundreds or thousands of dollars, it is those multipliers and discount rates that may lead to the misallocations of millions of dollars that go virtually unexamined.

Irving Kristol made this point in his discussion of the "injurious side of the muckraking syndrome in journalism" or the "passionate attention that newspapermen pay to the slightest hint of corrupt collusion between businessmen and public officials." He wrote,

> There would be nothing wrong with this—were it not for the fact that it leaves the newspapermen with so little time, energy, and curiosity to devote to larger, and more serious questions of, say, urban renewal. The journalist who exposes the fact that a city official steered a profitable urban renewal contract toward a friend, a relative, or a former business associate is sure to receive the appropriate honors and applause due a 'good reporter.' That this same journalist has never had anything intelligent to say about the urban renewal plan itself—that indeed he really understands nothing about this incredibly complicated subject—is deemed of little consequence. Yet the corruption probably involved the waste of tens of thousands of dollars of public funds, while the plan itself certainly the possible waste—innocent and uncorrupted waste—of tens of millions.[26]

It should also be noted that the adversarial relationship between journalists and officials is, as Fishman has noted, "circumscribed." That is, while there is much in the news and editorial columns that is critical of local officials, this criticism is limited when compared with the amount of information that is taken directly, and almost unquestioningly, from official bureaucratic sources. As Fishman has written, "Journalists see some agencies as more credible than others, and they know bureaucratic accounts can reflect errors and oversight, corruption and malfeasance, incompetence and inexperience. Thus, newsworkers will be critical of particular agencies or specific officials. But the governmental-bureaucratic structure cannot be doubted as a whole without radically upsetting the routines of newswork. Routine news leaves the existing political order intact, at the same time that it enumerates the flaws."[27]

Fragmented Beat Structures

The reliance on official sources for information, the reluctance to question quantitative estimates of costs and benefits, a concern for the sexiness quotient, and a narrow professional definition of public scandal all limit the analytical strength of coverage of new development projects. But the division of labor in the coverage of such projects also influences coverage. Typically, different aspects of the project come to be assigned to reporters on different beats at different times in the project's life span. While all journalists are influenced by certain common professional values, reporters on different beats tend to rely on different types of sources and to write for different types of audiences. Both the sources and specialized audiences for beat reporters' stories influence reporting, so that the story angle on a new development project will differ dramatically according to whose beat it is assigned. The beats that traditionally cover development projects and the angles they typically take on such coverage are described below.

The business beat. The coverage of major economic development projects is generally the primary responsibility of the business section of most metropolitan newspapers. These business sections have been greatly expanded in recent years in order to increase the newspaper's general appeal to suburbanites interested in the regional economy. While other sections of the newspaper tend to focus on "bad news" and to present critical reporting on the activities of public officials, these new business sections tend to be far more upbeat in their orientation. Their basic coverage focuses on regional economic trends and provides profiles of individual firms and business leaders. While they may examine the plight of a failing firm or a lawsuit alleging product liability, investigative reporting is generally not their mission.

In part, this orientation can be explained both by their sources and their particular audiences. Business reporters tend to rely on sources within the business community, and for the reasons of accessibility described in an earlier section, these business sources are often the heads of city-based rather than suburban corporations. Thus, the sources called upon by a business reporter to evaluate a new development policy initiative are often biased toward a progrowth—and in particular, a pro-city growth—mentality. Moreover, business reporters tend to write for an audience of upscale business leaders, which further encourages them to use progrowth angles in their coverage of proposals for new projects. While business reporters are generally more comfortable with data than journalists on other beats, they have little incentive to subject data to scrutiny in order to investigate major projects.

The City Hall beat. The city hall beat focuses on the actions of the mayor that relate to the project. For example, when the mayor takes a position on some controversy related to the project, the story is generally assigned to a city hall reporter. But in such cases, the focus of the story is often less on the project itself than on the politics of the project. For example, in the case of a dispute about the project's selection of contractors, a city hall reporter might focus on the question of how the controversy will affect the mayor's chances for reelection, rather than how the awarding of contracts will affect the cost of the project.

While city hall reporters are more apt to take an adversarial bent with local officials than are business reporters, they are not trained to evaluate whether such a project makes sense for the public interest. City hall reporters tend to be particularly weak on the coverage of the costs and benefits of projects, since their typical focus is on politics. Moreover, city hall reporters only cover the project when it relates to the mayor; they therefore have little understanding of the complexities of the issues surrounding the project's projected costs and benefits.

The city council beat. The project's debate before the city's legislative branch is often covered by a reporter on a separate city council beat. This beat is similar to city hall, in that reporters tend to focus on the political battles surrounding the project's approval rather than issues of whether the project itself makes economic sense. And also similar to the city hall beat, city council reporters have often not covered the project before it got to the council; they therefore have little insight into the original rationale and claims for the project.

State government. Major development projects generally require state as well as local funding and so eventually are considered by state legislatures, where they are covered by reporters on the state government beat. Here again, a reporter is covering an issue that he or she has not had previous experience with, and once again, the focus of coverage is on politics rather than policy evaluation. Coverage of debates in state legislatures touches less on the arguments for and against the project than on the political battles waged by different legislators. In particular, state coverage tends to focus on city-suburban political conflict and city-versus-rest-of-the-state clashes. Like other city-oriented local reporters, state reporters introduce a city bias into their coverage. Passage of a project for a downtown redevelopment project becomes a clear-cut "victory" while rejection is considered a "defeat."

The neighborhood beat. Some newspapers in recent years have instituted a neighborhood beat to cover issues affecting "the little guy" living or working in the city's black or ethnic neighborhoods. Reporters on a neighborhood beat get assigned to coverage of a development project when a protest is organized by residents or businesses affected by a new project. Because the reporter on the neighborhood beat relies largely on neighborhood residents or small businesses opposed to a new development for sources, the resulting coverage is often quite sympathetic to the project's protesters. Stories about "the plight of the little guy" are not uncommon. While this coverage tends to reflect an anti-project perspective, the opposition it describes is limited to the interests of those immediately affected by a large development scheme rather than a more general evaluation of the project. Often, the so-called "sob stories" about relocatees that are written by reporters on this beat simply have the effect of raising the level of compensation afforded these groups—and thus the cost of the project to the general public.

The architecture critic. Another attempt to attract the upscale, suburban reader to the metropolitan newspaper has been the addition of architectural critics to many newspapers' ranks. These critics often examine proposals for new development projects as part of their missions. Because their specific charge is to criticize rather than to simply report, they are far less likely to approach their evaluations from the perspective of a booster, as is the case with the business reporter. And unlike the city hall or city council or state government beats, they have little interest in the politics of a proposed new project. They also present a marked contrast to reporters who base their coverage on information disseminated largely by official sources, since the architecture critic tends to use his own critical skills to evaluate a new project.

These evaluations, however, are restricted largely to the realm of the aesthetic: that is, how will the project look or how will it impact on the visual environment of the downtown. The architectural critic may at times touch on the question of whether an unaesthetic project is actually needed, but generally he is ill-equipped and uninterested in the question of the evaluation of economic costs and benefits or in providing a general policy evaluation of the new initiative.

The editorial board. Editorial writers, like the architecture critic, are also free to evaluate a new project. But editorialists are heavily lobbied by city officials and business leaders to support new projects for the city and editorials on downtown development projects generally reflect this lobbying with a tendency to be quite supportive. The editorial page is also one of the places in a newspaper where the subtle progrowth interests of the newspaper's owners may be passed down to editorial page editors and editorial writers. While editorialists may be free to criticize the president, the governor, the mayor, and the city council, major city development projects viewed as representing "progress" for the city are often the sacred cows that go relatively uncriticized. Moreover, once the editorial board has a history of supporting a development project, they may be reluctant to change their position even though emerging opposition later points up problems with the project.

The practice of assigning coverage of urban development coverage to many different beats, therefore, tends to weaken news coverage of these projects, rather than improving it. Because the coverage of projects is sliced up among many different beats, often a reporter covering one stage of a project is unfamiliar with previous stages and the claims and rationales of local officials that came earlier. Moreover, those beats where reporters tend to be critical and investigative concerning the activities of public officials—like the city hall reporter or the architecture critic—have neither the skills for nor the interest in investigating the basic need for a project. And those reporters who might be capable of carrying out such an analysis, such as the business reporters, do not have an incentive to do so, since it is unlikely to please the editors of their sections seeking businessmen as their audiences.

In addition, overlapping responsibilities across beats often leads to turf battles. A reporter may not undertake an investigation into a project if he or she feels it will be viewed as an infringement by another reporter within whose beat the story technically falls. Therefore, while the coverage of an urban development project comes under the purview of many different beats on a newspaper, no one beat or reporter has the incentive or the expertise to evaluate the project's need through a thorough examination of costs and benefits. And often, with fragmented beat structures, no single reporter has an understanding of the intergovernmental relationships that often play a key role in such projects as well as in other local government programs.

Lack of Release Time and Weak Institutional Memory

Two other professional factors influence the coverage of urban development: the difficulty individual reporters face in gaining release time to investigate development projects and the turnover among reporters on individual beats, which hampers the institutional memory of the newspaper concerning the project. While some reporters do express interest in investigating major development projects, they claim they cannot do so because their editors often will not give them release time to carry out such investigations. This failure to give release time reflects the newspaper's priorities to cover the day-to-day flow of news and a recognition that the public is not terribly interested in the question of whether or not projects make economic sense. But without such time, reporters are unable to get beyond the superficial coverage of official descriptions of a project's costs and benefits.

In addition, there is the problem of weak institutional memories. Reporters covering projects over a period of years often do not remember the initial claims made by officials, such as the arguments in favor of building it or the original cost and benefit estimates, and therefore are unable to challenge those officials as they shift these claims. This problem becomes even more significant when reporters are regularly rotated among beats. While computerization of newspaper libraries facilitates information search, urban development projects often have hundreds of articles written about them by the time a new reporter is assigned to the beat. It is virtually impossible for the reporter to read everything that has been written about the project when he or she begins responsibility for its coverage. Therefore, local officials may shift their claims and estimates with little fear that a reporter will call them on what they originally said about the costs and benefits of a proposed project.

Local Journalist Bias: The "Luring the Teams" Case

Many of the factors that influence the local journalist's coverage of development issues can be observed in a specific case involving the threatened relocation of two Philadelphia sports teams. In 1989, the owners of the Philadelphia 76ers basketball team and the Flyers hockey team threatened to leave the Spectrum in Philadelphia to move to a new stadium across the Delaware River in Camden, New Jersey. The coverage of the teams' potential relocation was not limited to the sports sections of newspapers or local newscasts. Rather, it was covered on front pages and played prominently in the lineup of television and radio news stories, since it was precisely the kind of issue that could interest the entire regional audience. Moreover, it was an issue that involved prominent political actors in the two states and cities, as well as the well-known owners of the two teams.

In covering the proposed move, the horse-race theme was overriding, with most news coverage focusing on what each side was doing to woo the teams and who was likely to win. For example, in the *Philadelphia Inquirer* some of the typical headlines included, "N. J. Sweetens Offer on Arena for Sixers, Flyers,"[28] "Pa. Refuses to Raise Ante for Teams,"[29] and "Sixers' Owner Threatens to Seek His Own Deal on New Sports Arena."[30] A coterie of reporters from beats ranging from the two state governments to city hall and the sports staff attempted to provide the latest on the details of the different offers and on which offer was currently the most attractive to the teams' owners. By focusing on the question of who was likely to win, however, the coverage virtually ignored a more basic policy question: just what were the economic impacts of the teams on their local economies and did such impacts justify the expenditure of funds being proposed to win them?

It was not that reporters failed to cover the economic aspects of the plans being proposed for both states, but rather that their "fear of numbers" and sensitivity to the "sexiness quotient" led them to accept with little question the financial estimates and development prospects their sources provided, estimates that suggested that the benefits of "luring" the teams to New Jersey were worth the cost. For example, the *Inquirer* analyzed New Jersey's proposal to attract the teams in an article headlined, "A Critical Decision on Bid to Teams Confronts Florio." The first three paragraphs of this story illustrate the kind of news themes that are common to development coverage and that dominate the important opening of stories:

> Governor Florio has repeatedly said he stands ready to make the hard decisions. Thanks to a pair of Philadelphia sports franchises with wanderlust, he faces one now.
>
> Only weeks after taking office, the Democratic governor must make a critical decision: How sweet should he make the offer to lure the Flyers and the 76ers to Camden, the wretchedly poor city within Florio's own former Congressional district?
>
> Capturing the teams could help rejuvenate Camden, providing jobs and new development and reversing its troubled image in one stroke. It could also deliver an enormous political payoff to Florio, who may need an early victory in a year in which he faces a draining, no-win fight over tax increases. At the same time, Florio's ability to be generous with public money is limited by a newly reported $550 million budget shortfall.

Drama, political intrigue, and the strong pathos of the plight of the "wretchedly poor city" make for a lively beginning to this policy story.

The article went on to describe the state's proposal to subsidize part of the cost of the new arena with bonds that would be paid off by the use of local taxes generated from the new arena. It mentioned, in the thirteenth paragraph, that a second bond issue might be required to help the South Jersey Port Corp., which would lose half of its land to a new stadium and would have to relocate its operations, and that this second bond issue would have to be supported by "shrinking tax revenues." At the very end of the lengthy article, another concern is raised: that twenty-three firms, employing about six hundred people, would be displaced by the arena, workers who one business owner notes disgruntledly "make a hell of a lot more wages than stadium help."[31]

While appearing to analyze the financial elements of New Jersey's proposal and the "tough decision" facing Florio, the article actually reinforced the idea that the teams would be a financial boon for both the city of Camden and the state of New Jersey. It never addressed the question of what the net benefits of the new arena would be to Camden and New Jersey after the two bonds were issued, the property and sales taxes generated by the new arena used to pay off the first bond issue, and the state budget used to pay the cost of relocating the Port and relocating the twenty-three businesses. Rather, it simply accepted (and placed high in the story) the notion that "capturing" the teams would "help rejuvenate Camden, providing jobs and new development and reversing its troubled image in one stroke."

In a later article, which focused on the transportation problems Camden would face in providing access to the new arena, the same values that were apparent in the coverage of the Urban Renewal Program of the 1960s—the attraction by middle-class reporters to "wiping out vice-ridden hovels"—were still apparent. The story, which examined the attempt of Pennsylvania members of the regional port authority to block new highway ramps and train routes to the arena, noted (in the tenth paragraph) that Camden was considering razing some one hundred forty rowhouses in order to broaden one of the roads leading to the new stadium. Later in the article this plan is detailed:

> [Camden Mayor] Thompson and other city officials said Camden was considering a plan to knock down the rowhouses, many of them vacant, in a small and dilapidated neighborhood on the eastern edge of the site. The homes would be razed within a four-block area defined by Broadway and Sixth Street and Woodland and Fairview Streets.
>
> Thomas A. Roberts 2nd, executive director of the Camden Re-development Authority, said the city would help both homeowners and renters find new homes. It would compensate owners for their properties at "existing market value," he said.
>
> Roberts described the neighborhood as an isolated enclave, troubled by prostitution, drug-dealing and irreparable housing decay. He said the move would ultimately provide residents with a better place to live.
>
> At least one resident said he would welcome city help in moving, preferably out of Camden, he said.
>
> "We wouldn't give them any problem as long as we got a decent settlement," said Joseph Steinmacher, owner of a home in the 500 block of Lester Terrace.
>
> "There's drugs around here, and the houses are all messed up," he said. "Not only that, we can't even bring my grandson or our daughter up because it's so bad."[32]

Just as coverage of Urban Renewal in the 1960s had relied on the pronouncements of redevelopment officials who claimed that glamorous new plans would improve the areas being reclaimed, this article from 1990 makes the same assumptions. The need to relocate residents of 140 homes is treated as a minor detail of the grander competition to "lure the teams" and an interview with one willing resident is taken as evidence that all residents will be happy to move in the interest of economic progress.

Interestingly, a few months later the *Inquirer* ran a front-page story headlined, "When Sports Teams Have Moved, Economic Growth Hasn't Followed." [33] The article was based on academic studies of team relocations in other cities which showed that "acquiring the big city's sports teams provides the smaller community with some limited benefits from the jobs and tax revenues directly generated by the arena. But in terms of economic stimulation, the impact tends to be small." While an interesting article that was quite relevant to the current policy issue, the story did not directly address the question of how Camden would be affected by the new arena. The only direct consideration of the specifics of the Camden case came in the following paragraph: "As for Camden, some economists note that having a new state-of-the-art arena, with two major league teams, can't very well hurt the city, especially if the arena is built and operated with private funds. And, of course, it is possible that Camden would fare better than other communities have in converting a successful sports arena into broader economic development." In this summary of the Camden case, no mention is made of the second bond that would have to be issued to finance relocation of the Port's activities, of the twenty-three businesses and six hundred employees that would have to be relocated, or of the economic and social costs involved in demolishing the one hundred forty rowhouses that might have to give way for the new arena. Instead, the article suggests that the new stadium will bear no public cost. It would appear that this simplified description of the financing of the new stadium resulted from the fragmented beat structure used to cover the story: the authors of this story did not include the Trenton bureau staffer who had provided the more detailed coverage of the New Jersey proposal. And the fact that the experts interviewed for the study had not actually researched the Camden case and that the reporters themselves could not investigate the economic impacts in New Jersey led to the question of the actual impact of the teams on Camden to be set aside.

The article's concluding paragraphs suggest that the story was written less to examine the degree to which the Sixers and Flyers would help Camden versus Philadelphia, or to suggest whether public funds should be spent by either state to try to lure or retain the teams, than to serve as a justification for the teams to stay in the city of Philadelphia. Colored by the "city myopia" so evident in much regional development coverage, the article concludes:

There is one final irony. As the Flyers and Sixers ponder leaving the core city, the national trend appears to be in the opposite direction.

In Baltimore, the baseball Orioles will soon move from an old stadium in a residential neighborhood to a new one being built downtown.

In Cleveland, the Cavaliers are negotiating with city officials to move to a new arena that would be downtown.

And in Buffalo, the Bills' owner has announced the team will abandon Orchard Park when the lease expires, in 1998. His goal is to get a new domed stadium built downtown.

With the issue of costs and benefits and development potential in Camden swept aside, the story has now become once again a reaffirmation of cities and, in particular, their downtowns as the center of regional activity.

As this case has pointed out, the professional values of reporters, when constrained to meet the economic imperative of their newspapers, at times distort the consideration of regional issues and the evaluation of proposals for new development projects. The city myopia of metropolitan journalists leads to coverage that often distorts the importance of city development projects to the region. The reliance on eager official sources for information, the lack of quantitative expertise, the need for sexy angles to stories, and the fragmented beat structure of metropolitan newspapers all combine to prevent journalists from presenting the public with a balanced presentation of the pros and cons of new policy initiatives.

The initial coverage of a new and often glamorous development will tend to emphasize the positive sides of the project and its need. Reporters will tend to accept without question the estimates of the project's costs and benefits handed to them by local officials pushing for the project's approval and will not seek out independent sources to offer additional evaluations. Rather, whatever evaluations take place will tend to focus on the symbolic benefits of the project—its impact on the image of the city—or on its aesthetic characteristics, and whatever investigations are carried out will be limited to private greed or public violations of ethics.

4 Local Television News

At six o'clock each evening, some one-half million television sets in Philadelphia are tuned in to Channel 6, listening as the familiar theme song begins and the video montage of local scenes in the Delaware Valley flashes across the screen. "Action News," the announcer proclaims in a resounding voice, "The Delaware Valley's leading news program. With Don Tollefson, Dave Roberts, and Jim Gardner." Gardner, the silver-haired anchor for over a decade, greets his audience on a typical evening with an affable smile: "Tuesday night, authorities find more bones in Tacony Creek Park and Frank Rizzo says he will run for Mayor . . . maybe. But the big story on Action News tonight is a busy and important day in Harrisburg. On the agenda today, the Governor's budget and that all-important auto insurance reform plan. Suzanne LaFrankie is live in Harrisburg . . ."

Local news programs like Action News reach millions of viewers nationwide, many of whom use television as their main source of news[1] and trust it more than their local newspapers.[2] Although television news stories range from a mere twenty seconds to a few minutes in length, they often convey vivid messages about local problems and the actions of local public officials. But despite a growing importance in policy issues, local television news has received more ridicule than serious analysis. In general, there has been little attention to the criteria that are used each day to select, order, and flesh out local television news stories. Why, for instance, does a typical news program begin with a tease about bones in city parks and speculation about a city mayoral race over a year away before turning to the coverage of major state legislation? And when complex policy issues are covered, how well are they explained within the restrictive time frame of a news program?

This chapter probes behind the stereotyped images of local television news to learn how news is selected and presented and in particular, how government and policy issues are covered by local newscasts.[3] A number of factors, including the importance of local news anchors, the constraints of the broadcast's time and format, the limited number of reporters and their lack of beat assignments, and the need for effective video and sound bites, lead to news that often distorts the public's understanding of local policy issues.[4]

The Evolution of Local Television News

While local newspapers in America trace their roots back to the earliest days of the colonies, local television news is a relatively young medium, with the first programs beginning in the late 1940s. Originally, the reporting of news on television was a response to the Federal Communications Commission (FCC) requirement that a certain portion of programming be devoted to the public interest. In order to inexpensively fulfill this requirement, many local stations began news programs, using a "rip and read" formula featuring a staff announcer reading news items taken from an Associated Press radio wire. Early local news shows were often just a few minutes in length, and until the 1960s, even the longest local news shows were no longer than fifteen minutes.[5]

In the 1970s, however, many station managers began to recognize the profit potential of local news. While a major portion of advertising revenues collected during network programming had to be returned to the networks, a station could retain, in full, earnings from local programming. The production of news became attractive because it was inexpensive as compared with entertainment programming[6] and because news shows proved to draw large audiences. As one observer put it, "The cheapest program to produce generated the highest demand for commercials and the biggest audiences; little wonder, then, that local stations couldn't get enough news."[7] While network news remained only thirty minutes in length (affiliates resisted their expansion into local programming times), many local news operations began to expand their early evening news to an hour, or even an hour-and-one-half, and added news shows at noon, and ten or eleven o'clock, and early in the morning.[8]

As local news programs began to be viewed as money-makers for stations, the size of audiences that could be sold to advertisers became an important measure of success. The Nielsen and Arbitron services began to provide statistical estimates—referred to as "ratings"—of the numbers of households watching particular television programs. Advertisers could then buy access to audiences on particular stations according to program ratings. In recent years, the cost of advertising time has been determined four times a year—February, May, July, and November—which are referred to as "sweeps" months, during which time the ratings figures determine advertising rates for the coming quarter of the year.

While competition between major metropolitan newspapers has steadily declined in the twentieth century with the emergence of many "one-newspaper" cities, most local television markets in the country are intensely competitive. Network affiliates compete with each other and with an increasing number of independent and cable stations for audiences and advertisers. This competition has become particularly strong among the stations' newscasts, which compete fiercely to raise their ratings—and their ranking among their competitors—in order to increase their advertising revenues. Because news is the primary revenue-producing operation for the local station, the production of news and its ratings tends to be even more important for local stations than for the networks. The difference in a rating point can mean hundreds of thousands of dollars of revenues to a station.

The local television newscast's drive for ratings is primarily a drive for mass of households, regardless of the age, income, or educational status of their members. While metropolitan newspapers have become more concerned with the demographics of their audience—targeting their news and features increasingly to a more affluent and educated audience—television news tends to attract advertisers who are concerned more with mass than demographics. As a result, local television news gears itself to a less-educated and less-affluent mass audience than does the metropolitan newspaper. There is some targeting to particular audience segments according to the time of day of the broadcast. In general, local news broadcasts at noon and between five and half past six attract an older audience with a larger number of females than does the late news. In addition, late night news attracts more of the professional audience who arrive home too late to watch earlier television news shows.

Geographically, local television markets tend to be much larger than metropolitan areas (the basic market unit of most metropolitan newspapers), since broadcasts can reach over a wider geographic span than can physical delivery of a newspaper. For advertising purposes, the United States is divided by the Arbitron Company into 212 mutually exclusive television markets called "Areas of Dominant Influence" or ADI's, defined as encompassing "all counties in which the home market stations receive a preponderance of viewing."[9] The typical metropolitan ADI extends beyond city and suburb, often covering more than one state and a multitude of counties. This wide geographic span means that central-city viewers represent a smaller percentage of the typical local television news market than of the metropolitan newspaper's market.[10]

In the 1980s, increased use of satellite newsgathering and Ku-band uplinks allowed local news stations to increase their coverage of remote locations and, along with the increasing use of video tape instead of film, has increased coverage from outside the studio.[11] The ability of local news stations to beam reports back to their viewers, whether from distant parts of their regional market or from other parts of the nation or world, has led local stations to become competitive with network news for the presentation of national and even international news.[12] In combination with the use of helicopters in the larger markets, the new technology has allowed local news stations to expand the size of their markets and cover the news of ever larger territories.

In recent years, competitive forces have led many local news operations to call in outside consultants to evaluate their broadcasts on the basis of market research. These consultants have been criticized for focusing more on the look of the news than on its content and for bringing to local news broadcasts techniques of audience appeal developed in entertainment programming.[13] The advice of these consultants, along with intense competitive pressures, have led local television stations to structure their operations around certain key factors, creating a news product that, as Westin has put it, "has started to take on a texture of its own—one distinctively different from network programming."[14]

Local News Anchors and the "Cult of Personality"

Television viewers are often said to choose one local news broadcast over another not because of the content of the news but rather because of the personalities of the anchors and on-air reporters.[15] In an early analysis of the importance of the anchor's personality, Horton and Wohl claimed that viewers enter into a "para-social relationship" with television personalities, regarding them as they would friends.[16] Levy later described the para-social relationship between viewers and television news anchors as "a new form of social interaction . . . 'intimacy at a distance' in which the audience experiences the illusion of face-to-face communication with actually remote mass media communicators."[17] Market research undertaken by individual stations confirms these theories and suggests that viewers are closely attuned to the relationships between on-air personalities. As one local television anchor said, "If we show anything negative on the air, people become concerned. Our research shows that conviviality is extraordinarily important to viewers."[18]

As a result of such research, many local stations have tried to raise their ratings by hiring attractive and charismatic news anchors, relying on extensive audience research to tell them which anchors have the most appeal to viewers.[19] The emphasis on the importance of the anchor and the competition between stations for "stars" has led to increasingly high salaries being paid to the men and women who sit behind the anchor's desk. As one observer noted in describing the salary trends for both network and local news anchors, "Where they were once like newspaper reporters, only a little better-paid and better-known, they came more closely to resemble Hollywood stars, with the kind of celebrity and earning power a print reporter can only dream about."[20] As Philadelphia anchor Jim Gardner commented in an interview, "I'd say 99 percent of my salary is paid for what goes on in the studio, in front of the camera, while 99 percent of my work is in the newsroom."[21]

The "cult of personality" surrounding anchors has also led to increasingly expensive promotional campaigns that market on-air talent as local personalities. These promotions have come under fire from critics for blurring the boundaries between fact and fiction. For example, after promotional ads for local television anchors in New York and Philadelphia used actors to simulate newsmakers, one local columnist asked, "When a news organization knowingly presents a fictionalized version of what it does, how can it expect us to tell the difference when it says it's telling the truth in newscasts?"[22] Of equal concern, however, is the fact that expensive promotional campaigns together with high anchor salaries take resources away from covering the news itself, diverting money that could be used to hire additional reporters or researchers. In addition, promotional campaigns are often subtly integrated into the body of the newscast and may take already scarce time away from the coverage of local news.

Finding Local News: The Local Television News Reporter

While most public attention focuses on the local news anchor, the day-to-day newsgathering of the local television station is carried out with relatively little involvement by the men and women who sit at the anchor's desk. Anchors may write or edit the copy for their lead-ins and voice-overs, provide input on the order or play of stories, or veto particularly graphic video, but the ongoing search for news is conducted by others. As Smith has described it, a hierarchy exists in the local television newsroom, in which "reporters gather news, producers make the majority of news and production decisions on a day-to-day basis, and news directors set policies that determine the criteria for those decisions."[23] In addition, in most large local television operations, assignment editors are responsible for finding potential news stories.

Because of the high cost of anchor salaries and promotions and the continual need to update expensive technological equipment, the budget that remains for the people who actually report television news is relatively small. While metropolitan newspapers may have hundreds of reporters, and network news is put out by a legion of researchers and producers, local television news stations, even in the largest markets, rarely employ more than a handful of reporters on any given day. The limited number of staff means that most reporters are "general assignment" and that there are rarely any beat reporters.[24] (The exception is the increasing use of reporters specializing in consumer or health reporting.) As a result, television reporters often have little of the in-depth background information of print reporters who cover a beat and can therefore ask more informed questions of local officials. As one local television reporter described her experiences covering local news in Philadelphia:

> Theoretically, at least, I needed to be constantly prepared to cover important events—not just in Philadelphia but in three states. But often I arrived at the scene of a story wondering what was going on and who the principal players were. Sometimes I would just be given an address over the two-way radio in the news van; details were withheld in case the other stations were listening in.
>
> It's nerve-wracking to just 'drop-in' on events—on the important or lengthy trial coming to an unexpectedly abrupt conclusion, on the hastily called news conference in the mayor's office, dealing with a subject you know little or nothing about. I was frequently armed with nothing more than information I could recall from memory."[25]

There are also the problems of high turnover and contracts that discourage reporters from changing jobs from one local station to another station in the same city. Typically, local news reporters move from television market to market, living a "nomadic existence" as Westin called it,[26] ascending the ranking of markets as they gain experience. While this kind of hopping around from city to city spells success for the reporter, it hampers his or her ability to understand the nature of the locality and the complexity of the issues that confront it. Reporters and anchors may try to sell themselves as part of "the hometown team," but they often give away their lack of knowledge of an area by their mispronunciations of place names.[27]

The limited number of reporters and the lack of a beat structure makes local television news reporters particularly dependent on easily accessible sources for their story ideas. While some local television news reporters may cultivate governmental sources in much the same way that their print counterparts do, in general they are dealt out their story subjects by officebound assignment editors. The assignment editor, in turn, relies on five main sources of stories: (1) police and fire scanners or phone checks; (2) press releases announcing press conferences, protests or demonstrations, or other media events; (3) wire service stories and the wire service "day books," which list major local events for the day; (4) tips from viewers; and (5) the local newspaper or newspapers in the city.[28]

Berkowitz has found local television journalists have a higher reliance on these routine news channels than do print journalists, raising the concern that "sources who best understand the needs of the television newsmaking process stand the best chance of influencing the news agenda."[29] The small number of television reporters, working as general assignment reporters under extreme time pressures, are often incapable of giving independent scrutiny to official actions concerning local policy issues. To a far greater degree than newspaper reporters, television reporters are dependent on routine news channels to find local news and on the press release or press briefing to summarize a complex new policy.

The Importance of Video and the Sound Bite

While newspapers have increasingly tried to improve their visual appearance by adding color, graphics, and expanded use of photographs, visual images in the print media have continued to be used to supplement the news, not determine it. However, in local television news, critics have argued that "visual hype" calls rather than follows the tune.[30] Instead of simply helping convey the news, the need for good video and "sound bites," as interview comments are called, often determines what events will become stories and dictates the order of stories, the length of time devoted to particular stories, and the angle or method of presentation of the story.

Some news stories will be rejected altogether from coverage on local television because they are "video-poor," or lacking in effective video to accompany the reporter's words. For example, in one local news station a suggestion for a story on the difficulty of the working poor to secure health insurance was rejected by a news director because no one could think of compelling video to accompany the story. In other cases, the quality of the video, not the importance of the story, determines its ranking in the newscast: the story with the best video and sound bites often becomes the lead. As one television journalist said, "In many cases, the pictures are more important than the words. Oftentimes, stories will take on a larger role in the newscast because the pictures are dramatic. It is less so than it used to be, but it is still there."[31] Or, as another reporter noted, "You always start with your best shot."

While one television reporter claimed that leading with the best video was simply a technique "to get people hooked and interested" in order to present important information, the need for effective video may influence the angle of a story and alter the meaning of the news. As one reporter presented the problem, "I have to have a beginning, a middle, and an end to my stories and that's not always easy. You have to use the best video first and that often makes for a very convoluted story." Another local television journalist described the difference between a newspaper story and a television news story: "Instead of an inverted paragraph order in the newspaper, where the most important information comes first, television news stories have the formula of a mini-drama, with rising action, climax and denouement. Television stories stress action, not background facts."

One local television reporter wryly described the stress placed on video by management in the news hierarchy with a hypothetical situation: "Suppose I had this great story, an exclusive from the Pope saying that God was a Woman, and I'm the only reporter to get the Pope on tape making this pronouncement. You know what my news director would say to me after my package aired? 'Good story, definitely a winner, but you spent too much time on the Pope talking. The package really needed some video of God."

The need for good sound bites also influences the way local television covers the news. Often, the sound bite which makes it to the air is not the comment that best summarizes the speaker's position, but the one which captures the most emotional, dramatic, or controversial remarks. "Catchy" comments are often taken out of context, with the result that positions may be distorted and peripheral points may get more coverage than central arguments in a policy debate. The need for appealing sound bites also affects which local public officials are covered by local television news. Reporters come to gravitate to those officials who can be counted on to make their positions clear and colorful in twenty-second sound bites and, if possible, avoid those they consider long-winded or boring.

The search for the sexy sound bite can be particularly important in affecting the nature of local election coverage. As one local broadcast journalist in Philadelphia pointed out, in the 1987 Republican mayoral primary between the charismatic former Mayor Frank Rizzo and his more dispassionate opponent, John Egan, television reporters tended to give more air time to Rizzo than to Egan simply because the former offered them more effective sound bites. Even though reporters consciously tried to balance the time allotted to each candidate, they found it difficult to ignore differences in the appeal of the two men's sound bites. As a result of such tendencies, colorful and charismatic politicians often come to be covered more extensively—and taken more seriously by the public—than their election chances warrant.

Mass Appeal and the Use of Drama and Emotion

The need for effective video and sound bites—as well as the need to appeal to a mass audience—also leads local television news to search for news stories and approaches to the news that stress emotion and drama. When anchor Jim Gardner appeared before a group of university students in the winter of 1987, he touched on the need for mass appeal when asked why his newscast gave so much coverage to dramatic and emotional stories. In particular, Gardner was asked about the extensive coverage of the recent murder case of Gary Heidnik, who had allegedly imprisoned, tortured, and murdered women in his basement. Gardner turned to the young woman who asked the question and said,

> "Valerie, I assume you got at least 1300 on your SAT's, am I right? Let me ask you a question. What story would you rather hear about—Heidnik or the latest snag in the Geneva arms talks?"
>
> (The student, laughing, answered, the Heidnik story.)
>
> Gardner continued, "Exactly. You understand what I'm saying? There are stories we do because we think people should know about them. But there are stories we do because people are interested in them. A story like Baby Phillip Worthington [a case where a newborn was abducted from his mother's hospital room and later returned] is not going to change the world, but it is gripping and it does bring people to TV and yes, raises our ratings. We do them without guilt because they have tremendous impact and people want to know about them—even you in between your Proust and Kierkegaard."[32]

Another reporter similarly pointed out the importance of mass appeal in relaying the instructions of her news director: "Find the lowest common denominator and then shoot below it."

The search for emotion-packed reports with mass appeal has led local television news to give extensive coverage to tragedies like murders, deaths in fires, or plane crashes, in which they often interview survivors of victims about "how they feel." Arlen described a case in New York City where a WCBS reporter covering a Harlem tenement fire that had killed a six-month-old baby asked both the babysitter who had left the child and the dead child's mother how they felt about the fire. The reporter, Arlen notes, was not eliciting any information beyond the obvious, but seemed to ask the questions to try to get a sense of the "feel" of the event.[33]

Local television reporters are often criticized for invading the privacy of victims with such questioning, and many local television reporters privately express displeasure at being required to perform such interviews. For example, Philadelphia reporter Robin Mackintosh described as "one of the more unpleasant aspects of the job" his interview with the young daughter of a policeman who had been murdered hours before.[34] But even when individual reporters express qualms about such interviewing, they are forced by the competitive pressures of local television news to continue. As Bob Teague, former reporter for WNBC-TV in New York City described the pressures:

> If I failed to do it for dear old Channel 4, some other streetwalker made of sterner stuff would certainly do it for dear old Channel 2, Channel 5, or Channel 7. And if my masters saw that kind of pathos on a competing station—they all had a shelf full of TV monitors in their offices—they would ask me, "Where were you when Channel Blank was getting the good stuff?"

Teague recounts an incident where he tricked the mother of a young suicide into speaking to the cameras by claiming he would otherwise air information he had that the boy killed himself because he was a drug addict. Teague writes, "My excuse was: Who knows what Ch. 2 or Ch. 7 might have filmed before I reached the scene some three hours later?"[35]

Some television news reporters defend such practices by claiming that many survivors want to talk after a tragedy and feel flattered that television reporters care how they feel. As one television journalist noted, "Many times when we seem to be intrusive, we've been invited in by victims to tell their story." Other journalists claim that in some cases relatives of victims use the media to try to apprehend killers still at-large or to urge public officials to take action to prevent recurrences of the tragedy. Even Teague was able to rationalize his intrusive interviewing, citing a case where he spoke to a widow and her two small children after a man had been gunned down in Greenwich Village. Describing the widow's eagerness to talk to him, he writes,

> Reluctantly, I shoved the microphone under her quivering, freshly painted lips. She wailed about the loss of her husband, wept without embarrassment. Great TV. Some of her tears fell on my hand. That's when I got the message: she, as well as her kids, wanted the whole damn world to share their grief.
>
> Experiences in that vein allowed me to feel more comfortable in my television role. There was a quid pro quo that mitigated my indiscretions to some degree. Just as I used people to suit my purposes, they used me. Why not? Television belonged to everybody.[36]

Despite the apparent eagerness of tragedy victims to speak to local news cameras, reporters and their stations often exploit the confusion and grief of survivors and use the public's fascination with television to invade the privacy of such sources. For whatever reasons victims choose to answer television reporters' questions about their feelings and experiences, the dramatic and emotional results often displace more dispassionate news about local government and policy.

Brevity and Timeliness: The One-Minute Story and the "Update"

Although local newscasts have expanded the length of time that they broadcast, longer local news broadcasts have not necessarily meant increasing time for local news coverage of government and policy. Rather, the tendency has been for the additional time to be filled with what have been called "back-of-the-book" news items and features, such as consumer and health news, the economy or personal finance, gossip and entertainment, as well as sports and weather.[37] The news itself in a half-hour broadcast is typically reduced to between eight and twelve minutes, and the length of a news story ranges from twenty or thirty seconds for a story read by the anchor to a package assembled by a reporter of one to three minutes.

Different formats adopted by local news stations also have affected the time available for the presentation of the news. In the 1970s, many stations experimented with the so-called "happy talk" format, in which anchors, reporters, and other on-air personalities engaged in friendly banter and joking while presenting the news. While many stations have since pulled back from the "happy talk" approach, the style of informal conversation between anchors and reporters has continued to be a hallmark of local news, with even some network news shows adopting the repartee.[38] Although news organizations maintain that viewers enjoy the informality of the conversational approach, such comments and joking take away from the already limited time available for reporting the news.

Some stations have adopted a format with rapid pacing, adding the number of news stories covered while simultaneously reducing the amount of time for each piece. In some cases, the premium is said to be placed on giving the impression of covering a great deal of news while actually providing little information about any one story. In addition, the newshole itself has shrunk because of the increasing use of time for stories that tie in with entertainment programming being broadcast on the affiliate's network. In particular, late night local news shows have tried to bolster ratings by luring their lead-in audiences with news segments linked to a topic covered on the previous entertainment program. Such entertainment tie-ins, while often successful in boosting ratings, further reduce the time available to the news itself.

The need to appear to present timely news also has an impact on the way news is selected and presented. While all journalists want to get news stories ahead of their competitors, local television news stations are particularly concerned about which station presents news of a tragedy or disaster first. In most newsrooms, news directors and other staff watch their own newscasts with an eye to what their competition is airing at the same time and bemoan missing a story another station got first. Far less if any attention is given to how well the other stations covered a particular story. As Schudson has noted, "Getting the story first is a matter of journalistic pride, but one that has little to do with journalistic quality or public service." In explaining the importance of such timeliness considerations, he argues, "The insistence on getting the latest news and getting it first, the head-long lunge, the competitive rush that comes with a breaking story, all this is an effort to deny and escape the humdrum of daily journalism. Moreover, the race for news—a race whose winner can easily be determined by a clock—affords a cheap, convenient, democratic measure of journalistic 'quality.' "[39]

112

This "race for news" and the importance of timeliness to local television news is particularly relevant for news selection for the late evening broadcast. Since typically television staff and crews are reduced in number between the early and late evening broadcast, much of the late broadcast is devoted to edited versions of the earlier broadcasts. However, an attempt is made to cover and give priority to stories that have occurred between the early and late night programs—even if those stories have less importance than other local, national, or international events which occurred earlier in the day. Since most of the "breaking" news that occurs in the evening concerns accidents, crimes and fires, stories with relatively small significance to the general viewing audience may take precedence over government or policy stories that occurred during business hours earlier in the day.

Local Television Coverage of Government and Policy Issues

Local television news is defended by its practitioners as serving as an "electronic front page," providing an overview to the day's important events and serving as a kind of "headline service." But does it actually serve this function? A content analysis of one city's local newscasts indicates that local television news does not stand as an abbreviated version of the metropolitan newspaper, but rather as a unique representation of the local environment. The need to appeal to a mass audience, the cult of personality, the limited number of reporters and their reliance on routine channels of information, the importance of dramatic video and sound bites, and the element of timeliness, all lead to a distinctive definition of what is "local news."

The content analysis looked at the order and time allotment of stories in the early and late evening broadcasts of the three network affiliates in Philadelphia for two single-week periods.[40] All news stories were grouped into one of five general categories: "government," which included local, state, and national government stories; "occurrences," which included crimes and trials, accidents, disasters, and fires; "private institutions," which included news of business and private educational and religious institutions; "features," including consumer investigations, celebrity stories, and other miscellaneous features; and "world news," which included events occurring in other nations. Stories were also categorized by geography, that is, where they occurred or what unit of government they concerned, including international, national, regional, central city or urban, and suburban.

In addition to looking at how much time was devoted to different classes of

113

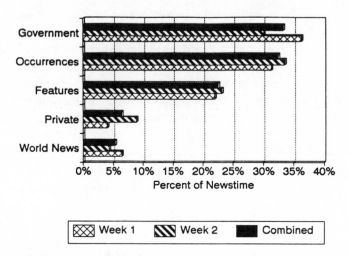

FIGURE 4.1   Newstime by Category and Week

stories in the newscasts, specific policy-related stories were analyzed in comparison to newspaper stories on the same subject. Interviews were also conducted with local broadcast journalists to gain the insider's view of how local television news goes about the business of covering government and policy stories. In general, a number of observations were drawn.

- **The coverage of isolated crimes, accidents, and fires is allocated equal or greater prominence than the coverage of government and policy.**

For the two-week sample, while 33 percent of local newstime[41] for all three stations was accorded to government stories, 32 percent of newstime went to occurrence stories.[42] This proportion varied slightly from the first week of the sample to the second. In the first week, when a major piece of state legislation and a state budget were announced, coverage of government represented 36 percent of newstime as compared to 31 percent for occurrences. However, in the second week, 34 percent of newstime went to occurrences, as compared with 30 percent for governmental stories (see figure 4.1). Looking at the number of news stories for the total two-week period, 36 percent of all stories focused on occurrences, while 33 percent focused on government. In week one, occurrences and government both were allocated 37 percent of total news sto-

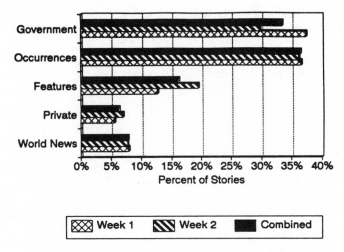

FIGURE 4.2   News Stories by Category and Week

ries, while in week two, occurrences were accorded 36 percent of total news stories, as compared with 30 percent for government (see figure 4.2).

It was also interesting to see how the different categories of news stories were allocated resources: that is, whether they were covered as "packages" (PKG), stories of one to three minutes in length, where reporters have been sent to file the story, "voice-overs" (VO), where the anchor reads the story while video is shown, "voice-over sound on tape" (VSOT), where the anchor reads the story but video and sound bites are included, and "reader" (READ) stories, where an anchor reads a story with no video or sound bites. In examining the allocation of packages, the division between government and occurrences was virtually equal and remarkably similar among the three stations. WCAU-TV allocated the same percentage of package time to both news categories—29 percent to occurrences and government each—as did WPVI-TV, with 35 percent of package time going to government and to occurrences. KYW-TV allocated slightly more time to packages on occurrences (33 percent to occurrences, as compared with 29 percent for government). (See table 4.1.)

These findings indicate how similar are the news decisions of all local television stations in a market, reflecting a common objective to balance government stories almost equally with stories about crimes, fires, and accidents (see figure 4.3). Importantly, this balance between government and occurrences coverage was as prevalent in week one, in which major government news oc-

TABLE 4.1   Percentage of Newstime by Category, Story Class, and Station

Station	Class	Government	Occurrences	Features	Private	World News
10	PKG	29	29	38	3	2
10	READ	67	14	5	13	0
10	VO	29	34	15	12	10
10	VSOT	44	25	20	8	3
Channel 10		33	28	30	6	3
3	PKG	29	33	31	6	1
3	READ	37	41	22	0	0
3	VO	25	42	14	5	14
3	VSOT	40	26	16	11	7
Channel 3		31	34	24	6	6
6	PKG	35	35	16	9	5
6	READ	40	15	13	13	19
6	VO	34	41	9	5	11
6	VSOT	48	21	19	0	12
Channel 6		36	35	14	7	7

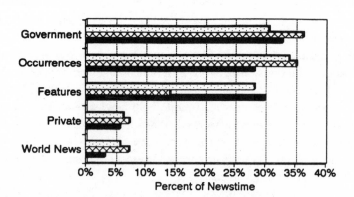

FIGURE 4.3   Newstime by Category and Station

116

curred, as in week two when no such initiatives were undertaken. No matter how important local government and policy issues may be, or how significant their effect for large portions of the television market, time for the coverage of government and policy is always balanced with time for what are typically isolated crimes, accidents, and fires, all of which have relatively limited effects.

Within individual broadcasts, relatively minor although dramatic incidents were often covered higher up in the story order and allotted more time than major local governmental issues. For example, on the day when Governor Robert Casey announced the details of his new budget proposal for Pennsylvania, KYW-TV covered the story as a 35-second voice-over in the sixth spot in its six o'clock broadcast. Preceding the budget story was a two-minute package on whether or not Frank Rizzo was going to run for Mayor of Philadelphia in the Republican primary over a year away; a 35-second voice-over on the announcement that prisoners would be reimbursed for belongings lost in the Camp Hill prison riot; a 45-second VSOT about possible cult practices in a neighborhood park; a 20-second VO about a suburban fire, and another two-minute package covering the arrest of a suspect in the case of a kidnapping of a suburban child.[43]

This emphasis on kidnappings, cults, and blazes, at the expense of stories like budget allocations, and the general balancing of government stories with occurrences can be explained by several factors. In addition to being easy to find and simple to report, crime, fire, and accident stories lend themselves to the visual medium of television, providing more opportunities for dramatic video than do government stories. Shots of flames billowing, cars mangled in highway accidents, or suspects being led away in handcuffs make for better television than officials standing at podiums. As one local television journalist admitted, local development issues are often dropped from the lineup on local television news because they are "more difficult to show on TV . . . all you get are people talking." In addition, crimes and fires produce more emotional sound bites than do government stories.

For example, in the KYW newscast described above, the governor's budget address was summarized by the anchor, but the story about the cult practices featured a police detective saying: "What we found at the scene were approximately four black and white roosters, two decapitated black dogs, the legs of approximately two goats or lambs. All were caked with assorted beans and pennies." Similarly, the story about the capture of a kidnapping suspect offered video of the eighteen-month old boy being cradled by his parents, shots of the bruises the mother had received while run over by a car trying to rescue her son, and an emotional comment from the mother that "he would wake up in the middle of the night just screaming and we couldn't get him to calm down."[44]

While the importance of video and sound bites plays a large role in elevating the coverage of crimes, fires, and accidents over government, so does the fragmentation of political jurisdictions in the typical metropolitan television market. Network television news, also a mass medium dependent on effective video and sound bites, can focus its government news on the President, Congress, and national agencies. But local television news has a more difficult problem: interesting an audience that encompasses not simply citydwellers affected by city officials and institutions, but residents of suburban, exurban, and often some rural jurisdictions. While a particularly gory crime can be interesting to anyone in the region, local government news has a much narrower sphere of interest. As a result, government news comes to be balanced or even submerged by other more sensational topics. As one local television news reporter commented, "Government stories are thought of as really low priority by TV."

- **Government stories become further de-emphasized between the early and late night news shows.**

Because of the importance placed on timeliness, most television news shows try to update their late-night newscasts to reflect events that have occurred throughout the evening hours. Since government offices close at five o'clock, this need for timely stories means that crimes, fires, and accidents will be the major source of new stories between the early and late night newscast and that such stories will take precedence over earlier lead stories. The content analysis for the two-week period revealed that for each of the three stations, the percentage of time allotted to news of government dropped significantly from the six to the eleven o'clock broadcast. Specifically, where WCAU-TV allocated 43 percent of its newstime to local government at six o'clock, that percentage fell to 21 percent at eleven. Similarly, WPVI-TV's 46 percent of newstime on government at six fell to 25 percent at eleven, while KYW-TV's 34 percent at six fell to 27 percent at eleven.[45] In all of the late night broadcasts, coverage of occurrences took up a larger percentage of newstime than did coverage of government (see table 4.2).

Government stories were also consistently lower in the story order and reduced in time between six and eleven o'clock, supplanted by news of crimes,

TABLE 4.2   Station Newstime Distributed by Time Slot and News Category

Station	Time Slot	(%) Government	(%) Occurrences	(%) Features	(%) Private	(%) World News
3	6:00	34	32	24	9	0
3	11:00	27	36	22	3	12
Station Total		31	34	24	6	6
6	6:00	46	34	11	9	0
6	11:00	25	36	18	6	15
Station Total		36	35	14	7	7
10	6:00	43	29	23	6	0
10	11:00	21	27	39	6	7
Station Total		33	28	30	6	3
Overall Total		33	32	23	6	5

fires, and accidents.[46] For example, on the evening of the announcement of a major auto insurance reform bill in Pennsylvania, each station led its six o'clock newscast with packages about the new plan, hailed as lowering rates for motorists in the state. However, by the eleven o'clock newscast, the story had lost its prominence on all three stations. One station pushed the story back to a 30-second voice-over in its number three spot, [47] while a second reduced it to a 40-second VSOT in the fifteenth story slot.[48] A third station put the story fourth as a one-minute VSOT; it led its broadcast with a two-minute-forty-five second package called "Back from the Dead," featuring an exclusive interview with a mother who had been falsely informed that her daughter had been killed the day before.[49] In the hours between six and eleven o'clock, the auto insurance legislation was judged to have lost its status as the most important news of the day.

When new policy-related stories are covered by late-night local news, they are either evening meetings or protests and demonstrations. However, unless they provide dramatic video, such gatherings will be given relatively little time in the line-up. For example, a meeting of a new local coalition for better health care for the poor was covered as a voice-over of twenty seconds on one station[50] and thirty-five seconds on another[51] with little information about the specific problems the group hoped to address or the policies they would work to enact.

In contrast, on a different night, an evening demonstration against the proposed building of a new White Castle restaurant in a Philadelphia neighborhood—with protesters marching with placards and offering strong denunciation of the proposal—was awarded a one-minute-forty-five second VSOT. As a result of such play, small-scale evening demonstrations often seem more important than either citizen parlays or major government proposals made earlier in the day.

- **When government and policy is covered, the need to adopt a "sexy" or "humanistic" angle may displace important information.**

Since government stories are competing with gory murders, emotional testimony at the trials of crime bosses, or sobbing survivors in the aftermath of fires, they have to be dramatic to get on the air and high up on the story list. This kind of competition leads reporters to try to highlight the sexiest part of their stories to get on the air, often focusing on conflict, demonstrations, or people with colorful personalities. As one local television reporter described it, "TV is willing to take major government stories—as long as you can get a debate. If I don't have sexy stories coming out of City Hall, I'm in jeopardy. The station has one eye out for ratings, one for journalism."[52] News directors often push reporters covering government plans or policies to "humanize" their stories. One television reporter described the instructions of her news director as she went out to cover the press conference of a city official announcing a proposal for a major capital investment: "We don't want facts and figures for the story. We want to humanize it." Another reporter commented, "The operative principle we think about all the time is people, people, people. If I'm telling you a tax story that's kind of dry and boring, I want to tell how it's going to affect you." However, often the effects that television reporters tell their viewers about are the superficial, short-term, and obvious impacts of new legislation. For example, when New Jersey Governor James Florio announced a major plan to revise state taxes, all three stations sent reporters to supermarkets to describe how a higher sales tax would increase the cost of household goods, like toilet paper. Almost no attention was given to the more complex plan to revise the state's property tax, which might have eased many viewers' tax burdens.

In other cases, the need to "humanize" government stories leads to scarce time being used for appealing video rather than for the presentation of important information. For example, one reporter told of how a story on budget cuts was "humanized" by a visit to a health center whose funding would be reduced and where video of a six-year-old's check-up was collected. When time for the package was reduced shortly before airtime, the reporter was forced to cut out the middle section of the report that explained which city departments would have their funds cut and which would remain unaffected. But the six-year-old stepping onto the scale remained untouched in the package's opening, and the reporter was congratulated by newsroom staff for putting together an excellent story.

Local television's requirement for good video and sound bites can also affect the way public issues are cast. For example, in covering city council hearings on subway crime, the dispassionate comments of the police commissioner and the transit authority's general manager were downplayed as compared to coverage of the Guardian Angels who had come to town to patrol the subways. In one report, the station's anchor described the officials' comments at the hearing in a 30-second voice-over: "Gambaccini testified that historically the city has offered less police help for subway safety than most other cities. But Williams claimed that subway crime is not as bad as it's being described." In contrast, the same station devoted one minute and forty seconds to a reporter's tour of the subway's "worst trouble spots," where a representative of the Guardian Angels notes, "I guarantee that [right now] someone's getting their face smacked," and later, "If they suck concrete until the police comes, hey, I'm not concerned about the muggers' rights, I'm concerned about the victims' rights."[53]

In contrast to the television reports, the *Philadelphia Inquirer* article on the hearings was headlined "The safety of subways is debated." Its lead paragraph read "SEPTA general manager Louis Gambaccini told City Council yesterday that despite a recent surge in robberies and muggings in the city's subways, the crime rate in Philadelphia's tunnels is considerably lower than in most other major cities." An accompanying graphic showed how Philadelphia's crimes per 100,000 passengers in 1989 was .87, lower than Chicago's (1.27), Boston's (1.36), Atlanta's (1.49) and New York's (.94). While the *Inquirer* article also covered comments by a Guardian Angel, they noted Commissioner Williams' criticism of the Angels' as "a publicity-seeking group whose commitment rarely outlasts the media fanfare."[54] Where the newspaper article clearly presented the debate about the severity of subway crime, the television reports accepted it as a given, using the Guardian Angels' sound bites to confirm viewer fears.

The need for good video and sound bites may also lead to the coverage of demonstrations in opposition to policies, no matter how small. As a result, many private interest groups, from neighborhood residents opposing a new trash disposal plant to environmentalists fighting a major polluter, have learned to stage visual events that appeal to television cameras, media events to which often only television reporters are invited.[55] At times, the coverage of such protests may inadvertently give momentum to what may be a small minority in opposition to a policy rather than to the "silent majority" that may be supporting it. As one local official commented, "If you want local television to cover you, get twenty people to march in a circle." Many local officials find it particularly disturbing that in giving prominent coverage to such small demonstrations, local television news tends to exaggerate the size of the opposition.

- **"Sexy" versus "snoozer" government stories receive more play.**

While most local television stations embrace a multitude of local governmental units—from one or more state governments to hundreds of local jurisdictions—the ongoing business of government receives relatively little coverage by local television newscasts. Rather, when government is covered, it is more likely to be the "sexy" story rather than drier news which may have greater significance for viewers. By far the largest percentage of time allotted to governmental news in the two-week period, 24.5 percent, was linked to crime—including crime-related government policy or legislation, the corruption of public officials, and drug-related stories. Another 12 percent dealt with election campaigning, with stories focusing almost entirely on the candidates' ranking in the race rather than their positions on issues. In contrast, governmental policy linked to health received 7 percent of government newstime, schools 4 percent, and housing policy received 1 percent of news time. (Almost 17 percent of newstime for government was devoted to coverage linked to transportation, reflecting the coverage of the major auto insurance bill for Pennsylvania that was announced in week one—see table 4.3.)

The tendency for local television news to focus on sexy government stories was evident on the evening when New Jersey Governor James Florio made his budget speech to the legislature announcing a major increase in the state sales tax, among other sweeping tax changes. While one station led its broadcast with a two-minute-fifteen-second package about the plan, almost equal time was allotted to another "government" story, a package concerning whether the "Rocky Statue" (cast for the Sylvester Stallone movie) should remain on the Philadelphia Art Museum steps and whether an urban riding school should be

TABLE 4.3   Governmental Newstime by Substantive Area

Substantive Area	Newstime	
	seconds	percent
Abortion	65	0.4
Budget	1,355	9.1
Census	1,190	8.0
Consumer	795	5.3
Corruption	830	5.6
Crime	2,380	16.0
Disaster	185	1.2
Drugs	130	0.9
Economic development	370	2.5
Election	1,810	12.1
Environmental	100	0.7
Health	995	6.7
Housing	210	1.4
National	515	3.5
New policy	15	0.1
Personnel change	145	1.0
Plant closings	120	0.8
Protest	40	0.3
Regional issues	260	1.7
Schools	570	3.8
Sports teams	340	2.3
Transportation	2,500	16.8
Governmental Total	14,920	100.0

allowed to remain in Fairmount Park.[56] A particularly revealing example of how local television covers government came a night later.[57] One station's early broadcast opened with a package on the latest attempts by convicted murderer and former high school principal Jay Smith to be released from prison. It then followed with voice-over stories about: a city murder probe, a jailed robber, a fire in Camden, a fire in North Philadelphia, and the aftermath of a small plane crash in a city park. The seventh, eighth, and ninth stories then turned to governmental issues. The first story was a package about a group of state representatives who took a ride on the Market-Frankford Elevated train to demonstrate that the El was safe after a fatal crash the week before. The second story was a report that Congressman Bill Gray was introducing legislation in Congress that would force the state of Pennsylvania to create a dedicated funding base for the regional transit system. The third story concerned the protest by a neighborhood group to get a traffic signal.

The media event orchestrated by the state representatives, most of whom were up for reelection that year, contained little substantive information but was nevertheless covered as a one-minute-twenty-five-second package. The story about Bill Gray's proposal—a plan that addressed the severe funding problems of the entire regional transit system—was covered as a 20-second voice-over. The traffic-light protest was allotted thirty seconds. In contrast, the newspapers made a very different judgment of which government news stories were most important. The *Philadelphia Daily News* covered its tabloid front page the next day with the headline "Heat's on Pa. to Aid SEPTA" concerning the Gray proposal, while on an inside page the newspaper derided the El-train ride with the headline "Reps' Trip on SEPTA One EL of a Charade . . . Politicians Take the Press for a Ride." [58] The traffic light protest was not covered at all by the newspaper.

- **Local television news reporters are more likely to accept sources' viewpoints on policy initiatives than are print reporters.**

Because of limited time when covering complex government stories like new legislation or budget announcements, local television reporters often rely heavily on the press briefings of the initiating official. As a result, their reports come to present the policy largely from the perspective of the official. For example, in covering the budget announcement speech of Pennsylvania's Governor, two of the three news stations reported that Casey's plan would raise the minimum starting salary for the state's public teachers from $18,000 to $25,000. One station described the proposal: "Education will also benefit from Casey's election year budget. He wants to boost the minimum teacher's salary from $18,500 to $21,500," accompanied by the graphic "Casey Budget: Teachers' Salaries Minimum Up From $18,500 to $21,000." At eleven o'clock, the station ran the message, "Some of the winners in the 12.3 billion dollar spending plan: teachers, Casey proposing an increase in their minimum starting salary from $18,500 to $21,000." [59]

However, the *Philadelphia Inquirer,* in its following day's analysis of the budget, pointed out the proposed boost was like "pull[ing] some rabbits from hats." The reporter noted "that looks terrific, except when you consider that it would directly affect only an estimated 1,590 of the state's 104,850 teachers in the 1990–91 school year . . . Also, the state doesn't plan to reimburse school districts for mandated raises until the following year, 1991–92. In other words, money for raising minimum teacher salaries isn't in this budget at all."[60]

A similar case concerned television coverage of Casey's proposal for education in general. One station's anchor announced at six o'clock, "The Casey budget does boost spending for basic and higher education," accompanied by a graphic that read, "Increased Funding for Education." At eleven o'clock, the message was similar: "The total budget comes to 22.4 billion dollars but the main segment, the general fund, equals just over 12 billion dollars. Of that figure, a big chunk goes for basic and higher education," with the accompanying graphic, "Basic education $4.6 billion, higher education $1.3 billion."[61] The newspaper report the next day told a somewhat different story:

> The budget does contain some nifty illusions: Budget Secretary Michael H. Herschock during a news conference named basic education as the recipient of the biggest new chunk of state money. When asked what entity would take the biggest hit in terms of a smaller increase than the current year, his answer remained the same—basic education.
>
> Casey ballyhooed "an $84 million increase over the current year" for basic-education subsidies, or 3.2 percent. That sounds pretty good until you look at what the state is sending the schools this school year—a $154 million increase over the previous year, or 6.1 percent.[62]

Television reporters will look for opposition to official policies, but because of time limitations opponents' comments are typically limited to a five-to twenty-second sound bite, which does not leave much time for criticism of a complex plan. And because of the premium placed on drama and emotion, often the sound bites selected do not summarize the speaker's major criticisms so much as offer the most emotionally charged comments. For example, a consumer advocate interviewed about his opposition to a state auto insurance plan was quoted as saying: "Well, I think Pennsylvania has messed up its auto insurance reform once again. They've done it twice before and this is the third time."[63] While giving the appearance of presenting a balanced evaluation of the new legislation, this five-second sound bite offered no substantive reasons for the opposition.

Similarly, the only station to cover Republican reaction to the Democratic governor's budget plan used the following sound bite from a state legislator: "This man can't do what he wants to do without additional state taxes. And it's up to him to bite the bullet and start telling the public the truth about what went on in that room just now. I'm annoyed about it. I think it was dishonest and I don't think it was fair to the General Assembly."[64] In contrast, the next day's *Inquirer* covered Republican claims that the governor did not fully fund the state's drug fight, criticisms about the use of $207 million from the state workers' compensation fund to contribute to the general fund budget, and charges that a proposal to use bond money for economic development programs previously included in the general fund would "mortgage the future to pay for today."[65]

Local television's need to "humanize" government stories has also led to major government proposals being commented on by the typical "man-on-the-street." While such "MOS" interviews, as they are called, can at times be informative in providing the flavor of how ordinary citizens feel about a policy debate, they are often relatively uninformative emotional comments that take away from the time that could be used by a reporter, or a more informed participant, to explain the pros or cons in a policy debate.

- **Coverage of local politics and government focuses almost exclusively on city and state, as opposed to suburban, governments.**

Local television news coverage displays the same kind of "city myopia" evident in the metropolitan newspaper, despite the fact that television markets include even more nonurban jurisdictions. While 37 percent of all newstime for the two-week period went to coverage of the city of Philadelphia or other urban centers (such as Camden, Trenton, or Chester), only 18 percent was allocated to suburban news (see table 4.4). Looking specifically at the coverage of government, while 54 percent of all government stories focused on the central city, only 1 percent focused on suburban areas (see table 4.5). Perhaps even more revealing is a look at what categories of suburban stories get covered. Of all newstime devoted to suburban stories, 73 percent of that time is devoted to stories about accidents, crimes, and fires; 20 percent is allocated to features; and only 2 percent is devoted to stories about politics or government. In contrast, while 40 percent of central-city stories focused on occurrences, 48 percent concerned governmental news (see table 4.6).

Why are city politics and government covered so extensively and suburban

TABLE 4.4   Newstime by Geographic Area and Station

Geographic Area	Channel 10 (%)	Channel 3 (%)	Channel 6 (%)	Total
Central city	36	33	42	37
Suburban	14	25	15	18
Regional	28	15	19	21
State	8	11	11	10
Other city	2	2	2	2
National	9	8	6	8
International	3	6	6	5
Total	100	100	100	100

TABLE 4.5   News Categories' Newstime Distributed by Geographic Area

Category	Central City (%)	Suburban (%)	Regional (%)	State (%)	Other City (%)	National (%)	International (%)	All Areas (%)
Government	54	1	6	29	1	8	2	100
Occurrences	46	40	4	0	6	2	2	100
Feature	12	16	56	0	0	16	0	100
Private	23	13	52	0	0	12	0	100
World news	0	0	30	0	0	0	70	100
Combined	37	18	21	10	2	8	5	100

TABLE 4.6   Geographic Areas' Newstime Distributed by News Category

Category	Central City (%)	Suburban (%)	Regional (%)	State (%)	Other City (%)	National (%)	International (%)	Combined Areas
Government	48	2	9	100	12	33	12	33
Occurrences	40	73	6	0	88	10	11	32
Feature	7	20	61	0	0	46	2	23
Private	4	5	16	0	0	11	0	6
World News	0	0	8	0	0	0	75	5
All Categories	100	100	100	100	100	100	100	100

government ignored by local television news? As with the print media, the answer lies largely in the accessibility of city government news and the fragmentation of the multitude of small suburban jurisdictions. In addition, the players in the local city government game tend to be more colorful and charismatic than suburban executives and legislators.[66] In the two weeks of local news observed, only one local story concerned suburban politics or government: the report, carried by one station only, of a major change in the political leadership of a suburban county of Philadelphia. In contrast, the question of whether Frank Rizzo would run for Mayor of the city of Philadelphia in an election over a year away was covered in a number of packages on all the local news stations.

When the rare suburban political story is covered, it tends to be limited in time and relatively low in the story order. For example, on a night not included in the observed sample, one station covered the vote by Democrats in a suburban township to oppose Governor Casey's reelection bid because of his stance on abortion. However, in contrast to the packages about Frank Rizzo's election chances, which often led broadcasts, the suburban story was a VSOT and the tenth story to be aired in the newscast. It trailed behind such local stories as a shooting in North Philadelphia, the latest on the condition of a suburban policeman wounded the night before, the report of a hepatitis case in Allentown, and a package on the reaction in Atlantic City to the news that millionaire developer Donald Trump and his wife were ending their marriage.[67] The story about changing political leadership in the suburban county was the seventh story on the eleven o'clock broadcast, occupying 45 seconds.[68]

By far the most time devoted to any suburban news story in the two weeks of broadcasts focused on a foul odor sickening students in a small elementary school. The odor turned out to be caused by emissions from a nearby chemical plant, and all three television stations did daily packages featuring comments from the children describing the smell and interviews with angry parents demanding that the problem be solved. While a serious issue to the parents involved, the story had relatively few implications for the suburban audience as a whole as compared with other more pervasive environmental threats such as lead poisoning or radon gases, which received no mention in the two-week period.

While accidents were the largest category of suburban stories covered, the most common category of city coverage was crime. Of all occurrence newstime on the stations in the sample, 46 percent was used for those occurring in cities. Looking exclusively at stories about crimes and fires, 62 percent concerned

128

those occurring in urban areas. In total, 13 percent of all newstime was occupied by stories about urban crimes and fires taking place largely in the poor neighborhoods of the central and satellite cities. In general, the two weeks' of viewing pointed out the disturbing practice of relying on the tragedies of poor, urban victims—and in particular children—to provide the emotional video and sound bites that draw audiences to television news. Often these reports seemed to be masquerading as a public service while in fact doing little more than allowing the audience to voyeuristically enjoy the tragedy of others, and particularly others living in poverty.

- **Increasing emphasis on features and promotions further reduces time for government and policy news.**

An increasing emphasis on features was evident in the two weeks in reports from health and consumer issues to entertainment and gossip about celebrities. In some cases, such reports provided useful information to viewers, presenting the simple warning signs of common diseases or providing financial or tax tips to viewers. Many of the features observed, however, were devoid of important information beyond the obvious, as when a report on children's ear infections suggested that parents whose children complain of hearing problems take them to their doctors. More common was the entertainment-oriented feature, which displaced or reduced time for important policy stories. As a case in point, on the day of Governor Casey's budget announcement, KYW-TV allocated less than one minute to the budget story, while three and one-half minutes were devoted to a feature about the Mercer museum in Doylestown, a piece that was part of the station's "Pride of Philadelphia" promotional campaign.[69]

In some cases, features are thinly veiled promotions for the newscast or the station's entertainment programming. For example, during the first week of the analysis, which fell in a "sweeps" month, two of the stations sent their own reporters to Hollywood for stories about entertainment shows. The stories just happened to be about prime-time programs being carried that evening on the affiliate's station. In one case, the reporter's feature on "The Loveboat" aired at 6:00, serving to promote the show that would appear later that evening.[70] In a second case at another station, a piece on the set of "L.A. Law" was aired in the 11:00 newscast and heavily promoted during the show itself, which preceded the newscast.[71] While such features are presented as news (described as "our report from Hollywood"), they use up chunks of a broadcast that could be devoted to serious journalism.

In addition, many of the serious investigations pursued by local television stations, particularly during "sweeps" months, distort issues by focusing on the unusual and extreme rather than the more common problem. For example, WPVI-TV aired a special report about children caught in the cross fire of drug violence,[72] calling attention to a problem far less prevalent and pervasive than inadequate health care for poor children or the public school drop-out rate. A similar focus on the tragic but unusual case was evident in a series that aired in February of 1989 at WCAU-TV called "Mothers Who Kill." Rather than focus on postpartum depression, which affects many women, the series chose to address the very rare psychotic syndrome that was claimed to be the cause of a recent murder case in the city. The series focused less on the medical or legal issues involved in the case than on interviews with imprisoned women who had murdered their children. While the reporter was careful to note at one point that postpartum psychosis was quite rare, she concluded her report with a warning to the audience to watch their mothers, daughters, wives, or sisters for symptoms of the disease.

In summary, local television news tends to give relatively low priority and limited time to governmental news and to focus on the relatively sensational aspects of government stories when they are covered. Complicated budgetary stories are reduced to packages of a few minutes in length or, when lacking in effective video, to stories read by anchors in less than a minute. Television reporters are less interested in probing whether new proposals are sound than in capturing an emotional sound bite on camera or covering an activity-filled demonstration, no matter how small in numbers.

The Increasing Role of Local Television News

In recent years, satellite technology has allowed local television news stations to increase their coverage of remote regional, national, and even international stories. In addition, more and more local stations are entering into cooperative newsgathering systems, such as Conus and Newsfeed, in which member stations uplink local stories for satellite transmission to other stations on the system. These satellite newsgathering capabilities are allowing local stations to decrease their reliance on network news coverage and to change the relations between affiliates and networks. In some cases, affiliates have become powerful competitors for networks, with larger numbers of viewers for local than network news. On the other hand, affiliate audience size is also a key contributor to the size of network news audiences in a local market, since the local news feeds the network news.[73]

The increasing independence of local stations has both positive and negative implications. On the positive side, the increasing ability of local television stations to broadcast from remote locales has allowed stations to provide a unique local perspective on national and international affairs. Local television stations routinely interview the areas' senators and congressmen via satellite from Washington to determine how they stand on national and international issues of interest to their local constituents. In national elections, local broadcasters cover the appearances of national candidates in the area and often query them on issues important to the local population. In such cases, local television news may be able to provide an important and useful local angle that is missing from national reporting.

In addition, local news stations are able to tailor national and international news coverage to the particular tastes of the local population. For example, in 1981, KYW-TV used the satellite feed system to gather reactions across the country to the attempted assassination of the Pope, staying on the air far longer than the networks. The extended coverage reflected the interests of the Philadelphia market's large Catholic population.[74] Similarly, in the spring of 1984, WDAF-TV in Kansas City, Missouri, sent a crew to El Salvador to cover the U.S. team that was monitoring the local elections because the team was headed by Kansas Senator Nancy Katzenbaum. Also in that year, a Seattle news station sent a crew to cover a natural gas explosion in Mexico City, for the benefit of one-fourth of its audience that is Hispanic.[75] In the two-week sample observed for this analysis, there were a number of instances in which reporters interviewed local experts about world events or talked to recent émigrés about conditions in their home countries, thus providing an interesting local angle to seemingly remote occurrences.

On the negative side, however, local television news reporters may be less qualified at subjecting national figures to tough questioning and scrutinizing their policies than national network journalists. Indeed, many national candidates have developed media strategies that allow them to make live appearances on local television programs, where they are more likely to get favorable coverage than on the network news. Local journalists, lacking regular beats and the reporting experience of their national counterparts, may offer far less incisive reporting than national news reporters. Even with their coverage of local officials, such as governors or area senators and congressmen, live satellite interviews generally represent a better opportunity for the official to present a prepackaged answer to brief questions rather than having to respond to tough probing by television reporters.

Therefore, while local television news is taking on an ever-expanding role in informing citizens about their localities and the world, the typical newscast's coverage of both national and local public affairs is often weakened by the constraints of the medium and by the need to meet competitive demands. With vast resources going into paying anchor salaries and investment in new technologies, the news-seeking function itself is often underfunded. The small number of reporters, working without beats and under strong time limitations, are often kept from investigating the claims of the public officials they cover. In addition, the need for effective video and sound bites and for drama and emotion leads to a distortion of some news and, in general, to the de-emphasis of governmental news in favor of crimes, fires, accidents, and disasters. When local television does cover government, it is often the sexier government stories or the more humanistic angles of government plans that are reported, frequently at the expense of more important information.

5 Alternative Voices in the Local Media

[While metropolitan newspapers and local television news serve as the mass media of the local news environment, there are many other smaller communications outlets that provide news and information to only a subset of the local community./From city magazines and urban newsweeklies to the black, ethnic, and gay press, from community newspapers to talk radio stations, the specialized media serve many important functions for their often intensely loyal audiences and offer information not found in the larger local media. With the decline in the number of metropolitan newspapers, particularly in the nation's large cities, these specialized media have come to flourish, attracting not simply larger audiences but increasingly sophisticated journalists as well.

This chapter looks at the changing nature of the specialized local media and considers the roles they play in influencing urban, regional, and national policy agendas. How much influence do these alternative media hold in molding public opinion within their communities and in affecting the actions of public officials and the direction of public policy? And, most important, do these media serve as true alternative voices in the region, presenting different perspectives on local issues from either metropolitan newspaper or local television news?

The Evolution of City Magazines: From Boosterism to Consumerism

While city magazines with their "ten-best" lists of local restaurants and romantic weekend getaways may seem a recent arrival on the local media scene, the concept of a local magazine has been in existence for almost a century. The first "city magazine" in America was a publication called *Town Topics*, founded by Colonel William Mann in New York City before 1900. Although the publication closed about thirty years later, it set the precedent for city magazines by providing a select audience of readers with "society news, gossip, and general light news."[1]

The next city magazine to emerge was the *New Yorker*, founded by Harold Ross in the 1920s. While intended to serve as a "metropolitan magazine," the *New Yorker* had certain hallmarks that characterized it from its beginnings to

133

current day: literary offerings from established and new authors and poets, satirical cartoons, and reviews of arts and entertainment in New York. While enjoying a large circulation in New York, the *New Yorker* soon gained a large national circulation. The *New Yorker* also had several imitators in other cities, including the *Senator* in 1939 in Washington, D.C., the *Chicagoan* in 1926, and *Parade* in Cleveland in 1931.[2]

In contrast to the literary style of the *New Yorker,* many city magazines were founded as organs of local chambers of commerce, strong on boosterism of the local economy and frequently offering guides to local hotels, restaurants, shows, museums, and other forms of entertainment. For example, magazines like *Boston Better Business* and *Greater Philadelphia* appeared as early as World War I to promote commerce in their respective regions.[3] In the 1960s, however, magazines that had been dismissed as chamber of commerce puff pieces began to take on a more activist and muckraking role. *Greater Philadelphia* became simply *Philadelphia* magazine and took on a new, more incisive approach to local journalism.

One observer described city magazines of this era as acting "more like civic gadflies than tame publicity purveyors."[4] An editor of a city magazine in the 1960s described the aim of his magazine: "Our job is to plug the city—and to attack the city and its problems . . . My city right and wrong."[5] Often these magazines tackled tough political and social issues before the metropolitan newspapers in their cities did and reported actively about those newspapers and their reporting standards.

New city magazines also appeared in the 1960s with *New York* magazine setting a standard for many others. Begun in April 1968 as a Sunday supplement to the now-defunct *New York Herald Tribune, New York* was a sophisticated commentator on both the New York and national and international scene. Clay Felker, the first editor, described the mission of his magazine in a written statement: "We want to cover everything in New York. We want to attack what is bad in this city and preserve and encourage what is new and good . . . We want to have a direct involvement in this city. We want to be inseparable from it. We want to be its voice, to capture what this city is about better than anyone else has."[6]

In the 1960s, many city magazines like *New York* were a combination of articles with social and political commentary and guides to enjoying the good life in the city and its surroundings. Some of the best, like *Philadelphia,* did both with a sometimes acerbic, sometimes witty style. An examination of the

134

cover stories of *Philadelphia* from 1968 indicates the kind of mix of articles the magazine featured in that era. While the March 1968 issue had a story titled, "How Much Riot Control?" and a September issue covered the new black establishment in the city, other issues focused on "Fun and Games on Long Beach Island"[7] and "Why Your Kids Can't Stand You."[8] This eclectic blend of politics, social analysis, and lifestyle advice could also be seen on the West Coast, where *Los Angeles* magazine in 1968 featured cover stories on "How Sick Is Our Health Care" in the same issue as "Love in Los Angeles: Is Romance Obsolete?"[9] or "A Civic Prescription to Ease Alienation and Violence" advertised on the same cover as "The Couples-Go-Round: Mating Games in the Suburbs."[10]

However, twenty years later, the covers of city magazines tended to reflect a general shift away from social and political criticism and toward a greater focus on consumerism. *Philadelphia*'s cover stories in 1988 included: "Dining Out Annual,"[11] "Don't Get Married Until You Read This,"[12] "The Best Places to Buy Homes,"[13] "The Essential Shore,"[14] "Getting In, Beating the College Crunch,"[15] and "Pregnant at Last."[16] *Los Angeles* magazine had embarked on a policy of running photos of Hollywood celebrities on its covers by 1988, including Cher heralding the "Annual Health and Beauty Guide,"[17] or Michael Tucker and Jill Eikenberry accompanying a cover story on "The Ultimate Wedding Planner: Fabulous Locales, Planners, Florists and the Works."[18] City magazine editors continued to run occasional serious articles about social or political issues but began to find that newsstand sales were best with guides-to and worst with "downbeat" stories, particularly those concerning crime and fear in the city.

By the late 1980s, city magazines in the large cities were enjoying a great deal of success and attracting an affluent audience with an average age of forty-five, with more readers located in the suburbs than in the city. While they continued to give some attention to politics and business trends in the city and region, their primary focus had turned to lifestyle and guides to consumption in the local area. When they did address political or policy issues, they tended to focus more on personalities and political intrigue than on the economic or social implications of the policy itself.

The Urban Newsweeklies: Roots in the Underground Press

In the 1950s and 1960s, at the same time that city magazines were beginning to flourish, many local areas saw the emergence of politically radical local media often referred to as the "underground press." The *Los Angeles Free Press*, founded in 1964, the *Seed* from Chicago, the *Avatar* from Boston, and the *Berkeley Barb*, among others, were targeted to a youthful population, from students on campuses to post-graduates in their twenties. Many of these papers started with a focus on local issues and grew to address the national political issues of the 1960s, such as civil rights, the Vietnam war, and the "military-industrial complex," as well as advocating radical lifestyles embracing sex, drugs, and rock music. As Johnson describes it, the underground press was different in a fundamental sense from the mainstream press: "As much as possible, its reporters were present and involved in the events they wrote about. They sought inside information rather than relying on hearsay or established press releases, and their journalism attempted to communicate factual material as well as a personal style of concern and participation. They had no pretensions to a so-called 'objectivity': for the most part they wrote about what they felt and witnessed." [19]

The newspapers practiced advocacy journalism, written by concerned journalists seeking to change society and influence the political arena. The newspapers served also as a kind of bulletin board of listings to advertise radical activities—the women's liberation meeting, the protest march, the be-ins and sit-ins of the era. The newspapers were operated on a shoestring budget and paid very little to their writers and editors. The advertising they received was often minimal, provided by purveyors of goods whose political philosophies were consistent with the editorial content of the newspaper: rock albums and music stores, stereo equipment, motorcycles, head shops, and a multitude of classifieds for personal services.

By the 1970s, many of these underground newspapers had died out, in part because causes like the Vietnam War and the draft had disappeared and the economy had tightened, in part because their readers had grown older, more conservative, and had new informational needs. Most underground newspapers went out of business in the 1970s, although the *Berkeley Barb* hung on until 1980. In its farewell issue of July 3, 1980, the *Barb* cited as the reasons for its closing two trends in the country, "the rise of a conservative backlash . . . and the overwhelming growth of political apathy among those who can't bring themselves to hop aboard the neo-conservative bandwagon." [20]

In their place grew a new kind of local publication that filled a niche left over from the underground papers. Still reaching out to the 18 to 35-year-olds, the "alternative" or "urban" weeklies—or "city papers" as they have come to be called—began to emerge to appeal to a youthful target population typically residing in inner-city neighborhoods. As Armstrong has described them, these newspapers served as "how-to guides for coping with and enjoying city life" targeted to "the Woodstock generation a decade later, looking for a condominium rather than a tab of LSD."[21]

As these so-called "alternative" weeklies moved into the 1980s, they became effective advertising vehicles for those retailers seeking access to a young audience with high disposable incomes—the singles or childless couples living in inner-city areas and looking for wide-ranging entertainment activities. Their audiences were generally younger and less affluent and more concentrated within cities than the audiences of city magazines. However, more and more of these newspapers have begun to distribute their newspapers in suburbs as well as cities as increasing numbers of young, affluent singles have relocated outside of the city.

The advertisers of these newspapers are typically small retailers—restaurants and clubs, boutiques, wine stores, fitness clubs, futon mattress stores—who have ample advertising budgets but who typically cannot afford the rates of the metropolitan daily. Increasingly, some of the more successful of these newspapers are also able to target national and regional advertisers who want to pinpoint a young, affluent demographic group. For example, the Philadelphia *City Paper* has begun to carry cigarette and liquor ads from national companies, as well as ads for regional furniture stores and multistore record chains.

Although some papers, like the *Boston Phoenix* and the Seattle *Weekly* have paid circulation, most have discovered the lucrative formula of free distribution, enlarging their audiences and hence their advertising revenues and avoiding the problem of having to pay distributors. The typical formula of these newspapers has been to lead with a few serious "news" articles and to follow with a heavy emphasis on entertainment and restaurant reviews and a stress on extensive listings of entertainment activities.

In some areas, alternative weeklies have grown large enough to rival the metropolitan newspapers for circulation. For example, in 1989, the *Phoenix New Times* had a circulation of 140,000 as compared with the *Arizona Republic* circulation of approximately 318,000 and the *Phoenix Gazette* circulation of 111,000.[22] Despite their success in gaining readers, many of these newspapers have come under criticism because of their editorial content. Some observers dispute the notion that the newspapers represent "alternative" voices in a metropolitan area, because of their emphasis on consumerism. For example, Armstrong has charged that while these newspapers "benefitted from their radical predecessors," which paved the way for changes in society that created a large singles population, they are instrumental in "helping to entice them away from the challenging world of radical politics."[23]

> By defining this community of interests in an intensely commercial context—the music, the bars, nightclubs, self-improvement centers, and physical therapy courses to which the upwardly mobile young moderns flocked were not free—the urban weeklies helped displace the corresponding community of interests provided by radical politics, which had generally existed in a less commercial context . . .
>
> The urban weeklies offer a very different agenda than did their radical predecessors: pleasure rather than struggle, status rather than the erasure of privilege, enjoyment of the world as it is rather than visions of the world as it might be.

Armstrong does admit that these newspapers serve as alternative voices "in the broadest sense":

> Many are cleanly designed, carefully edited periodicals that differ from conservative daily newspapers in several important ways: their relative ease of access for unknown or offbeat contributors; their use of the personal voice in writing; their willingness to do in-depth, magazine-style features about issues generally skimmed by daily newspapers and electronic media; their willingness to jab at the local power structure.[24]

But critics like Armstrong also contend that the urban weeklies tone down any temptation to radicalism so as not to offend advertisers, since, unlike the underground newspapers of the 1960s whose advertisers' views were often as radical as the newspapers, the advertisers of the weeklies want to encourage consumerism. In addition, as urban newsweeklies attract increasing advertising from tobacco, beer, and alcohol companies, they may shy away from editorial content that discusses the dangers of smoking and drinking.

Editors of these newsweeklies defend their mission and their status as "alternatives" by claiming that they often provide a different slant to local issues than the metropolitan dailies in their town, which are increasingly owned by conglomerates and which are often monopolies on the regional level. They claim they are less likely to be "practitioners of press release journalism" and purposely look for perspectives ignored by the major mainstream media. As the publisher of the Philadelphia *City Paper* described the function of his paper, "We are here to present news and ideas overlooked by other people . . . we poke around where the other media aren't allowed to surface."[25]

Some editors recognize that readers pick up the newspapers as they would shoppers, for their advertisements and listings, but may get drawn to some of the articles. "Seventy-five percent of people pick up these papers to see what to do on Saturday night," said an editor of one such paper. "That gives us as editors the freedom to write whatever we want in the editorial sections, which we gear to the 15 percent who do read." They also claim to act as "watchdogs on the watchdog," reporting on issues facing the big metropolitan newspapers and on the way those newspapers cover local issues. "We want to make people more wary of the information they get from other media," said one editor. And while some admit to putting more entertainment-oriented stories on the covers of their newspapers than politics and social issues, they argue they are following the interests of their audiences, as well as providing an alternative slant to those entertainment issues. "Yeh, we do a lot of lifestyle," said one editor, "because those things are fun. But hopefully we are transcending pure consumerism, remaining weird and crusty, cynical and cankered, and humorous and wry."[26]

There is considerable variation among papers in different cities in the emphasis they place on news, politics, and issue-oriented pieces as opposed to arts and entertainment features. In the same month as the *Bay Guardian* was running a cover story on "Who Owns San Francisco?"[27] the *Boston Phoenix* was featuring a cover story on the Boston Red Sox entitled "The Autumn Game,"[28] the Chicago *Reader* was doing a piece on minimum-security prisons,[29] the Baltimore *City Paper*'s cover heralded stories about David Letterman and *Spy Magazine*,[30] and the *Dallas Observer*'s cover story was "The Beast Awakens," described as a survey of "the area's burgeoning heavy metal scene."[31]

This variation in content is evident in the way editors of the papers describe their work. The editor of the Seattle *Weekly*, David Brewster, described the mission of his paper:

> The *Weekly* doesn't want to view itself as an "alternative" newspaper but rather as a "city weekly"—smarter, written better, a writer's paper, locally owned, locally rooted, downtown-oriented. Our aim is to reform the problems of print journalism, going back to an earlier tradition of good writing and concern with change rather than stenographic packaging of nonoffensive

139

material. For the major metro papers, a calculation is made that the fewer people you offend, the bigger market you reach.

Here, fairness is the goal, not objectivity. We want a range of ideas. Most journalism narrows debates: simplifies, stereotypes. We want interesting views from the right or the left, although our center of gravity is left of center, certainly. It is obviously a paper for young professionals in the city, but I like to think of it as a bridge paper, a bridge between ages, between city and suburb, hitting people with influence and yet the impatience of youth.

Brewster noted that the *Weekly* often takes a distinctly different approach to public policy issues than do the metropolitan newspapers and tends to be more critical of official sources of information than the mainstream press. In discussing an issue concerning the city's decision whether or not to offer incentives to attract a naval home-port to Seattle, he said, "The big papers printed these inflated numbers of how many jobs would be generated by the Navy. No one dares oppose the Navy. So a major debate doesn't take place. No one except the *Weekly* was there to take a position. The big papers wait for opponents. The *Weekly*'s impact lies in the fact that we embolden other reporters, release sources, create opposition."[32]

However, editors of other city papers seem to have less interest in promoting change in their cities and regions. The former editor of the Baltimore *City Paper,* while noting that city papers can be "a major player in town, particularly where there is a weak daily," described his objectives in different terms: "We're not trying to have an impact politically. Our purpose is to provide quality writing that won't find a place elsewhere."[33] These thoughts were echoed by the publisher of the Philadelphia *City Paper:* "We don't tell people what to vote for. We're not trying to simplify things to tell pople what to do."[34]

When these alternative newspapers do provide an alternative perspective on political and social issues in their cities, their impact seems to be somewhat limited. As Brewster noted, "We usually lose. But we do create bases for opposition and our analysis is often eventually accepted."[35] In part, their limited political impact is a result of their emphasis on listings and entertainment, which seems to have limited their credibility with their audience when serious political issues are tackled. In these cases, the readers often discount the more radical news writing, even as they use the papers as bibles of entertainment information. And in many cases, readers do not even read the political pieces, turning instead to the listings and ads, as they would with a common shopper.

With their increasing emphasis on entertainment rather than political stories, many of these newspapers fail to provide a consistent alternative voice on local policy debates.

The Specialized Press

In many American cities, specialized newspapers exist to serve specific subcommunities of the population and often come to play an important role in local political debates. Typically weeklies, but sometimes dailies, these newspapers target the black, Hispanic, Asian, Jewish, and other ethnic communities that abound in metropolitan areas and stand alongside the foreign-language press, which continues to flourish in cities with recent immigrants to the United States. In addition, in many cities there are local newspapers targeted to the gay population. While the economic viability of these newspapers varies considerably and their specific functions differ, the specialized press share certain common functions.

First, the specialized press fill a gap left by the metropolitan newspapers by providing in-depth coverage of local, national, and international news of particular interest to the specific group. Second, they play an advocacy role by attempting to marshal the support of the community in favor of certain political and social changes. Third, they provide an arena in which political candidates and elected officials can be evaluated from the perspective of how well their performance and campaign promises fulfill the needs of the specific community. That is, in many cases, candidates for public offices become known and judged on the basis of how they are covered (or advertised) in the specialized press.

In addition, the specialized press differ from the mainstream local media in that they are said to have more credibility with their readers than the mainstream media, both in terms of editorial and advertising content. A poll taken by the National Newspaper Publishers Association, a trade association of black newspapers, for example, found that 70 percent of readers of black newspapers believe what they read in those newspapers, as compared with 40 percent of readers of daily newspapers.[36] Similar to the black press, other specialized newspapers targeted to specific communities provide an important source of trusted information for their readers.

The Black Press

The first black newspaper in the United States was called *Freedom's Journal*, begun in 1827 in New York City to fight the proslavery stance of another New York newspaper and "to plead our own cause." Most black newspapers, however, were not founded until after 1920. Many of the black newspapers founded in the South were subsidized by political parties for the length of a particular campaign, serving as patronage vehicles through which black voters were urged to vote for particular candidates. Often these newspapers died soon after the election was over and their goal accomplished.[37]

In cities like New York, the large in-migration of literate blacks created a "golden age" for local black newspapers, which crusaded for causes like putting an end to lynching. Because of the segregation of society before the 1950s, many of these newspapers flourished with advertising from black businesses that served a growing black population. With the increasing integration of society, however, many black businesses suffered and often failed, which in turn hurt the black newspapers they had supported. Newspapers like the *Amsterdam News* in New York, which had a circulation of close to 90,000 in the 1950s, had dropped to closer to 50,000 in the 1980s.[38]

In 1989, there were approximately three hundred black newspapers in the United States, most of them weeklies.[39] They vary in size of circulation, penetration of their black market, and economic viability, with some black newspapers enjoying strong advertising revenues while others struggle to survive. In general, however, the readers of black newspapers tend to be skewed toward an older black population, according to the Scarborough Report on Black Newspaper Audience Readership, with the majority nationwide concentrated in the 35–54 age group and with 27 percent over the age of 55.[40] In the largest metropolitan areas, several black newspapers exist, often with different political perspectives. For example, in New York City, there are six black newspapers, the total circulation of which in 1989 was close to 400,000. In Chicago, there are seven black newspapers, totaling a circulation of 360,000. Philadelphia's *Tribune* had a circulation of close to 120,000 in 1989, almost half the size of the *Philadelphia Daily News,* the city's tabloid.[41]

While black newspapers vary in format, technical sophistication, and political perspective, they have in common several functions that they play for their readers. First, they present a black viewpoint, a "window on the community" as one editor put it, on local, national, and sometimes international events that may be missing from the mainstream media. In particular, they tend to give greater detail to events and issues of particular interest to blacks, while at the same time often giving a different perspective to those issues and events.

Second, black newspapers often fight for black causes and rights, rallying their readers in support of causes or in protest over injustices against blacks. From civil rights in the 1950s and 1960s to protests over charges of police brutality against blacks in the 1980s, the newspapers have taken an active advocacy position for their readers. They also represent a vehicle through which political leaders, black and white, may send messages to the black community. As the editor of the *Philadelphia Tribune* commented, "White politicians know that there are two vehicles with which to communicate to blacks: the church and the black media."[42] Most candidates for office actively court the major black newspapers in their cities and often advertise extensively in them before elections.

Black newspapers also serve a social function in providing a vehicle for positive stories about blacks and individuals who may serve as role models. Such positive stories are intended to dispel the stereotypes that emerge from the mainstream media, where, it is argued, blacks tend to be featured only when they commit or are victims of crimes. As the Kerner Commission noted, "Far too often the press acts and talks about Negroes as if Negroes do not read the newspapers or watch television, give birth, marry, die, and go to PTA meetings."[43] More recent critics argue similarly that "news about black organizations, achievements of individual blacks, even ordinary birth, marriage, and death news about blacks was generally ignored by newspapers . . . although the same kinds of news about white organizations and individuals was run."[44] Black newspapers often cover just those social events and highlight the everyday lives of black Americans, covering weddings, debutante parties, obituaries, and society news.

However, as a result of such coverage and because of the functions many have historically played as a "vanity press," black newspapers have come under criticism for being overly positive, "covering the bourgeoisie to the exclusion of the poor," and for being "more concerned with the social life of the few than the political life of the many."[45] At the same time, some black newspapers have been criticized for breeding ill will between the races and increasing segregation. In addition, some black newspapers have been faulted for their poor editorial quality, for accepting too much public relations copy, for providing inadequate news coverage and interpretation, and for their poor technical quality.[46] This legacy of poor technical production value has been found responsible for the tendency of younger blacks to reject these newspapers in favor of mainstream dailies or black-oriented radio and television.[47]

In part, the lack of sophistication in production value can be traced to a major

problem of black newspapers and the black media in general: difficulty in securing advertising from non-black businesses. The editor of the *Amsterdam
News,* William Tatum, has been quoted as saying, "Try as we might, we have
not been able to explain the true importance of the black press and the $200
billion-plus that we represent in sales in this country . . . Advertising agencies
and corporate representatives believe that a very small percentage of their advertising dollars overall should be assigned to black media."[48] Other black publishers and editors agree with this statement, claiming that they must aggressively struggle to convince individual businesses and large advertising agencies
that there is a black consumer market with considerable disposable income.

In recent years, many black publishers have been investing considerable capital in transforming existing publications or starting new ones that offer pol-
ished, professional journalism with sophisticated use of graphics and color and
incisive local news reporting. The *St. Louis American,* the *Winston-Salem
Chronicle* in North Carolina, and the *Miami Times* are among those black newspapers which have been cited for their aggressive coverage of issues of interest
to the black communities in their cities. For example, in St. Louis, publisher
Donald Suggs redesigned his *American,* changed it from paid circulation to free
distribution, and expanded its coverage from the city to suburban areas with
middle-class black populations. The editorial content of Suggs's paper is typical of the new brand of black newspaper, which is trying to attract not just an
older population but the young black adult: the two-section paper contains local
and national news, church news, community events and editorials, as well as
arts and entertainment, social events, and a nostalgia column.[49]

Black newspapers have had a tradition of reporting on local issues that affect
the black community and in rallying the community behind political and social
action. For example, in 1987 in Phoenix, it was the *Arizona Informant* that
played a major role in the boycott to protest the state's decision not to observe
Martin Luther King's birthday.[50] Similarly, when a young black man was killed
while fleeing a gang of white youths in Howard Beach, Queens, it was the
outraged coverage of New York's black newspapers that helped spur an investigation. And in 1989, several black newspapers in New York City, though
varying in their political outlooks, worked to defeat Ed Koch in the mayoral
primary.

The political importance of black newspapers extends beyond their ability to
influence their own readers. Often, reporters from the mainstream media pick
up stories from the black press and transmit them to the larger community. In

cities like New York, the mainstream media have taken to reporting on the coverage of the black newspapers itself, particularly in trying to gauge the sentiments of the black community in local elections.

While black newspapers have often been criticized for failing to scrutinize the actions of black political leaders, some publications have begun to buck the trend. For example, the *City Sun,* based in Brooklyn, has been critical of politicians like Harlem Assemblyman Herman D. Farrell, and while endorsing David Dinkins in the New York City election in 1989, did so with conditions.[51] "If black officials and candidates for office are not doing what we think they should do, which is to serve their natural constituency, we don't give them ink," said *Sun* publisher Andrew Cooper.[52] Many black newspapers have also started covering more news concerning the problems facing the black community as a whole, such as drug abuse or child abuse, instead of trying to remain resolutely positive and upbeat as they did in an earlier era.

The Jewish Press

The Jewish press in America has its roots in both a thriving Anglo-Jewish press going back to the mid-nineteenth century and an equally flourishing Yiddish press that began with the Eastern European Jewish migration of the late nineteenth century. Yiddish dailies appeared in cities with the heaviest concentration of Jewish immigration, such as New York, Philadelphia, and Chicago, their objectives being to discuss political and social issues confronting the community, as well as to publish "belles lettres, literary criticism, and essays of broad cultural content, providing Yiddish writers, essayists, and propagandists with an influential forum."[53] Newspapers like the *Forward* in New York City crusaded aggressively for union-building to protect Jewish garment and hat makers and to create national social programs such as Social Security and Medicare.[54]

At its peak, an estimated two million people read the Jewish daily press, but with increasing assimilation into American life, readership gradually declined. In particular, with a dwindling population speaking Yiddish, many of whom relocated out of Northern cities in New York to the warmer climates of Florida, circulation of these newspapers plummeted. The *Forward,* once a daily paper with a circulation of 238,000 in 1917, had become by the late 1980s a weekly with a circulation of approximately 20,000.[55]

After World War II, the English-language Jewish press, in the form of weeklies in many metropolitan areas, began to witness an expansion in size and circulation. The function of these weeklies has been described as working toward "group survival at home and financial and political aid for Israel and for Jewish communities under stress abroad." At the same time, they have served to publicize social events and milestones in the local Jewish community, such as announcements of engagements, weddings, and bar and bat mitzvahs, as well as serving as a bulletin board for calendars of community events. The newspapers also contain articles on religious holidays and the occasional rabbinical commentary, as well as features on Jewish arts, entertainment, and travel.[56] Their function was described by one editor as serving as a "communal glue, a cohesive force. With physical dispersal, there has been more of a need for Jews to stay in touch with the community."[57]

In the past, many of the weekly Jewish newspapers suffered from a limited number of staff that prevented them from covering news in an aggressive fashion. Most national and international news related to Israel and Jews in other countries came from the Jewish Telegraphic Agency (JTA), which is supported by Jewish philanthropic funds. For their local news, many were dependent on press releases from local Jewish organizations. While many Jewish newspapers continue to rely on the JTA for international news, increasingly ample revenues from advertising targeted to a generally affluent readership has allowed for expansions of staff reporters. The *Jewish Exponent* in Philadelphia, for example, has a staff of ten reporters covering regional news.

The Jewish press has been criticized, however, for traditionally avoiding coverage of controversy within the Jewish community, particularly in those newspapers which are owned by the local Federation of Jewish charities, whose objective is to stimulate Jewish philanthropy.[58] Of the forty-eight weeklies published in 1985, eight were owned outright by the local federation of philanthropies and others received financial aid in one form or another from the federation. As one critic questioned, "Can a newspaper financially dependent on the federation afford to offend its sponsor?"[59]

In particular, critics claim that federation ownership stifles debate about Jewish leadership, about Israeli policy, and about how Jewish philanthropies should allocate their funds (for example, for non-Jewish institutions versus Jewish institutions, or toward the Jewish poor versus programs for the middle class). In general, there has appeared to be a tendency not to air conflicts of a religious or other nature between Jews, because the Jewish establishment might consider it "airing our dirty linen in public."[60]

In some cities, like Los Angeles, there have been bitter fights between independent Jewish weeklies and federation-owned newsletters. In the Los Angeles case, the local federation, feeling that the independent papers were not giving adequate coverage to their fundraising activities, tried to strengthen the coverage of their own newsletter, reporting news and soliciting advertising. Using their own mailing lists with which to distribute, they began to seriously challenge the independent newspaper in that city. In response, the independent newspaper filed a suit against the federation, arguing that a charitable institution should not be in the newspaper business. A similar conflict has arisen in New York, where an independent Jewish newspaper has claimed that a federation-connected newspaper paper has an unfair business advantage and represents an unfair use of funds raised by the community.

Despite criticisms of censorship of news by federations, many observers claim that the *Jewish Exponent,* which is owned by the local federation, is one of the best Jewish newspapers in the country. The *Exponent,* with a circulation of 70,000 and large advertising revenues, turns money over to the federation rather than vice versa, and has its own board of directors. While Al Erlick, the editor, noted that there is often a tension between serving as a "Jewish paper of record" and a "vehicle to achieve communal aims," he claimed that newspapers like his own present a balanced debate on issues concerning the Jewish community and Israel.

> Some people claim bad news doesn't belong in a Jewish newspaper, that the newspaper should be a purely cohesive device. I disagree. Some people say Jewish newspapers shouldn't be writing about the bad things Israel is doing, as the general press are, but I disagree . . . the Intefada, the excesses of the Israeli military, some of the horrors, it's our obligation to report those activities. But we also say—unlike the general press—that these activities were frowned upon by the government and punished.[61]

Despite criticisms of the Jewish press, there is no question that the Jewish weeklies hold considerable political influence, particularly in influencing local elections and in swaying the actions of national officials. (It is said that many Jewish newspapers are read in the White House, as well in other government and diplomatic offices.) While many Jewish newspapers, as federation-owned and therefore nonprofit organizations, may not make editorial endorsements, their news coverage and columns regularly discuss the actions and policies of elected officials that affect the Jewish community. For example, in the 1988 presidential election, Jewish newspapers uncovered a story about the Nazi leanings of certain campaign workers for George Bush, a story which was picked up and widely publicized by the mainstream press.

Perhaps the strongest area in which Jewish newspapers hold political influence lies in their coverage of American policy in the Mideast and of the policies of the Israeli government. Each week they offer to their readers a decidedly pro-Israel viewpoint on American diplomatic actions toward Israel and on the Israeli course in the Mideast. Jewish newspapers are quick to point out local officials' positions regarding the Jewish community and, in particular, the future of Israel. As an article in the *Baltimore Jewish Times* noted, "Representative Ron Wyden, a young Jewish Congressman with his eye on the Senate seat held for years by Sen. Mark Hatfield, a Republican, would seem a sure bet to win support from the pro-Israel community since he has a reputation as a strong supporter of Israel, and his opponent has long been a thorn in the side of many pro-Israel groups." [62]

Candidates for office also use Jewish newspapers for campaign advertising before elections, trying to cast themselves as friends of the Jewish community and sometimes attempting to cast aspersions on their opponents' records on issues of concern to Jewish people. In general, however, the targets of the Jewish press's news coverage and editorials have been more typically focused on Israel's interests than on the coverage of Jewish interests in the local area. For example, in the 1970s one critic pointed out that Boston's *Jewish Advocate* "provided feeble coverage of the most important chapter in Boston Jewish history"—the rapid change of the Mattapan neighborhood from a predominantly Jewish to a largely black population in the late 1960s and early 1970s. Altschiller notes that the story called out for coverage in the Jewish press for a number of reasons:

> . . . the enormous exodus of a sizable Jewish community in a period of less than five years; the questionable role of the banks and even the Federal Housing Authority in creating a situation that eventually aroused such concern that the Senate Subcommittee on Antitrust and Monopoly convened a special hearing; and probably most significant of all, the almost total indifference of the Jewish Establishment, e.g., the Combined Jewish Philanthropies, to the plight of one of the most thriving Jewish communities in New England . . . During the destruction of the Jewish

community in Mattapan, the *Advocate* failed to sufficiently alert its readers to the magnitude of the situation.[63]

But in the 1980s, with the increasing sophistication and expanded reporting resources of some of the larger Jewish newspapers, more coverage of local news pertaining to the Jewish community has become included in the Jewish press. For example, the *Atlanta Jewish Times* reported on a controversy over whether a Jewish religious institution, The Temple, should be designated by the local Urban Design Commission as a historic landmark. The article reported the case in favor of such designation as well as the arguments by the Temple's officers and board of trustees that landmark status would restrict their ability to relocate their congregation in the future.[64]

The Immigrant and the Foreign-Language Press

Traditionally the immigrant press has been viewed as playing many informational functions, from reporting on the group's country of origin and on the progress of the group in other parts of the country and in the local community to "express[ing] a group's values, heritage and changing sense of identity."[65] Park described the functions of the immigrant press in his pioneering 1922 study as helping to acculturate immigrants to the new way of life, allowing them for the first time to enjoy not only the political liberation but a social and intellectual liberation as well as to read their native language in the new country.[66] The foreign language press had its largest circulation in the period of 1900 to 1930. Between 1930 and 1960, non-English dailies declined by 57 percent while weeklies declined by 63 percent.[67]

However, since that time, foreign-language newspapers in localities have been on the upswing, following waves of recent immigration to the United States. In New York City, for example, there are at least twelve foreign-language dailies and scores of weeklies and other papers, including the *Korea Herald,* the *Irish Echo,* the *Polish Daily News, Il Progresso* for the Italian population and *Il Diario* for the Hispanic community. These newspapers typically devote considerable coverage to news of the homeland, such as economic development and foreign relations, as well as to issues facing the ethnic community locally. As one observer describing New York's ethnic newspapers put it, the newspapers have "one eye trained on the mother country and the other on the mayor's office." Like the English-language ethnic newspapers, the foreign-language press is used by public officials and candidates as a vehicle for communicating to particular constituencies. For example, the *Sing Tao Daily News,* a Chinese newspaper in New York City, often runs paid advertisements from elected officials, offering proclamations wishing the Chinese community good will on certain holidays or anniversaries.[68]

Perhaps the largest foreign-language media in the country is the Spanish-language or Hispanic media. The Hispanic population of the United States in the 1980s numbered 18 million, or 7.5 percent of the country's total population. The largest component of the Hispanic population is Mexican, followed by Puerto Ricans and Cubans, with the remainder coming from the Caribbean islands and Latin America. The Hispanic population is concentrated in a number of metropolitan areas: Los Angeles, New York, Miami, San Antonio, San Francisco, Chicago, Houston, McAllen/Brownsville, El Paso, and Albuquerque. While Hispanics differ considerably by nationalities, they have language as their common denominator, which draws them to the Spanish-language media.[69]

There are five major daily Hispanic newspapers in the United States, located in Los Angeles, New York, and Miami, as well as hundreds of weeklies and monthlies in regions of the country where the Hispanic population is concentrated. In Miami, where the Spanish language daily *Diario Las Americas* has operated since 1953, the *Miami Herald* decided in 1976 to publish a Spanish-language insert in its newspaper. The newspaper's later decision to publish a Spanish-language sister publication arose because of the general affluence level of Miami Hispanics and the fact that that population seemed to be retaining its Spanish language more so than anywhere else.[70] Like the other foreign-language press, the local Hispanic news media carry out three major functions: to provide Latin American news in greater detail than mainstream press, to provide extensive coverage of local Latin communities, and to serve an advocacy function for Hispanic issues such as immigration, bilingual education, and housing.

The Gay Press

While there are a number of nationally distributed gay newspapers and periodicals, in most major metropolitan areas in the United States there may be found one or more gay newspapers focused on local issues and aimed at "the dissemination of information within the local gay subculture." Some of these periodicals are little more than mimeographed newsletters listing the name and phone numbers of local gay organizations, advertisements by gay businesses, and calendars of events of interest to gays, but in many cities the newspapers provide extensive coverage of regional and local news, as well as national news, affecting the gay population.[71]

Many gay newspapers, like black newspapers, have a problem gaining advertising from businesses which do not cater exclusively to that community. With the gay community, however, part of the problem comes from the embarrassment of businesses to deal with a gay newspaper. As the publisher of the *Philadelphia Gay News* commented, despite the fact that his newspaper's audience is relatively affluent and with large disposable incomes, many companies, such as major department stores, banks and casinos, will not advertise with them. "With gays, advertisers are embarrassed to even deal with the newspaper," he claimed in an interview. However, many gay newspapers like the *Philadelphia Gay News* are trying to change that perception, commissioning Simmons market research to produce demographic profiles of their readership and marketing themselves as "the most potentially profitable untapped market" in the country.[72]

Gay newspapers provide a number of functions for their readers: they attempt to provide positive images of homosexuals and to facilitate the "coming out process," they serve as a source of social support for individuals who have assumed a gay identity, and they help create an awareness of local gay organizations and events in the community.[73] They also play an active political role, through their coverage of local and national policy actions which affect gays. In particular, many gay newspapers track the record of local officials on legislation and programs affecting homosexuals and communicate this information to their readers, particularly before elections. For example, the *Gay Community News,* published in Boston, reported a front-page story headlined "Mass. gay rights bill clears another hurdle" describing the progress of a gay and lesbian civil rights bill in the Massachusetts legislature, noting which legislators were proposing and supporting the legislation.[74]

Gay newspapers have also tracked the treatment of gays by local police vice squads and in turn have examined how law officers have prosecuted crimes against gays. For example, the *Philadelphia Gay News* reported on a meeting with federal, state, and local officials for a "public policy roundtable on anti-gay violence," clearly noting the promises of the local officials and their representatives on actions that would be taken as a result of the meeting.[75] Other local political issues affecting gays have also been closely monitored. In San Francisco, for example, gay newspapers reported extensively on a 1989 city election proposition referred to as the "Domestic Partnership Ordinance," which provided for a number of benefits for unmarried partners in both heterosexual and homosexual relationships.

As with the black and Jewish presses, the gay press features prominent ads by candidates for office before elections. For example, the *Philadelphia Gay News* featured two ads for candidates for district attorney and city controller before elections in 1989. In addition, the gay political action committee in the city took out an ad in the same issue, endorsing candidates on the basis of their records with respect to gay issues. Incumbent District Attorney Ron Castille was endorsed with the accompanying statement that he "has assisted in the effort to pass Pennsylvania's Hate Crimes Amendment. His office let it be known that it would not allow violence against gays, by putting Thomas Duffy on trial for gaybashing. Castille has made numerous appearances in the gay community, and when he first announced his intention to run for D.A. four years ago, he courted the gay/lesbian vote."[76]

Summary: The Role of the Local Specialized Press

Although only a few of the local specialized presses have been examined, many more exist, from the Armenian newspapers in Massachusetts to the Japanese-American newspapers in Los Angeles.[77] In general, the specialized press have in common the objective of providing detailed information to their subcommunities concerning local, national, or international events that affect the community, written from the perspective of the community's interests. Unlike the mainstream media, these newspapers tend not to claim they are objective in their reporting, but rather openly admit that their mission is advocacy for the community and its specific interests. Moreover, while economic survival and profitability are clearly goals for most of these newspapers, political and social objectives tend to be stronger than the commercial ones. As Robert Park noted in describing the publishers of the foreign-language press in the early twentieth century, "Very few . . . have learned to take the detached and impersonal attitude of the American newspaper man toward the contents of the paper they print."[78]

It should be noted, however, that within all the specialized presses, conflicts do arise within the community concerning editorial content and the extent internal debates should be publicized. With the black press, there is disagreement over whether negative stories about black crime should be included and whether black officials should be openly criticized. With the Jewish press, there is disagreement over the extent to which criticism of Israel, the effectiveness of Jewish leadership, or debates about "who is a Jew" should be publicized. With the gay press, there have been conflicts over the extent to which newspapers should cover the AIDS epidemic, with some factions claiming an emphasis on the disease perpetuates stereotypes and is too downbeat in a vehicle that should be promoting positive self-images of gays.

Despite such conflicts, however, it is clear that the specialized press often play an important role in influencing local, national, and even international policy debates by informing their readers about social and political issues and, in particular, by providing them with evaluations of the performance of public officials on issues of particular concern to the community. Because of this influence, the specialized press has become a vehicle through which elected officials and candidates communicate their policies, positions, or simply images to particular communities.

To some extent, the specialized newspapers' power to affect specific policy issues rivals that of the metropolitan newspaper because of the ability to marshall the support or opposition of an audience that may feel particularly strongly about an issue. Should a gay newspaper decide to target a local official for defeat in an election because of his legislative record, that newspaper, despite a modest circulation, may be very effective in stimulating a strong gay turnout at the polls. Moreover, the specialized press tends to enjoy a high degree of credibility with its audience, lending it that much more power to influence the political actions of its readers. And the role of the specialized press may often extend beyond the information they transmit directly to their readers, for often their stories—and perspectives—are picked up by the metropolitan daily newspapers, which increasingly turn to these specialized newspapers to take the pulse of particular constituencies.

The Community Press

The development of the community press has been traced to the decentralization of the central business district and the development of secondary retail shopping districts throughout cities and their suburban areas.[79] While city neighborhood newspapers typically were started anew, many suburban newspapers grew out of smaller rural outlets that were transformed after rapid population influx as a result of suburbanization. In the early 1960s, Byerly described the roles played by community newspapers, citing a number of functions that hold for the same newspapers three decades later:

1. Reports local news items that appear in no other newspaper.
2. Reports details of local news that are not included in stories used by other newspapers.
3. Aids local shoppers, and serves as an advertising medium for a town's merchants and other business firms.
4. Promotes local welfare and projects.
5. Gives recognition to those who work on community programs, further helping promote such projects.
6. Creates interest in government and elections, serving to make the former better and the latter more effective.
7. Stimulates thinking, particularly on local problems and projects.
8. Instructs, entertains, and informs.
9. Serves as a unifying force in a community.[80]

Janowitz's study, also undertaken in the 1960s, found that most community newspapers had a "promotional flavor" because they served as "instruments of the local merchants and their associations." He claimed that "as an outgrowth of its origin and because of its main sources of revenue, the community newspaper's interest and the interests of the secondary shopping center are usually identical."[81] Janowitz found many instances in which community newspaper editors helped change policies and procedures of local government, both through writing about problems and using personal influence. But he also noted that there was a certain pressure on them to put the best face on happenings in the community. "Editors and publishers constantly relate instances of socially disapproved behavior in the local community which they are asked to suppress."[82]

Many community newspapers of the late 1980s exhibit the characteristics ascribed to them by Janowitz, strong on neighborhood shopping advertisements but relying heavily on press releases for editorial content. However, many other community newspapers see themselves as playing a more important journalistic role and view their mission as coverage of problems in the community, in particular crime. In Philadelphia, for example, the *Chestnut Hill Local,* published for over two decades in its affluent suburbanlike community, and the *Westside Weekly,* a newly started community newspaper in a black working-class neighborhood, are very different newspapers, but both give careful attention to the problems of crime in their neighborhoods, whether burglaries in the expensive village shops or drug dealing on the corners. As the editor of the *Local* commented, local newspapers are crucial because "the only place you can still get community news is in your community newspaper."[83] Because they are often carefully read by the residents of their communities, these weekly newspapers tend to be carefully watched by elected officials and candidates for office and can be very effective in campaigns for policy changes. Like the specialized press, many community newspapers are used by politicians for advertising before elections.

The typical weekly community newspaper, whether in city or suburb, tries to balance its hard news with upbeat stories, on its front page as well as throughout its issue. For example, the front page of one issue of the *Villadom News*, serving communities in northern New Jersey, was dominated by a large photograph of two preschoolers preparing for Thanksgiving. The news summary accompanying the photo, however, offered glimpses of more serious policy-related stories, like the proposal from a local church to seek a zoning variance for senior housing and a proposal for changes in a local school's schedule.[84] As Sachsman and Sloat point out, the suburban newspapers in New Jersey "offer a form of countercoverage, emphasizing those areas of news coverage that are virtually ignored by the New York and Philadelphia papers. Local and regional coverage is given top priority, statehouse reporting is a serious matter, and "lifestyle" coverage centers on suburban family living."[85]

The *Bellevue Journal-American*, a small suburban newspaper serving communities on the outskirts of Seattle, was similarly described by one of its former reporters as "really in touch with their community. They play to the hilt their role as community leader . . . The *Journal-American* does the kind of coverage that big-city newspapers find demeaning. It isn't embarrassed to cover prep sports, and those communities identify with their high school teams. There's lots of civic pride out there. They do bulletin board type lists, they're not embarrassed to do community journalism. Development is a major story in a suburban newspaper, unlike in Seattle. People moved out there to avoid the masses so they are concerned with development."

With major technological breakthroughs in production, like offset printing and computer typesetting, many small-scale entrepreneurs are finding they are able to start weekly papers with a relatively small capital investment. As the editor of the *Westside Weekly* said, "The MacIntosh makes editors of us all."[86] However, as weekly papers in both city and suburbs have become profitable vehicles for carrying local advertising, they have become attractive properties for chains to acquire. In 1989, it was estimated that half of the nation's 7,600 weeklies were owned by chains, where a decade earlier, some 70 percent were independent. Many weeklies offer advertisers total market coverage, through either total or partial free distribution. And as chains increasingly acquire many of the weeklies in a regional market, they have become capable of offering advertisers smaller or larger portions of the regional market, often at prices lower than those at the metropolitan daily.[87]

In many ways, the community press can be viewed as similar to the specialized press, in that they present news of interest to only a limited part of a metropolitan area—in this case, a geographically circumscribed area. They tend to present in great detail news that the metropolitan daily or regional television news stations find too inconsequential to cover. Many also serve an advocacy function, much in the way of the specialized press, trying to uncover and highlight problems in the community in order to muster political support to push local policy makers into instituting change. And like the specialized press, there are often debates internal to the community concerning how much "bad" news to include in the newspaper, as opposed to the more upbeat items that instill pride in community members.

Local Radio

In an era when automobile commuting has largely replaced mass transit for the journey to work, local radio stations have come to enjoy high ratings, particularly in the lucrative morning and afternoon "drive-time" slots. While most local radio stations offer more music than news and information, in many regions of the country all-news and talk-radio stations have begun to play an increasingly influential role in local policy debates. Most of the country's local news and talk radio shows are found on the A.M. band. In 1989, 163 of the 2,954 total radio stations in the nation's top 175 markets—with over two million listeners—were programmed in the news/talk format. Approximately 10 percent of all radio listeners in those markets were tuned to news or talk stations. Moreover, listenership to news/talk stations has been steadily increasing over the last decade, a particularly noteworthy trend since the audiences for A.M. radio in other formats have been shrinking.[88]

Within the growing "all-news" or "news-information" format, the programming formula has varied. Some radio industry analysts have claimed that all-news stations have increasingly become "briefing services," spending more and more time on weather, traffic, and time checks, with news summarized briefly as headlines and "bottom-line summaries" of what's happening.[89] However, staff members at stations like KIRO in Seattle or KRLD in Dallas–Fort Worth maintain that although their stations may have a quick pace, they continue to provide listeners with background analyses of local, national, and international issues. And stations like KIRO have added call-in segments with experts, including, during an election year, segments in which officeholders and candidates answer listener questions. But editors at stations like WINS in New York, take a somewhat different perspective:

> Some people may think of an all-news station as a newspaper of the air that should include plenty of time on depth analysis and explaining the historical background leading up to today's events. But we're not a newspaper. In terms of a news consumer's time, he or she can flip through a paper and read only those items that interest him. He doesn't have to read everything. But in radio, he usually has to wait through a portion of each of our full 22-minute reports before we get to those items he wants to hear about.[90]

All-news radio stations see themselves as having three groups of listeners: people who tune in for short periods a few times a day for updates on the news, people who listen for an hour or more, and people who tune in only in crisis situations to hear more details. In order to increase the second group, more and more local radio all-news formats are increasingly including consumer features—often with call-in experts answering questions—in such areas as health, fitness, finances, investment, and real estate. As a result, like local television news, radio news has only limited time available for the consideration of local policy issues. Also like local television, news on radio is equally dependent on the sexy sound bite in reporting on issues of government and policy.

In recent years, increasing attention has been paid to the role of "talk" or "call-in" radio in the discussion of local as well as national and international issues. Often hosted by controversial personalities—some politically liberal, some conservative—call-in shows focus on a wide variety of topics, from local sports issues to the merits of the death penalty. Talk radio shows have been in existence for several decades and have been viewed as serving several important functions for both callers and listeners, such as the need for interpersonal communication and support for listener beliefs.[91] While some analysts have argued that talk radio serves as a public forum providing access to public officials for lower-middle-class and working people,[92] particularly those who feel alienated and disaffected from the large bureaucracies of their governments,[93]

157

other studies have shown that many talk radio shows increasingly appeal to college-educated and upwardly mobile groups.[94]

While most scholarly analysis has focused on the functions of talk radio, less attention has been devoted to their political influence. However, in 1989, the influence of call-in radio shows gained popular attention when an alliance of thirty talk-show hosts organized what turned out to be a successful assault against a proposed 51 percent congressional pay raise. Other talk radio initiatives have been targeted to local policy issues. For example, Mike Siegel of Seattle's KING–AM led a fight to improve police efforts to fight drug activity and, in an earlier position at a Miami station, used his radio show to help defeat a proposed rate increase by the local telephone company. Jerry Williams of WRKO in Boston campaigned against Massachusetts' mandatory seat belt law, helping to collect 40,000 signatures for a petition asking for a referendum, which led to the law's repeal.[95]

The power of talk-radio to rouse interest in policy issues and rally support for positions has been praised by some observers and criticized by others. Consumer activist Ralph Nader has described talk radio as "the working people's medium. There's no ticket of admission. You only have to dial," and a Massachusetts congressman has claimed that the shows are "in touch with the anger and hostility and frustrations that people feel with respect to government in their daily lives." However, other observers have cautioned against the dangers of powerful hosts who come to influence large blocks of citizens, particularly when those hosts may be more concerned with boosting their ratings than with acting in the public interest.[96]

The other arena in which radio plays an important role in policy issues is in the communication of news and information that takes place on black and Spanish radio stations. In 1989, data for the 175 rated radio markets showed 193 "black/urban" radio stations and 104 Spanish radio stations, representing 8 and 2 percent, respectively, of listeners in those markets. Many black radio stations, in addition to playing music, offer news and information that is specifically targeted to their black listeners. One station manager described the role of black radio stations as particularly important in many medium and smaller markets, where there is often no other source for "the kind of information black adults need than one radio station geared to the 25–49 black listener with a steady job, and a regular pay check to spend."[97] In New York City, WLIB–AM, the country's only all-black news and talk format station in 1989, was viewed by many public officials and community leaders as an important outlet for reaching the local black community and as a place to turn to gain reaction to positions.[98] In Philadelphia, WHAT–FM has organized voter registration campaigns at election times and aired a number of programs in which community and political leaders discuss local issues.

Spanish-language radio stations also attract a sizable audience and play an important role in communicating information to their communities. While most of Hispanic radio stations feature music programming, some, as in the Miami area, are focused on news and talk shows. Spanish-language television stations have also proliferated under the aegis of two national networks of Spanish-language affiliate stations, Univision and Telemundo.

Summary

City magazines, alternative weeklies, the specialized press, and the weekly community press all provide detailed local news to a particular demographic segment of the regional population and, in a sense, serve as alternative voices providing perspectives on local issues differing from that of the metropolitan daily newspaper or regional television newscast. Some have argued that the existence of such media serves as a safeguard against the potential abuses of "monopoly" newspapers in one-newspaper cities, protecting against censorship or limited perspectives on local issues.

While these more specialized local media play many important functions for their audiences and may influence voting behavior and the direction of policy, they do not warrant a description as true alternative voices in the metropolitan area. Where city magazines and alternative weeklies once focused on serious social and political issues and challenged the coverage of metropolitan newspapers, by the beginning of the 1990s, most have turned their attention to lifestyle and consumer issues. In contrast, the specialized press has remained focused on those political and social issues that hold key importance to their communities and carefully follow the records of local officials on these issues. However, the specialized press and community weeklies have not challenged the metropolitan newspaper's news and editorial coverage of major urban and regional issues. In general, none of the smaller local media have attempted to provide a consistent alternative voice to the metropolitan newspaper's coverage of the kind of major development issues that involve the expenditure of millions of dollars in public funds.

6 Local Government Officials as News Sources

For over four decades, one local official named Robert Moses was able to dramatically reshape the physical environment of New York City by attaining a power base unmatched by other elected or appointed officials of his time. While some of that power would have gone to anyone holding the positions of park commissioner or construction coordinator, Moses' unique stronghold rested on the power of the public's opinion of him, as molded by the New York news media. It was the image that the media projected of Moses as a brilliant and selfless local hero that for decades kept him almost completely immune from attempts by mayors, governors, and even presidents to control his actions.

Robert Moses' adulation by the New York news media was no accident. As Robert Caro points out in *The Power Broker*,[1] Moses learned early in his career that the most skillfully crafted plans were useless without the kind of strong public support that could only be achieved through positive press coverage. Moses was able to get that kind of coverage because he understood—better than almost any of his contemporaries—how to deal with the local news media so as to get himself and his plans covered positively. We now turn to a consideration of how local public officials like Robert Moses come to be covered by the metropolitan news media and how different media strategies influence that coverage.

The Importance of Local News Coverage to Public Officials

Local public officials are among the most avid consumers of local news and attend to the media's messages far more closely than the average citizen. As Dunn pointed out in his study of the press and state government, public officials often begin their days by examining the local newspaper for stories about themselves and other officials and agencies, "comb[ing] it daily for messages about their work."[2] Twenty years after Dunn's study, officials follow the news just as closely, although now that monitoring often includes reviewing videotapes of the previous evening's local newscasts. Why is the news so important to public officials? The answer varies according to the position in government involved and the objectives that motivate the official's actions.

160

Elected Officials

News coverage is important to elected officials for both political and policy reasons. In order to get reelected or elected to higher office, a public official must keep his name before the public and inform constituents about his activities, positions, and policies. There are three channels through which such information can be communicated: (1) campaign advertising and mailings; (2) public appearances; and (3) news coverage.[3] The use of advertising, direct mail, and appearances is important because it allows candidates to carefully control their messages and images. However, news coverage has certain other important advantages: unlike advertising and mailings, it is costless, and in contrast to public appearances, it is capable of reaching masses of people. Even more important, news coverage carries with it greater legitimacy than advertising and consequently may play a stronger role in creating a general positive image for an official.

News coverage is also important to elected officials in sending messages about specific actions and positions to particular constituencies. The congressman who is influential in securing federal funding for a new highway project wants to make sure the local business community and union workers learn about his role in the awarding of the grant. Similarly, the mayor who orders more police patrols for a particular section of a city will want news of his actions to reach residents of those neighborhoods. At other times, elected officials use news coverage to shift blame, so as not to take the political heat for unpopular actions. For example, the governor may call a press conference to state that cutbacks in education funding are not his doing, but rather a result of the reductions in federal appropriations.

While news coverage is crucial to the political aspirations of elected officials, it is also important because of its effects on policy. In particular, many officials rely on news coverage to help them coalesce groups in support of a new policy. In trying to institute a policy change, a public official needs to disseminate information to the media that will help sway the opinion of the public in general and of private interest groups in particular to support the policy.[4] As one official said, "Whether we like it or not, people read newspapers and watch TV, and people form impressions from what they read and see. The media is a good tool to convince the public of the need for a new policy."[5]

Because news coverage often produces public concern or outcry, it may be used by one official to lobby other governmental officials to support or defeat a policy. In other words, an official may release information to the news media that indicates the existence of a crisis in order to put pressure on other officials to support a new initiative. As Sigal has written in his study of the relation between national news coverage and federal officials, "the test of a good policy is its ability to muster and maintain support among officialdom." He points out that many officials use news coverage to inform themselves and other officials about policy needs in the external environment, as well as to serve as a barometer to public opinion.[6] Similarly, Dunn notes that officials use news coverage as a way of measuring both general public interest and the reactions of specific interest groups to proposals or policy needs. He writes,

> [The official] reads the papers to see how the press plays government activities. This gives him some idea, he believes, of how his constituents (who may be groups inside or outside government) are viewing the situation. He deduces what he thinks his constituents' reaction will be and adapts his behavior accordingly. He may adopt a certain stance on a proposal. Or he may introduce new symbols into the communication channel to change the message presently being transmitted. Public officials often act as though they believe everyone is reading newspapers and reacting as they themselves do to what they read.[7]

In many cases, news and editorials serve to communicate information among a relatively small number of decision makers. As one official observed, "It's amazing how few of the general populace read newspaper articles about controversies within public agencies. Even fewer read editorials about the matter. But the people who do read editorials are very important, and they often wield tremendous influence. The Governor reads the editorial page, so does the Mayor, so do the County Commissioners. And believe me, they respond to what those editorials say."[8] While some officials say they respond to editorials because their recommendations make sense, others admit they sometimes react reluctantly, out of fear. As one official put it, "Sometimes newspapers force us to do some things irresponsibly. They create a public clamor, and yes, you do react." Another observer pointed out that "politicians are influenced by the press more than the public is. The press likes to point out the dumb things politicians do, so politicians try to anticipate that."

Some officials also use the news media to "float trial balloons," releasing hints of new policy directions to determine the reaction of other officials, interest groups, and the public before committing to the policy.[9] If news of a potential initiative prompts other groups to publicly denounce the move, the official may refrain from actually introducing the policy. In other cases, officials release information so as to awaken public opposition to a policy change they want to see nixed. According to Sigal, "What observers may mistake for a trial balloon is frequently a premature disclosure of a policy option—or a deliberately distorted version of it—designed to kill it off by arousing opponents before the arguments in its favor are fully articulated or its potential supporters mobilized."[10] News coverage may also help determine the timing of a new proposal, either hastening or delaying an announcement, depending on what other events are being covered at the time, or what Dunn has called the "support climate" of related news.[11]

Officials who are members of local legislative bodies or agency boards also note the important role media coverage plays in communicating information about minority positions. As a Republican city councilwoman described her aggressive use of press conferences to introduce legislation to Philadelphia's-Democratic-dominated council, "My press conferences were the way I got information out to reporters. It is important to me as a minority member of Council that I build a constituency in the press for my legislation."[12] A similar function was pointed to by a member of a regional transit board who had successfully fought to have a national search for the system's new director. "As a minority on the board I would lose every vote. I needed to enlist an external ally and that ally was the press." Once the board member had convinced the local media of the importance of an open search, and the press had editorialized in favor of it, he said it was difficult for other board members to openly oppose the position.[13]

News coverage may also be important as an instrument of communicating information for the implementation of a new policy to the public. For example, Philadelphia's district attorney relayed how he had used the media to communicate a new tough enforcement policy on credit card fraud by using television news to reach the teenagers who typically commit such crimes. In this case, news coverage was the only way of publicizing the new policy, short of a costly advertising campaign. The district attorney noted that this use of the media was particularly important in the criminal justice system for the purpose of deterrence of crime.[14]

Appointed Officials

Although they do not need the media to win elections, appointed officials are dependent on news coverage for other reasons. The media image of appointed officials and their departments affects both job tenure and budget allocations, since decisions on hiring and firing and appropriations are made by officials who are elected and therefore sensitive to public opinion. As Sayre and Kaufman noted in an early study of the relation between local government agencies and the press, "the evidence strongly suggests that the Mayor, the Board of Estimate, the City Council, the Bureau of the Budget, and other important legislative, executive, and financial institutions of the city government hesitate to refuse requests for appropriations and power by agencies in high popular favor."[15] In a similar way, news coverage may affect an agency head's negotiations with a union, with a positive image helping to win concessions, while a negative image strengthens the union's position.

Like elected officials, appointed officials also need news coverage to coalesce groups in support of policy changes. News coverage of inadequate police patrols on city streets may help a police commissioner institute a new policy of using civilians to replace patrolmen in carrying out police department paperwork. Officials whose agencies must deal with the private sector are also concerned with positive news coverage in order to ease the way for negotiations and cooperative ventures. As the director of Philadelphia's City Planning Commission Craig Schelter noted, "Everybody tells you how the press is biased and how you can't believe anything you read in the newspaper. But the same people who read articles about themselves and think how wrong they are, then read articles about some other agency and believe it is fact. So if the press says something bad about you, or makes you look bad, people believe it, and you're hurt. Press can be enormously useful if it's on your side and devastating if it's against you."[16] This statement was echoed by a planning official in another city who described how the press's inaccurate reflection of his position had alienated officials in his city's housing department and hampered cooperation on subsequent new programs.

Middle-level Leakers

Middle managers within local government are also concerned with news coverage of their agencies. Often, it is staff in these middle-level positions who release information to the media that contradicts the views of agency heads. Their incentive to leak negative information about an agency may be political: they want to discredit the current administration in order to bring in a new political regime or even to succeed superiors in their jobs. In other cases, however, middle managers leak because they disagree with the policies of top management. Unsuccessful in arguing their case internally, they release to the media information that puts pressure on the top official to alter his course. The importance of "leaking" information, rather than releasing it on the record, is to keep from alienating superiors. As Sigal has put it, "The fear of reprisal forces official opposition underground. Dissenters must leak; they dare not do otherwise." [17]

Many beat reporters say they cultivate sources among these middle managers in order to obtain information about problems in an agency or the less positive viewpoint on its objectives. As one reporter noted, "You need sources at various levels of an organization. People in management at the top two levels of an agency—the director, the deputy directors—are loathe to tell you anything negative, so what you need to do is cultivate people on the next two levels." [18] Or, as another reporter said, "Sources are the middle-level bureaucrats who see a lot and hear a lot. That's where your best tips come from." However, reporters observe that in many government departments, staff members are often reluctant to leak, either because of fear of reprisals if found out, or because they do not believe that talking to the press will result in a policy change. In many public agencies, top officials institute strict policies against the release of information by subordinates. Staff who are discovered to leak may be fired or, when protected by civil service regulations, "punished" by a transfer.

Private Interest Groups

Other actors in the local policy arena also may have an incentive to become sources for the media in order to satisfy a range of objectives. Goldenberg's study of how "resource-poor" citizen groups seek access to the metropolitan press pointed out a number of reasons why news coverage was actively sought: to establish legitimacy as spokesmen for a particular group, to convey information that helps attract members and support (including donations) from third parties, and to put pressure on public officials to change policy or introduce new legislation. [19] Her study and others which followed have shown how such resource-poor groups face difficulties in influencing news coverage because of journalists' routine dependence on authoritative sources like government officials. However, since Goldenberg's study was undertaken in the late

1960s and early 1970s, private interest groups have increasingly turned to local television news to gain public attention. From neighborhood residents protesting a new land-use or fighting for a new traffic signal to union laborers marching in favor of a new public construction project, many groups have attempted to attract the attention of local television reporters and, in turn, a mass audience.

Union leaders also typically serve as willing sources for the media, eager to comment on the policies of management in order to gain public support for salary demands, benefits packages, and work rules. By getting their positions across in the media, union leaders gain political capital that may help them at contract negotiation time. The business community and private developers may also be concerned with news coverage, both to communicate among themselves and to influence public opinion. Some private businessmen say they think of the metropolitan newspaper as a kind of "trade newsletter," in which they communicate with each other about their activities. In other cases, where a business or developer may be affected by a local public body (such as a zoning board), they may be eager to convey a positive image for themselves as well as for their projects in order to gain the necessary approvals.

For public officials as well as other local sources, different local media become important for different policy purposes. Positive coverage and editorial support from the region's metropolitan newspaper may be essential in gaining support for a new policy from a region's upscale audience, as well as from its business and opinion leadership. However, more specialized media are also important in communicating to specific constituencies. For example, officials may actively seek to communicate to the city's black, Hispanic, Jewish, Asian, and gay press, among others, in order to reach those particular subgroups of the population.

Although many local officials spend a great deal of time preparing information for the local print media, most officials—particularly those in city government—emphasize the importance of local television news in molding public opinion. "If it didn't happen on the six o'clock news, it didn't happen," was the maxim repeated by officials as they pointed out that television news reaches the great mass of people within a city, many of whom do not read newspapers. As one official said, "The influence of columnists and editorials is overrated. Only one thing is not overrated—TV, because of its enormous audience. TV is it, by and large." [20] Although negative coverage on the evening news cannot be sent around city government the way a newspaper clipping can be, officials say that it has a powerful impact on viewers and on the public officials who monitor television news coverage in order to gauge public opinion.

At the other end of the spectrum, officials, whether in city government, regional agencies, or state legislatures, noted the strategy of going around the metropolitanwide press and television stations to communicate messages directly to community and suburban newspapers. The rationale was that the local press was less likely to be hostile than the metropolitan media and more willing to transmit positive information about official activities and policies. As one suburban state legislator said, "It is much easier to get your point across in the local papers. They take the time, the fifteen, twenty, thirty minutes, until they understand what you are saying. Big-city papers are looking for headlines, not understanding. Also, in local papers I find little that tends to be negative . . . the reporters know you and when you know people, they treat you better. And local reporters are less cynical than the downtown press. They're less likely to be looking for the negative headlines that lead to advancement."[21]

Local Officials as Sources and Symbols

While local officials and other actors in the policy arena need media coverage, reporters and their organizations, in turn, need local officials both to provide information and to serve as objects of audience interest, enlivening what may otherwise be dull policy-related stories. Local government officials become particularly interesting when their actions allow journalists to turn them into larger-than-life figures cast in the roles of hero or villain. Reporters may not set out consciously to create such heroes and villains, but they recognize that colorful figures who inspire admiration, outrage, or simple amusement in their audience make their stories more interesting and that emphasizing the role of certain personalities in their stories may give them greater play.

The creation of local "knowns"[22] is particularly important to the metropolitan media because they come to serve as symbols of a unified regional identity. Unlike the national news media, which rely on the president, congressmen, cabinet officials, and agency directors to draw on for their personalities, the local news media have relatively few figures who are recognizable to the entire region. In most metropolitan areas, it is the big-city mayor who becomes the most important "known" for the local news media. Despite the fact that the city's top official represents the minority of the population in most areas, he or she still towers over the average county commissioner in perceived importance and may serve as an attractive draw for the regional audience. As one reporter covering the 1987 Philadelphia mayoral race between Frank Rizzo and Wilson Goode noted, even suburbanites who would be relatively unaffected by the outcome of the election would find the coverage interesting because of the two "larger-than-life figures."

Because of the importance of the city's chief executive as a local known, the mayor and the local media come to engage in a strange symbiosis. The mayor needs the media to communicate with his city-based constituency, while the media need the mayor as one of the prime local personalities who can engage the interest of their largely suburban audience. While the mayor hopes to create a positive image, the local news media benefit from a mayor who can be depicted as either very good or very bad—or very outrageous. For example, one editor in Detroit claimed that coverage of Mayor Coleman Young was one of the reasons many suburbanites still turned to the Detroit newspapers. "The mayor here is very confrontational, controversial. The readership may like that. They like to see what a fool he is. They like to read about him and about the city because it makes them realize how glad they are they left."

Within the local policy arena, reporters often try to inject interest into their stories by personalizing policy issues with heroes and villains taken from local agencies and departments. For example, in Philadelphia, the regional mass transit agency, the Southeastern Pennsylvania Transit Authority (SEPTA) had suffered from a poor funding base and weak management for years, with relatively little media attention. But when a new general manager was brought in and resigned five weeks later after a battle with the board chairman, the story made front-page headlines. The news coverage, rather than focusing on the substantive problems of the agency, tended to exaggerate the personal battle and create an image of the new general manager as local hero and the old board chairman as local foe.[23] One of the reporters covering the transit agency when the controversy erupted commented on why the issue of SEPTA's management hadn't been covered prominently in the previous years: "I don't think people find transit systems that interesting. When you get a battle between personalities, people get interested."

Similarly, in 1988, coverage of children dying of child abuse while under the supervision of Philadelphia's Department of Human Services began to focus predominantly on the management style of the department's director rather than describing the complex web of factors—including changing federal regulations regarding removal of children from families and inadequate funding from the state and federal government—that contributed to the problem. Reporters noted that stories about problems in the system of dealing with abused children were not considered as "sexy" as stories about an agency "screwup" or the management problems of the director. Although such examples suggest that individual reporters and their news organizations often use local public figures as heroes or villains to increase the interest of their coverage, the strategies of the officials themselves have much to do with whether an official will be viewed positively, negatively—or ignored—by the local news media.

Media Styles and Strategies

Many studies of the relation between public officials and the media have noted the symbiosis that exists between reporters and officials, with both parties needing each other to perform their jobs. But in this symbiosis or "dance," most analysts argue that more often than not, sources do the leading. In other words, reporters are said to be manipulated by the officials they cover.[24] While there is some truth to this claim, the argument exaggerates the ability of public officials, particularly at the local level, to control the kind of media they receive. If officials manipulate reporters so well, why does one regularly see local officeholders skewered in the media? How can the ubiquitous media criticism of local officials be explained if those officials are so adept at controlling their news coverage?

The answer is that there is great variation in the media skills of both appointed and elected officials, particularly at the local level. As one reporter noted, "My feeling is not that the press get manipulated but that most city officials, with the possible exception of the mayor, have a very poor idea of press relations and don't know how to use the press. They just don't release things." In other words, while some local officials are very adept at gaining positive coverage, many more have little or no understanding of how to influence the media. The head of the transit authority or the commissioner of police are appointed to their positions because of their technical or managerial expertise—not necessarily because of their ability to deal effectively with reporters. Even elected officials who have used the media effectively during their campaigns often have trouble controlling the coverage of their policy moves once in office.

In examining the relation between officials and the media, therefore, we need to distinguish among types of officials according to the "media styles" they adopt, sometimes unwittingly, in their day-to-day dealings with reporters. The officials who succeed in gaining positive coverage are those who understand the objectives, requirements, and constraints of local news firms and work within them to meet their own objectives. Other officials, however, make the mistake of frustrating the objectives of journalists, ignoring their constraints, or providing them with information that makes the official or his policies look bad. The misconceptions of local officials are reflected in the following media styles.[25]

Foibles and Follies

The paranoid media-avoider. Some local government officials believe that the press are simply out to get the goods on anyone in government and that reporters will write or broadcast anything, no matter how slanted, in order to create the kind of scandal that sells newspapers or raises television ratings. Because of this belief, the paranoid official's media strategy is avoidance: the official rarely puts out his own press releases, holds press conferences, or speaks informally to individual reporters concerning the routine activities of his office because he is fearful of inviting press scrutiny. In turn, when possible he avoids responding to reporters' requests for information, believing that his comments will be misquoted and misinterpreted. "Not available for comment," is the message he passes on to the media through his representatives.

While some officials begin their public careers by being relatively open with the news media, after a negative article or editorial or misquote, they retreat and become "paranoid media-avoiders." One reporter described these kind of officials as having "a bunker mentality . . . They feel like everyone's out to get them, so they hunker down and don't let anyone near them."[26] This notion was echoed by an official who commented, "For a long time, if I thought a reporter wasn't going to do a positive story, I wouldn't talk."

The paranoid media-avoider recognizes the media's need to use scandal and impropriety as a means to capture audiences, but fails to recognize an even more fundamental need of reporters: to gather information, much of it relatively uncontroversial, as the basis for a continual stream of stories. The paranoid media-avoider's basic inaccessibility to reporters frustrates the reporter by denying him what he needs most to do his job: information. This inaccessibility leads the reporter to go around the official and look for another source of information, often going to a source who is hostile to the official.

In the long run, this kind of inaccessibility tends to arouse the reporter's suspicions. Should the official later propose a new initiative, sources will be sought to discredit it and should charges be leveled against the official by critics, the reporter will be more willing to air them publicly. As one reporter described it, "When someone's inaccessible, reporters figure they have something to hide, and they are more likely to attack the person."

The naive professional. A different misconception characterizes other local officials, particularly those appointed rather than elected to office. Often, a technically skilled agency head regards the media more benignly, assuming that a well-crafted rational plan is bound to gain media support. The naive professional produces thick reports on new initiatives and hopes that reporters will take the trouble to wade through pages of technical explanations in order to appreciate the soundness of the plan. These officials believe it is not their job to spoon-feed information to reporters or to engage in glitzy media events in order to sell what they consider sound proposals. Rather, professional expertise is all they believe is required for policy success. Many others do not even deal with reporters, conducting the agency's business without regard for trying to disseminate information to the media and the public.

When the naive professional does deal with the media, he has a tendency to speak to reporters as he would with a friend or business associate, without an understanding of how offhand remarks, doubts, qualms, or politically sensitive charges and claims will become translated into 20-second sound bites on the six o'clock news and headlines in the newspaper. This kind of behavior often results in comments being taken out of the context in which they were intended; in particular, offhand remarks may receive an importance not intended, invoking the wrath of political enemies or the opposition of citizen groups awakened to block a new initiative.

The naive professional errs in failing to recognize the limitations on time and technical expertise that confront the daily journalist. Most reporters do not have the freedom to spend days and months poring over technical reports for in-depth reporting—and those who do, devote their digging to areas where they suspect scandal or impropriety. In addition, reporters often lack the technical expertise to digest and translate highly technical policy reports. For this reason, the naive professional who fails to take account of the reporters' time constraints and technical limitations often has his reports ignored, or worse, sensationalized by reporters seizing on simple fragments of them. Similarly, reporters looking for controversial stories will sometimes exaggerate offhand remarks, as long as they are on the record, that will have the effect of stirring the political waters.

The ribbon cutter. A quite different style is exhibited by elected officials who are more conscious of the need to court the media and often try to control their news coverage by eagerly trying to meet the media's needs. The strategy of these politicians could be called ribbon-cutting: filling their schedules with the kind of public appearances or "media events" that will attract the attention of both print and broadcast journalists. The ribbon-cutter sets media attention at the top of his agenda, donning hardhats and fire gear to appear at groundbreakings and four-alarm fires, to maximize his public exposure and visibility.

While the ribbon-cutter does succeed in gaining visibility for himself, particularly on television news where there is a continual appetite for visual media events, he eventually raises the suspicion of reporters who begin to feel used. Even as he meets their short-term needs for stories, the official leaves reporters wondering if there is any substance behind the media events. In the resulting news coverage, the image of the official begins to look frivolous and shallow, failing to raise the kind of political capital that will allow the official to succeed when he makes controversial policy proposals. The mistake of the ribbon-cutter is in providing media events that fail to create the kind of substantive image for himself and his office necessary to succeed in subsequent policy-making efforts.

The dancing marionette. A related but somewhat different strategy is followed by those officials who closely follow the investigations and editorials of the local media and formulate policy proposals and responses on the basis of them. These officials know they will receive prominent—and usually favorable—coverage by the journalists pursuing the issue, since the politician's response points out the efficacy of the media crusade. It is not unusual for a television consumer reporter's three-part series on health hazards in waste dumps to be followed by a state representative's press conference to announce a new bill to prohibit such dumping. Similarly, the newspaper's investigative reporting pointing out health violations in public housing projects generally prompts some officials to demand changes in the city's housing agency.

Most officials are sensitive to media investigations and editorial positions, and indeed see a response as part of their elected responsibility to protect the public. However, some officials gain a reputation as being "dancing marionettes" because they only respond to media causes and do not often initiate their own proposals and recommendations. Moreover, these officials tend to propose whatever the media has argued for or against, failing to add their own perspectives to the issues.

This media style of prompt response to media investigations and crusades does result in prominent coverage of the official, since the reporter's need for accessible, suitable information are being met, and the newspaper's or television station's own prestige is raised by showing that they have affected change through their reporting. However, like the ribbon-cutter, the dancing marionette fails to create an effective image for himself in the process. He comes across as a follower, not a leader, responsive, yet too obviously "grabbing for headlines." As a result, his motives for proposing a new initiative may become suspect in the public eye.

The colorful quotables. Among local officials and candidates for local office, there are always a few that delight reporters by the colorful, amusing, and often outrageous quotes they offer concerning the issues of the day. Unlike the paranoid media-avoiders, the colorful quotables actively court local media attention, enjoying the center stage on which they can hold forth. The quotables also differ from the ribbon-cutters in that they engage less in media events than in media statements that make for entertaining newspaper quotes and colorful television and radio sound bites. The colorful quotables are also distinguished from both the ribbon-cutter and the dancing marionettes because the former are seen as active, rather than passive, and because their colorful quotes often reflect tough and sometimes controversial stances about substantive public issues.

It should be little surprise that many of the nation's big-city mayors could be described as colorful quotables, for the strategy is successful in gaining prominent attention in the metropolitan media and for winning citywide elections, where image and name recognition often count for more than particular stands on issues. However, the colorful quotable strategy may also be viewed as a media mistake because often the strategy leads the official to make statements which appeal to the media but wind up alienating large segments of the official's constituency. Reporters may love to cover the campaign of a charismatic old-style pol and audiences may lap up the outrageous comments he makes—but those same comments may fail to get him elected when it comes time for voters to go to the polls.

The liar. Some officials hope to avoid negative news coverage by trying to hide from the media any occurrences that make the official or the agency look incompetent, ineffective, or unethical. Unlike the paranoid media-avoider, these officials will respond to reporters' inquiries about controversial issues by providing incorrect information that makes them look good. The strategy involves simply hoping that no other source will come forward to provide the media with contradictory information. Sometimes, officials succeed in hiding negative information from the media. In particular, when the information being obscured is highly technical or based on quantitative information the reporter cannot secure or understand, a policy of obfuscation may work. For example, as pointed out in chapter 3, a local official could exaggerate the benefits of a new development project or underestimate the costs with little chance of being challenged by reporters ignorant of economic analysis.

However, in other less technical areas, there are great risks involved in lying to the media, particularly in cases where other sources, because of their own objectives, are capable of pointing out the lie to reporters. For example, the head of a city labor union may know about and have an incentive to reveal cases of misinformation that discredit management and make labor look more positive. In other cases, it will be someone in the official's office or agency—a middle-level manager or professional—who may want to leak information to reporters about misinformation at the top of his organization. As one local official put it, "The media can find out anything [about the department] including what kind of socks I have on in the morning."

In those cases where reporters learn that they have been lied to, the results are often calamitous for the official. Journalists who are heavily dependent on their sources to report the news feel betrayed and angered when they learn the source knowingly misled them and will tend to work subsequently to discredit that official in their reporting. Moreover, any public initiative the official makes in the future will be subjected to intense scrutiny not given to other officials. When the official makes a new proposal, the reporter, suspicions aroused, will seek out critics of the proposal and often place their criticisms before the proposal itself in the resulting story. Leaks about the official and his office that might have been shrugged off in the past will be followed up assiduously.

Therefore, while each of these strategies or styles has some logic to it, they all lead more often than not to negative coverage of the official who pursues them. Even more importantly, none of these strategies succeeds in gaining for an official the kind media coverage necessary to successfully sell a controversial new policy initiative. A successful strategy is only forged by those officials who understand how to meet the needs of the local media without pandering to them, who help the individual journalist to do his or her job and the news firm to meet its economic objectives, but who do so in a way that conveys an image of the official as an active and effective leader.

The Successful Media Strategy of the Local Official

Officials create long-standing positive images for themselves not by engaging in media events or responding willy-nilly to every media crusade, but by continually providing reporters with the kinds of information they need to produce what journalists consider good stories. There are three basic elements involved in becoming and remaining an effective source: (1) establishing an initial media image for the official or agency or revamping a previously tarnished image; (2) producing an ongoing stream of information for reporters, both about the agency or office, its victories and problems, as well as about other parts of government; and (3) neutralizing criticisms, problems, and other negative coverage.

Establishing an initial image or refurbishing a tarnished image. Almost every official entering public life—whether after an election or an appointment—enjoys a "honeymoon" period during which media treatment is relatively uncritical. But as time goes on, and an official begins to make decisions that meet opposition, more critical coverage may ensue. However, some officials try to protect themselves against that stage of controversy by building up an initial image—directly with reporters and indirectly with the public—of honesty and efficacy. The mistake that many newly appointed officials make is in moving too quickly with major new policy initiatives, before they have established a trustworthy image for themselves and their organization or agency. This image-creation phase is even more urgent in those cases where an official is brought in to clean up a troubled agency or office. In those cases, the new official must take steps to distinguish his management from what came before without insulting or alienating employees who remain from the old regime.

Providing reporters with information. Officials improve their chances of getting their positions across effectively by maintaining accessibility and providing the information reporters need to do their jobs: returning journalists' phone calls, holding frequent press conferences, allowing subordinates to respond to reporters' requests for information. As one reporter commented, "Accessibility is the main operative force. People who return phone calls and hold press conferences get their points across."[27] Officials may also actively suggest story ideas which appeal to journalists while at the same time making the official or agency look positive and effective. A new project to help the disabled, the release of a study showing improvement in school children's test scores, the new transit program to assist the elderly all make for interesting stories that also make the agency or office look good. In particular, community newspapers and local television news are often eager for upbeat feature story ideas that appeal to their audiences.

Officials may also benefit from supplying reporters with less positive information, as when they "leak" information about problems in other parts of government or discuss frankly, if off the record, problems in their own department. As one beat reporter noted in describing his relationship with the top official he covered: "The thing I liked about him as a source was that, unlike his predecessors, who would answer my question, 'Why did you hire so-and-so?' with 'Because he's the best man for the job,' [this official] would talk to me off the record and tell it to me straight. Even though I couldn't use a lot of that, it helped me later in my reporting."[28] In such situations, officials have the opportunity to make clear to reporters which problems lie outside the jurisdiction of the agency or office. As one reporter pointed out about a local housing official, "He's very candid about what he can and can't do. He says to reporters, 'Don't expect my office to get rid of all the abandoned houses in this city.'

Some officials also take the time to talk with reporters off the record, simply to increase their understanding of the agency's problems and policies, so that when the reporter comes to write a story it is informed by an understanding of why an official took a certain position. As an official in Philadelphia's economic development agency said, "Many reporters really want to understand a situation or an issue and call you to discuss a matter off the record. I think it's important for officials to get reporters to understand why they are doing what they are doing."

In some cases, reporters are reluctant to criticize a source who has provided them with information in the past, for fear of alienating the source and stopping the flow of information. As one reporter described it, "Some officials are very clever people, they understand how to manipulate the media. They leak you some stuff you can use that's not too damaging to them and you become comfortable relying on them. Then you get dependent and you're reluctant to criticize them when you get something negative about them." Similarly, another reporter commented on the difficult position a reporter finds himself in when "you find something bad about a good source." Although most reporters interviewed said they would not hold back on a major negative story about one of their chief sources, some did suggest that minor transgressions might be overlooked.

Officials must also be sensitive to the needs of the different local media. While lengthy, regular background discussions with a beat reporter may be an effective strategy for dealing with the print media, television requires quite different skills, including the use of press conferences and visual events and the ability to formulate positions as sound bites. Many officials have begun to choose their public appearances so as to provide an effective visual backdrop for a television news appearance. For example, on the day of a major demonstration against a state bill banning assault weapons in New Jersey, Governor James Florio made an appearance before a state police ceremony. With the uniformed officers flanking him in the background, Florio told television reporters that he was in favor of the legislation and suggested that officers of the law were also.

Similarly, Philadelphia Police Commissioner Willie Williams described two distinct strategies for dealing with print and broadcast journalists. While he schedules regular briefings with the beat reporters from the two major newspapers and visits several times a year with their editorial boards, for television reporters he recognizes the important need to offer on-camera interviews with the Police Administration Building as the backdrop. In addition, the commissioner noted how his department had begun inviting television reporters to accompany police officers on drug busts. The television stations, eager for dramatic video for their reports, were only too willing to cover the events and, in the process, helped the police department convey to the citizens of Philadelphia—and in particular the residents of certain neighborhoods concerned about police action against drug activity—that strong steps were being taken to fight drugs.[29]

Although many local officials have begun to learn the importance of scheduling visual media events for local television cameras, some have difficulty meeting the other requirement of television: speaking in "sound bites." That is, officials need to be able to convey a position in the five to twenty seconds allotted for the interview in the television news package. If an official is incapable of speaking in sound bites, his interview comments will often be eliminated from the package and a voice-over will be used. As a result, the official will have less television exposure (and therefore gain less name and face recognition) and at the same time will be less certain of getting his position across effectively to the audience.

Neutralizing criticisms, scandals, and disasters. Perhaps the most difficult task for any official, no matter how skillful in dealing with the media, has to do with handling problems or occurrences which threaten to tarnish the image of the official or the agency.[30] In such situations, officials who are normally accessible and good at handing out press releases and scheduling media events often fall down because they do not know how to "neutralize" the criticism. In many cases, they make the mistake of either denying the problem, avoiding the media, or becoming defensive. In contrast, some officials succeed in weathering the storm because they maintain media contact, admit obvious mistakes, but try to put the best face on what has occurred. In the case of newspaper reporters, the strategy involves using established trust to talk at length to explain your side of the story and your argument. With television, it usually involves maintaining accessibility and framing a succinct defense.

A similar dilemma arises when an official is confronted with negative coverage he believes is based on incorrect information. In those situations, some officials have the tendency to get angry and retreat, "freezing out" the offending reporter for what is viewed as a deliberate sensationalizing error. However, other officials say they consciously stifle this urge, choosing instead to maintain contact with the offending reporter and attempting to correct the error. Philadelphia's Police Commissioner noted he ignored advice from his senior staff to call a press conference to denounce an article in one of the city's newspapers which claimed, in a front-page headline, that there was only one policeman on duty on each shift for every 3,052 people. Although the commissioner claimed the reporter had ignored information which indicated many more police on shifts, he said he thought a full-blown denouncement would be counterproductive. He chose instead to write a letter to the editor pointing out the factual errors of the story. "You don't want these things to take on a life of their own," he said.[31]

These three elements, establishing an initial image, maintaining accessibility, and neutralizing criticism, represent the three prongs of a successful media strategy for the local official. It is important to note that local officials who are successful in these three areas are often guided by experienced press secretaries or public affairs spokesmen. In contrast, officials and agencies that blunder and fall into the trap of making classic media mistakes are often those who have no press arm in their organizations and who accord little importance to public relations strategies.

Media Strategies for New Initiatives

Earlier chapters have shown how reporters and their news firms approach coverage of a major new policy initiative, particularly proposals for new downtown or regional development projects. Nonetheless, it is important to recognize that the local official's strategy for introducing such proposals plays a major role in how those plans come to be covered by the local media and ultimately whether the public supports or rejects them. There are three key junctures in the proposal of any new plan: the preproposal phase, when the official establishes his own image and reliability as a source and when the foundation is laid for the need for the new initiative; the actual announcement of the proposal itself, when the project's importance is argued; and the response to the opposition, when the arguments of the plan's foes are addressed.

Setting an Official Image

Crucial to the coverage of a new policy initiative is the image of the agency or official that has formulated the proposal, an image that has been established long before any press conferences are called to announce a new project. This image determines the way the official and his office are regarded, not simply as public servants, but as sources of information for the media. Because of the constraints on a reporter's time and expertise, an official with an image of being productive and efficient will tend to have his information accepted routinely, but an official who has a poor image, as either inefficient, unproductive, or unethical, is likely to have his proposals scrutinized in great detail. In other words, proposals for new policies or projects will be covered quite differently according to the degree of respectability—or suspicion—the official proposing them has earned in the months if not years that preceded the announcement.

For example, Robert Moses rarely had his proposals scrutinized by reporters, even though his projects often involved dislocating thousands of people whose homes stood in the way of proposed highways, bridges, and parks. While Moses' pronouncement on issues would be reported verbatim at the top of every article, his critics, even when they meticulously documented their objections, would rate a scarce paragraph at the very end of stories, if they were reported at all. As Caro writes, "Some reporters wanted to [investigate Moses] but were refused permission, in some cases because of their publisher's admiration for Moses, in most cases, simply because it seemed to editors a waste of time; where Moses was involved, they felt, there would be no scandal to be found; trying to find it would be a misuse of manpower that could be more profitably employed investigating politicians or bureaucrats." [32]

In contrast, an official or agency with a poor media image will find new initiatives subject to intense investigation. For example, in 1982, Houston's Metropolitan Transit Authority (Metro) set in motion plans to improve its bus fleet and construct a new rail system. In order to issue the bonds necessary to support the improvements, the agency had to hold a referendum to gain public approval. The mistake that the agency's director made, however, was in going forward with this referendum at a time when Metro still had a negative image left over from previous management as a result of common bus breakdowns and accidents. Even though the new director had an excellent reputation from a previous stint running Atlanta's transit system, and despite the fact that many felt there was a strong need for the capital improvements to relieve traffic congestion, Metro's plans continued to receive negative coverage in the pages of the *Houston Chronicle* and *Houston Post*. When the June 11, 1983, referendum was held, the bond issue was, not surprisingly, defeated. As a public relations consultant later told officials in the agency, "If I had looked at your clips, I would not have recommended a referendum in June." [33]

In contrast to Metro's problems, an agency or official with a positive media image accumulates political capital and will find it easier to gain public support for his initiatives and more difficult for his critics to assail him. As Philadelphia's District Attorney put it, "The more popular I am [as a result of news coverage], the better I am at lobbying with legislators. And if I can translate that popularity into getting people to contact their legislators, that also enhances the chances of getting legislation passed." [34] Similarly, Danielson and Doig have described how positive news coverage of economic development agencies such as the New York Port Authority helped the agencies to carry out their plans. "Stories that applauded the clearing of slums in Newark or New

York, and that spoke rapturously of the George Washington Bridge, the Narrows span, and the World Trade Center kept the general public a friendly audience, and made it difficult for opponents—those removed forcibly from homes and small shops, those who saw environmental decay in the rush toward new roadways—to gain wider sympathy." [35]

Laying the Foundation: "Educating the Media" and Media Events

Gaining support for a new policy initiative also involves focusing the media's attention on stories that emphasize the need for the new initiative. A proposal for a new policy or project that is announced with no preliminary work is less convincing than one for which the need has been established over a period of months or years. One of the first steps in laying the foundation for need consists of what some officials call "educating the media": holding meetings with editorial boards at newspapers and with senior staff at television and radio stations and going off the record with individual reporters to explain the reasons behind the policy change or new proposal before any official announcement is made. "Hopefully, the media will buy into what I'm doing and agree it's prudent," said Philadelphia Police Commissioner Kevin Tucker. "You have to do that, touch all your bases, before trying to implement any change." [36]

Officials also rely on media events to convince the public of a need for a new policy or proposal. As Dunn notes, "Officials design publicity to win support for a new policy by dramatizing the existence of a problem in dire need of solution. Then they present proposed solutions." [37] For example, Richard Ravitch, early in his tenure as board chairman of the Metropolitan Transit Agency in New York, was disappointed to see how little coverage he received when he called a press conference to announce a fourteen-billion-dollar capital improvement program for the MTA. Ravitch quickly learned not to call press conferences to discuss dry capital plans, but rather after there were breakdowns and delays on the subways—subjects that interested journalists and satisfied the needs of their news firms to find regional stories. Over a period of months, these media events created in the public mind a sense of the need for new financing to improve the MTA's equipment. And so when Ravitch embarked once again on a major capital plan, he got prominent attention in the media— and had secured public support in advance by paving the way in the news media. [38] As one official put it, "The best way to get money is to follow a bad story."

181

The Announcement of a New Proposal

When the time comes to announce a new proposal, officials often begin by scheduling a press conference for both print and broadcast media, creating the kind of media event that journalists are certain to cover. The power of the press conference in announcing a new proposal lies not simply in gaining attention for the proposal but in "getting there first": that is, the proponents of the proposal get to make their case to the media in a forum that excludes critics. Unless well-defined opposition to the proposal exists at that point, deadline pressure will often keep journalists from obtaining comment on the proposal from other actors with less of a vested interest in the project. Therefore, the press conference is often reported as a single-source story, particularly if the proposing official has a positive media image and there is no obvious, organized opposition to the initiative.

Second, officials often accompany their announcement with the release of numbers. Before proposing a new initiative, officials may commission a consultant's study of the need for the project and its estimated costs and benefits and use the results when announcing the project to the media. If the mayor announces that the new project will cost $5 million and generate $3 billion in tax revenues and 10,000 new jobs, those numbers will tend to be reported in the lead paragraph of the local newspaper story announcing the project's proposal. The reporter is not trained to question whether those numbers are realistic—whether, for instance, an inflated multiplier was used, or whether the city failed to use a discount rate when comparing present costs to future benefits. In addition, the numbers are given added legitimacy when they are said to originate from an "independent" consultant's study. Reporters consider such consultants to be unbiased sources of technical information, despite the fact that such consultants are paid by the city officials who want to see the project built.

The other major part of the announcement affecting the nature of news coverage involves the symbolic framing of the proposal. Officials may succeed in gaining positive coverage for their initiatives if they cast their proposal into terms that play on reporters' personal and professional values and the news media's overall economic imperative to appeal to a suburban audience. There are several themes that both appeal to the media and serve to paint the project in its most positive light:

The public versus the private interest. This theme stresses that the project will benefit the public as a whole rather than pointing out the groups who might benefit more directly than others.

Adopting a regional perspective. This strategy plays to the media's need for appeal to suburban audiences and the need to gain state funding by stressing the regional importance of the project and emphasizing that the economic benefits will cross city boundaries.

Blending nostalgia with progress. This type of announcement emphasizes that the project will help regain "an earlier glory" and bring the city and the region into the modern service-sector era.

Sounding the "horse race" theme. The competition between cities and interurban rivalry is played up in order to help enliven coverage about economic development and stimulate a sense of haste, which encourages public support for the expenditure of funds.

Forestalling the opposition. By painting opponents as "naysayers" or "obstructionists" who block progress for the sake of their own narrow self-interests, the official may not only gain positive coverage for the proposal, but may ensure future positive coverage in the face of criticism.

The way in which new initiatives are presented and framed for the media is particularly important in cases of policy differences among local officials, where there is jockeying to convey the wisdom of a position to the public. For example, in Seattle in 1984, state and congressional officials were eager to see the city of Seattle become the home port for a group of U.S. Navy battleships and advocated that the city actively court the Navy, including offering tax incentives and other perks. Seattle's Mayor Charles Royer, on the other hand, took the position that he would welcome the home port only if the costs of the concessions to the Navy were to be balanced by the benefits.

While both sides had reasonable positions, the pro–home port forces received far more extensive and positive news coverage because of the way they conveyed their position to the media. Washington's governor and the state's congressmen actively held press conferences at which they declared their unqualified support for the Navy and sounded the "horse race" theme of intercity competition, which the local media picked up and played prominently. Governor Spellman commissioned a study by his office that showed the positive employment and tax impacts of the home port, the results of which, though later proven to be inaccurate,[39] were given banner headline play in the *Seattle Times*. In contrast, Mayor Royer conveyed his position only when contacted by reporters and often let his press secretary speak for him. In addition, Royer's position was not framed in terms that were as symbolically appealing as that of the pro-Navy contingent. "My feeling is that the Navy's got to pay its own way . . . we will not get into a bidding war with Everett," Royer is quoted as saying.[40]

As a result, while the governor and congressmen saw their names and positions in headlines like, "Back Navy or lose base to California, Spellman warns,"[41] or "Dicks, Gorton, and Evans urge enthusiastic welcome for the Navy,"[42] the mayor and his position were referred to only negatively in headlines like, "Wright criticizes Royer for failing to encourage Navy."[43] When Royer did expound on his position, it was not at a press conference he himself called but in the course of a routine appearance at a union luncheon. As a result, his defense of his position did not appear until the last two paragraphs of a story headlined, "Workers to Royer: Go for Navy Base."[44] In effect, the opposing positions in the debate were given imbalanced consideration because of the different media strategies of the officials holding them. In particular, the differences in the coverage could be traced to the way those positions were framed to meet the local media's need for stories with symbolic interest to the regional audience.

The importance of symbols in the framing of policies is perhaps nowhere more evident than in the successful rise and later downfall of Robert Moses. One of Moses' original strengths lay in knowing how to cast his proposed projects in the most positive light, while providing the New York news media with the kinds of stories—and symbols—they needed to maintain their own local audience. The unveiling of one majestic project after another—Jones Beach, the Parkways, the Bridges, Lincoln Center—were used by Moses as occasions to herald pride in the New York region, thereby allowing the media the opportunity to reinforce a sense of shared local identity from Westchester to the Hamptons. At the same time, Moses was able to cast himself in the role of the local hero, remaining virtually immune to criticism for over thirty years.

When, in 1956, thirty years after his rise to power, Moses finally began to fall from grace—when the local news media's criticism of his policies began in earnest and the investigative tools of journalism finally turned on him—it was not because the man had changed his colors or that local news reporting had become more discerning. Rather, Robert Moses's media coverage changed when he somewhat callously tried to turn a small playground in the middle of Central Park into a parking lot. Compared with the negative impacts of some of his other projects, the Central Park episode was relatively minor. However, Moses' opponents, affluent, media-savvy residents of Manhattan, were able to triumph, because they, not Moses, were able to symbolically frame the issue in the kinds of terms that held appeal to the local news media. Moses was successfully cast as the defiler of one of the most symbolic local assets in New York, Central Park, and soon after began to lose his status as local hero.[45]

The Use and Misuse of the Media By Local Officials

We have seen how local officials may both succeed and blunder in their dealings with the media as they attempt to establish a general image for themselves and their offices and gain coverage for their initiatives. In any local arena, there are important differences among local officials in their understanding of how to interact with the media effectively; some are expert while many others fail in their attempts to get positive coverage for themselves or their initiatives. This imbalance affects more than political or professional aspirations; it comes to play a key role in determining the way policies and proposals are presented to the local audience. In concluding this chapter, it is important to recognize how the varying media skills of local officials affect the policy process. Specifically, a number of scenarios are possible.

Good plan, positive news coverage. The most sanguine cases occur when an effective public official is able to gain positive news coverage—and eventually public support—for sound policy initiatives. In these cases, public officials use news coverage of a new plan to effectively make the case for its need. Journalists and news firms, while meeting their own objectives for good stories, inform the public about policy needs or new opportunities and strategies for addressing them.

Unwise plan, negative news coverage. The public interest is also served when reporters succeed in exposing the claims of public officials who put forth plans that are likely to be ineffective, detrimental, or wasteful. Either because reporters themselves dissect the plan or because other sources (union leaders, middle managers, organized citizen groups) leak reporters damaging information, the downsides of the plan are exposed. In these cases, the public interest is also served while, again, journalists and news organizations get a good story.

Good plan, negative coverage. In more troublesome cases, officials at times receive negative coverage for themselves and for their initiatives largely because of their naivete in handling the media. As a result, the media, in their continual search for local villains and a common sense of outrage, help defeat a plan that might have been promising. A similar concern is raised when, in a policy debate, one position gets portrayed more prominently and positively than the opposing position, simply because of the unequal skills of the officials advancing them.

Bad plan, good coverage. Another disturbing scenario occurs when a media-savvy official gains positive coverage for an initiative which is overly costly or which will benefit only a narrow segment of the community. In this case, the official trades on an established capital with reporters to get good coverage of his initiatives, with little scrutiny. By providing reporters with the kind of information, story ideas, and symbols they need, the official succeeds in gaining positive public opinion and support for the proposal. Even when opposition appears to argue with the plan, it tends to be discredited by the power of the local "hero's" persuasion.

Symbolic diversion and lost capital. In other cases, officials may get positive news coverage for largely symbolic initiatives that have little substance behind them. The increasingly sophisticated use by some officials of media events may divert the media's and the public's attention from uncovering real problems or from subjecting the official's performance to scrutiny. The police department's move to invite television reporters and their cameramen to ride along for a drug bust may result in a positive story on the evening news but it will not say much about whether any substantive progress has been made on the drug problem. In addition, the planning and staging of media events themselves may take valuable time away from governing. For example, one state legislator noted that during campaign years, the need to get media attention involved staging activities which often forced aside follow-up work needed for pushing legislation through committees. "You can introduce 900,000 bills and get lots of positive coverage but if you don't have the time to push them through, you haven't really served your constituents," he remarked.[46]

In other cases, local officials with poor media skills lose the political capital with which they might have advanced good ideas and plans. The transit director who fails to take the time to educate the media and the public about certain needs will ultimately fail in his attempts to implement an innovative new transit plan or gain political support for a new tax to support an aging system. Equally disturbing, news coverage which focuses on the personal incompetence of officials often diverts attention from the real causes of social and economic problems and the need for substantive solutions that confront those problems. When local officials are hounded out of office by news coverage, the solution is often simply the appointment of a new official, with very little about the situation changing.

In all of these cases, there is cause for concern whenever policies, positions, and officials come to be evaluated more on the basis of media skills than on solid performance and when questions of personality come to override the consideration of underlying social and economic problems. It is not simply the media's economic imperative or journalists' professional values that color the coverage of new local policies, but the actions of local officials as well.

7 Philadelphia's New Convention Center: A Case Study

On June 30, 1989, Philadelphia's City Council voted to approve funding for a $523 million convention center in the heart of downtown Philadelphia on the site of the historic Reading Railroad train shed. The development, which would replace an older Civic Center located across the Schuylkill river in West Philadelphia, would be the largest single expenditure ever undertaken by the city of Philadelphia. First proposed by the administration of Mayor Bill Green in early 1983, the Convention Center proposal had taken six years to gain approval by both the Pennsylvania state legislature and the city council.

The decision to use public funds for the construction of a massive economic development project like Philadelphia's Convention Center was the result of the planning and lobbying efforts of a myriad of actors, from public officials to business leaders and organized citizen groups. But it was also critically influenced by the reporting of the city's news media. This chapter examines the role that the local news media play in weighing major development proposals, such as a new convention center. The case will illustrate how the economic objectives of the local media, the professional and personal values of local journalists, and the strategies of local sources come together to shape the reporting of a new initiative.[1]

The Background of the Convention Center Proposal

Philadelphia at the beginning of the 1980s was like many older northeastern cities, struggling to transform itself from a decaying manufacturing core to a revitalized center of the service economy. In the past thirty years, its population had declined by over 380,000, with a 13 percent decline from 1970 to 1980 alone. In that same decade, the city had lost over 100,000 jobs, with manufacturing employment declining from 237,000 in 1970 to 150,000 in 1980. While the number of service jobs were increasing, it was not sufficient to offset the loss in manufacturing. The city had just bid farewell to Mayor Frank Rizzo, a charismatic public figure beloved by many in the city but a man who was also frequently criticized for marring Philadelphia's image. The highly publicized allegations of police brutality under his leadership and his call for the national guard to help control potential disturbances at the city's Bicentennial celebration were often cited as hindering Philadelphia's attempts to attract tourists, conventions, and other service jobs.

The administration of the new mayor, Bill Green, set out to break with that image in order to stimulate service-sector development in the city. The center-piece of these efforts was a plan for a new downtown convention center. A project that had long been discussed among the city's hoteliers and tourism officials, the Convention Center was brought to center stage in 1982, when the city commissioned a consultant's study of the need for a new complex. City officials admitted privately that there was little doubt in their minds that the city needed a new convention center. The study was commissioned more to provide numbers that could justify the new center and be used for the cost and benefit estimates that would be taken to the bond market to begin financing of the project. The sense among many city officials was that it was a foregone conclusion that the city needed a new convention center. The only questions were when, where, and how big.

As with any major development project, there were powerful private interests supporting the city administration's attempts to push for a new convention center. After struggling for many years, Philadelphia's hotel industry in the early 1980s was still plagued with low occupancy rates. Hotel owners looked to expansion in the convention trade to help deal with problems created by a legacy of poor management and were eager to see a proposal to replace the existing convention facility with a new central-city complex. The Civic Center that was already in place was located about two miles from downtown and composed of a convention hall built in 1931 and two exhibition halls, one constructed in 1967, the other in 1978.

Two major developers were also eager to see a new downtown convention center, because they hoped it would be located on one of their sites. The first was the Reading Company, the real estate development company that was formed when the Reading Railroad went out of business and turned over its extensive real estate holdings and tax investment credits to a new company. Reading owned several blocks of real estate on the east side of City Hall, including a train shed and terminal that were soon to become obsolete with the city's completion of an underground commuter tunnel. Reading had a strong motive to see the Convention Center proposal approved: it would be the perfect use for its historically certified train shed, in addition to using a large amount of adjacent real estate also owned by the company.

Reading was not the only developer in town trying to find a major development use for its property. The Franklin Town Corporation also had a sizable parcel of real estate, to the northwest of downtown, acquired years before for a residential and commercial mini-town that had never been built. Like the Reading Company, the Franklin Town Corporation had a strong interest in seeing a new Convention Center proposal approved. Along with these two developers, and the city's hotel, restaurant, and retail owners, the local construction and trade unions would also potentially benefit from the construction and operation of a new center. It was into this climate of support that the announcement came in January of 1983 that the city administration was proposing the construction of a new convention center.

Initial News Coverage of the Proposal: The Estimation of Need

The most extensive and continuous coverage of the proposal for a new Convention Center came from the city's two newspapers, the *Philadelphia Inquirer* and the *Daily News*. Although the two newspapers are owned by the same company, Philadelphia Newspapers, Inc., which in turn is owned by the Knight-Ridder group, they maintain separate news and editorial staffs. The morning *Inquirer*, with a circulation at the time of close to 550,000, is targeted to a regional audience, with approximately 60 percent of its readers residing in the suburbs. The *Daily News*, in contrast, is an afternoon tabloid with a circulation in 1983 of roughly 290,000, sold predominantly at city newsstands, with a relatively small suburban readership. Both newspapers are extremely well regarded nationwide. The *Inquirer*, under editor Eugene L. Roberts, Jr., had won numerous Pulitzer Prizes for its investigative reporting and the *Daily News* was generally viewed as one of the best city tabloids in the country.

One of the first long discussions of the plan for a new convention center in either newspaper came in the *Inquirer* in a July 1982 column by editorial writer George Wilson headlined, "Convention center is a must for the area." Wilson's column began, "Does Philadelphia need a new convention center? Does the sun shine in the morning? The answer to both questions is the same and should be equally obvious." Wilson's column went on to stress the need for careful analysis of the costs and benefits of a new center by the consulting firm doing the feasibility study. "It is up to the consultants to separate the pie in the sky from the down to earth. Boosterism is fine but it doesn't pay the bills. What are the realities? How much convention business can Philadelphia expect to get in the remainder of the 20th century with existing facilities? How much additional business would it get with optimum facilities?" Despite such caveats, the column stressed the need for a new center, no matter what the numbers might turn out to say.[2]

A few months later, the question of whether Philadelphia should build a new convention center was examined in the *Inquirer*'s Sunday business section. Under the main headline, "Exhibiting a need for convention space," the question was posed, "Should Philadelphia jump on the bandwagon with a new convention center? The Civic Center's 382,000 square feet of exhibit space—it cost $40,000,000—make it competitive, but it is far from Center City hotels."[3] Despite this evenhanded beginning, the story itself revealed a subtle tilt. The first thirteen paragraphs, featuring comments from meetings planners who had cancelled plans for conventions in the city, all supported the need for a new center. It was not until midway through the article that other countervailing opinions appeared, such as "There has been too much 'me-tooism' as far as the building of convention centers," and later, "The [present] convention center needs a little work, but I think it's aesthetics as far as I'm concerned."

The article also made clear that the greatest problem Philadelphia had in attracting large conventions was not the weaknesses of the existing Civic Center, but the lack of a large convention hotel. And in the last few paragraphs of the article, a cautionary note is sounded by the reporter: "Most industry experts acknowledge that the growth in new facilities outpaces the growth in the industry itself, prompting many city officials to worry that they had saddled their municipalities with costly white elephants. Not only are convention centers expensive to build, but they require continual public subsidies to operate because they are seldom self-supporting." But these warnings were dwarfed by the story's long initial portion and its headline, which suggested that a need had been "exhibited."

All such caveats were missing when the newspaper came to cover the release of the feasibility study and the city administration's announcement of plans to go forward with the construction of a new convention center. On January 12, 1983, the *Inquirer* ran a front-page story headlined, "Big civic center a must, study says," based on the findings of a preliminary copy of the consultant's report.[4] The lead paragraph of the article states, "Philadelphia needs to build a new convention center in Center City with 300,000 square feet of convention space to remain competitive in the convention and meetings business, a private consulting firm has determined."

The story is drawn largely from the report's findings, which supported the construction of a new center. It also included comments from the general manager of a local hotel and a member of the city's Convention Center Steering Committee, a group of city officials and business leaders examining the need for a new center. Nowhere in the article is there a comment suggesting there was not a need for a new center, nor an interview with another source evaluating the accuracy of the findings of the city-hired consultants. The article does note again that the city's problems are not with the existing center so much as "its location and its proximity to the city's lean supply of hotels." A new downtown convention center was needed, it suggested, in order to stimulate the construction of a 1,000–1,200-room hotel.

When, two days later, the *Inquirer* reported the city's official announcement of plans for a new center, it was with a front-page story headlined, "City pushes convention center plan," which began,

> An effort to move quickly to build a four-square-block convention facility in Center City was put in motion yesterday by city officials and business leaders.
>
> The facility, which would be completed by 1987 at the earliest, is expected to cost more than $130 million, add more than $1 billion in city tax revenues over its 30-year life and pump more than $21 billion into the city's economy, City Commerce Director Richard A. Doran said yesterday.[5]

The only two sources used in the story were the commerce director and the consultant's study. Again, no comments were included to contradict Doran's claim that "Philadelphia's need for a new center was critical" or to dispute the estimates of the costs and benefits of the project as developed by the consulting firm.

The need for a new convention center received additional consideration by the newspaper the following Sunday in a longer piece in the review section of the paper headlined, "With center, city hopes to fix image."[6] This article, as the headline suggests, focused not on the economics of the new project but on the link between the new center and the city's image, a connection cited by the feasibility study. The beginning of the story summarized the estimates of the monetary costs and benefits of the project as if they were now facts:

> To be sure, the city—and the state—would receive a significant $1 billion boost in revenues from wage, sales, hotel occupancy and real-estate taxes.

> As many as 5,000 jobs would be created. And the construction
> of a convention center in Philadelphia is expected to spur other
> development projects. At least two major hotel chains have ex-
> pressed interest in erecting hotels near such a center.
>
> A new center is also expected to send $21 billion rippling
> through the region's economy in indirect spending over the 30-
> year life of the center.
>
> But perhaps the biggest benefit is the least tangible: Philadel-
> phia stands, once and for all, to correct the misperception that it
> is a drab, undesirable place to visit.

The article goes on to present the findings of the consultants' report that deal
with the poor image of the city found among meetings planners, leading to the
statement, "If the city built a major new convention facility closer to the city's
supply of hotels—its major drawback as a convention center—Philadelphia
would demonstrate to the nation that it was a 'progressive' and 'forward-
thinking' community, [the consulting firm] said." The article summarized other
results of the study and then went on to consider the three major sites being
considered for the center. Once again, no one who might dispute the claims of
the new center's backers was interviewed.

On the *Inquirer*'s editorial page, the outlook was even more positive. Soon
after the city's announcement, an editorial appeared with the headline, "A new
convention center: Do it now and do it right."[7] The editorial stated, in part,

> If there were any lingering doubts about the wisdom of the . . .
> recommendation, they should be swept aside in the latest find-
> ings. The . . . report . . . said a new convention center in Center
> City would generate more than $21 billion for the economy of
> the region in its first 30 years and contribute more than $1 billion
> in direct tax revenues to the city and state. That would be an ex-
> cellent return on an initial investment estimated at $133 million
> for construction plus whatever additional costs might be involved
> in site acquisitions and parking facilities.
>
> Conversely, failure to build a new convention center would
> condemn Philadelphia to second-class status as a convention city
> and perennial loss of convention revenues.

News coverage of the initial plans for a new convention center was similar,
although less prominently played, in the *Daily News*. The commerce director's
press conference announcing plans for the new center was reported in a page-4

story headlined, "Panel Has Sites Set on Convention Center."[8] Like the *Inquirer*'s story, the chief sources for the *Daily News* article were Doran and the consultant's study, with a few additional comments from two other city officials involved in the planning of the new center. The $133 million estimate of the price tag for the new center was repeated, as was the estimate that the facility would "bring the city $21 billion in additional convention business over the next 30 years." Doran is quoted in the fourth paragraph as saying, "I feel a great sense of urgency about this. . . We have no choice but to move in this direction—fast." No comments were offered which might contradict this view or question the consultant's estimates of costs and benefits.

While the *Daily News* did not offer an editorial concerning the new convention center soon after the announcement, as did the *Inquirer,* it did throw its editorial support behind the project several months later, after the Reading site had been selected for the center. Lauding the choice of the Reading site, the editorial stated,

> Whichever site would have been selected, the project brings jobs the city desperately needs. They'll come in construction, in tourism and in everything from hotel workers to vendors who sell little Liberty Bells, and to people who clean up after a convention is gone.
>
> The Civic Center is outmoded and out-of-the-way. It needed replacing, and now it will be replaced, once the difficult job of relocating businesses and residents displaced by the new project is completed. Reading Co.'s proposal looks like a good start on that relocation.
>
> We took our time as usual. But it looks like we did it right.[9]

This review of the initial coverage of the proposal for a new convention center in both of the city's major newspapers points out a number of ways in which the new project was being boosted.

Headlines were overwhelmingly positive. In the period preceding and immediately following the city administration's announcement of its plans to build a new convention center, the headlines of stories suggested a certainty that a new center was needed. Headlines of news articles, columns, and editorials such as, "As a convention center, Philadelphia lacks something," "Convention Center is a must for the area," "Big Civic Center a must, study says," "City pushes convention center plan," "Panel has sites set on Convention Center," "Modern Philadelphia Convention center a must," and "A new convention center: Do it now and do it right," conveyed a sense of urgency and a positive image for the project, masking some of the questioning statements within individual articles and columns.

Official estimates of costs and benefits were accepted unquestioningly. The *Inquirer* and the *Daily News* presented as attributed fact the estimate of the consulting firm and city officials that the cost of the project would be $130 million. Within a year, that cost estimate was revised to approximately $400 million, indicating a 300-million-dollar discrepancy with the original estimate. Similarly, the benefits of the center were accepted by the newspapers to be $21 billion in multiplier effects and $1 billion in taxes, figures challenged later in the approval process. No impartial sources were sought to verify the accuracy of the estimates.

The use of single-source or single-perspective articles was common. The stories reporting the city's plans for a new center were often single-source stories reporting only the claims of the city officials making the proposal and the findings of the report commissioned by the city. In other cases, where other sources were used, all of those interviewed had an interest in advancing the progress of the proposal. In addition, although the center was considered a regional project and would be financed in part by state funds, no suburban officials were interviewed for their opinions about the need for the new downtown project.

Questioning notes about the need for the center were often buried in articles and later entirely dropped. Both the *Inquirer*'s editorial columnist and the newspaper's reporter covering the proposal had balanced their stories about the need for a new center with information suggesting that renovation of the existing center might be adequate or that convention trade might not be a wise investment for the city. However, such cautionary notes were often overwhelmed by more positive comments and over time, such questioning began to disappear entirely from coverage of the proposal.

The logic of the consultant's assertions were not questioned. Reporters failed to question two key assertions made by the consultant's study, one that a new convention center would stimulate the construction of a 1,200-

room hotel and that such a center would succeed in changing the city's image. As the years passed, it became questionable whether a 1,200-room hotel would be built, since there was doubt that the city could support such a large hotel with regular business between conventions. And events like the city's disastrous confrontation with the radical group MOVE and rioting on a center city street on Easter Sunday in 1985 were to reveal that changing a city's image involved more than constructing a new convention center.

Larger policy issues regarding the expenditure of public funds were ignored. In considering the need for a new center, reporters and editorialists failed to devote much consideration to broad policy questions. For example, should the city and region focus so much money on trying to become a leader in the convention business when business downturns could reduce the number of conventions? Similarly, little attention was given to the question of whether, with so many other cities building new centers, there might be an oversupply of facilities in the future. Moreover, the larger question—whether several hundred million dollars could be invested in an economic development project with better returns—was never addressed.

Why was the initial coverage of a major new development project, a project that would turn out to represent the largest single expenditure of city funds and a major allocation of state funds, covered in this way? Why was greater emphasis given to the arguments in favor of a new center than to the notion that a new center was not needed? Some critics of the center argued that the newspapers served as shameless boosters for the project because they stood to benefit from the kind of economic growth such development projects engender. Some claimed that positive coverage was the result of the fact that the publisher of the two newspapers at the time, Sam McKeel, was a member of many local business groups and an active lobbyist for the convention center in the state capitol. It was suggested that McKeel particularly controlled the coverage of the influential *Inquirer,* so as to give a boost to a project supported by friends and business associates.

Most journalists interviewed, from both the *Inquirer* and *Daily News,* staunchly denied that McKeel influenced such news decisions and noted that Knight-Ridder newspapers have a strong reputation for publisher nonintervention regarding editorial decisions. Comments by reporters, editors, and outside observers suggested that the initial coverage of the center proposal was colored by other, more complex factors. First, the initial reporting seems to have been influenced by the nature of the story's appeal to each newspaper's target audience. For the *Inquirer,* a stress on the need for the center in early coverage served to increase the interest of a story that could hold a broad-based regional appeal to the paper's affluent, suburban audience. In contrast, stories examining the renovation of the existing Civic Center or the use of city and state funding for job training or tax incentive plans, would not be as interesting to their target audience.

By emphasizing the regional impacts of the project, the contribution of state funding, and the link between the project and the image of the entire region, the coverage could also help reinforce the sense that the suburbanite was still linked to the fortunes of the central city. In addition, the newspaper's positive perspective helped create an upbeat issue, which both strengthened the city as symbolic center of the region and balanced some of the negative stories being written about Philadelphia's crime, poverty, and corruption. As one observer noted in explaining the newspaper's positive editorial stance, "There was a sense that this was an 'up' project, an 'up' type problem that the city was facing that could be solved." Interestingly enough, the *Daily News,* while supporting the project, did not cover the proposal with the same fanfare as the *Inquirer.* As a city newspaper targeting a largely city audience, the *News* had at its disposal many more subjects of common audience interest.

The professional values of the reporters who covered the issue also may explain the initial coverage. Journalists, even those covering business issues, are typically not trained to evaluate quantitative estimates of costs and benefits and the complex financing of capital projects and, therefore, tend to accept official estimates. Even if those reporters wanted to check the estimates with a knowledgeable source, they would find it difficult to get such a check simply by phoning another source. An investigation into the accuracy of government estimates of the costs and benefits of a new project would need to go beyond the traditional methods that most reporters use to gather information. Therefore, lack of technical expertise may have led both newspapers' reporters in this case to simply accept the city's estimates of the costs and benefits of the proposed center.

In addition, reporters choose the angle of their stories so as to create audience interest and get prominent play for their stories. Emphasizing the position that the city needed a new convention center first in an article may have been seen as a way of writing a more interesting story by stressing the angle of the story that is most "new" in an attempt to get more prominent play in the newspaper. Similarly, the decision to focus the long Sunday review article on the issue of city image rather than the economics of the project suggests that the reporter considered the symbolic rather than the economic aspects of the project to be more interesting to her readers and perhaps to herself as well.

In effect, reporters' inability to delve into quantitative issues encourages them to focus on questions other than costs and benefits—such as city image and pride—encouraged by a sense that such issues make more palatable topics for their audiences. In addition, the personal values of reporters as "young urban professionals" might have also swayed the coverage. The reporters who covered the initial proposal may have been excited at the prospect of a new, modern convention center that would help clean up the city and make it more attractive to outsiders. They responded positively to the city officials' statements that the old Civic Center was "outmoded" and needed to be "updated" and that this project would be instrumental in turning Philadelphia into a world-class city.

At the same time, the role of sources was crucial. City officials ensured that the initial coverage of the center would be positive by: (1) commissioning a consultants' study to back up their proposal, knowing that journalists would view the consultant as an "independent" party; (2) announcing the proposal for the new center at a press conference, which would be covered as a single-source story; and (3) stressing certain themes, such as the "horse race" competition between cities, which reporters would be eager to pick up to make stories about the new proposal more interesting. Of equal importance was the lack of organized opposition to the center at the time of the proposal's announcement. Reporters with limited time to finish stories relied on sources who made themselves accessible rather than seeking out opposition where none forcibly presented itself. The only eager sources were those city officials, private businessmen, and city-hired consultants who had an incentive to supply the media with positive information about the need for the new center. Since the officials who proposed the center had untarnished reputations with reporters, the rationale for their proposal was accepted unquestioningly.

It should also be noted that although the *Inquirer*'s coverage stressed the regional nature of the project, the paper's reporter confined her interviews to city sources rather than suburban or regional officials who might have given an alternative view of the project's worth. For example, a suburban county commissioner or state representative might not have been as enthusiastic about the use of state funds for a project that would provide competition to a newly opened, although smaller, suburban convention center developed privately at Valley Forge. However, suburban officials are less familiar than city leaders to reporters on city-based newspapers and are rarely considered as sources for stories about city development projects.

In summary, positive initial coverage of the Convention Center proposal, particularly in the *Inquirer,* was most likely not the result of an order from the publisher to sway coverage. Rather, it is likely to have emerged as a result of the need to stress upbeat, symbolic issues of regional interest; the limits on reporters' abilities to investigate quantitative estimates and the incentive to emphasize the "sexy" aspects of policy coverage; and the fact that the most eager sources about the center were all proponents of the project. The effect of the initial positive coverage, particularly the positive headlines, was to create a climate of positive public opinion concerning the need for a new convention center and therefore to make public officials in the city's and state's legislative body more likely to approve funding for the project.

The Aesthetic Critique: The Viewpoint of
the Architecture Critic

Questioning notes on the project from the local media were sounded, however, in a column on Art/Architecture in the Sunday *Inquirer* called "Surroundings," written by reporter Thomas Hine. Early in the deliberations, Hine wrote two columns that offered a more skeptical appraisal of the center's value. The first column was titled, "Perfect site still eluding the planners," which began, "Finding a site for the new convention center is like locating a doghouse for Godzilla. Wherever it goes, it will be an imposition. And once the monster is in place, it will control all future decisions." [10] In this column, Hine emphasized that the city's problems in attracting conventions had less to do with the problems of the existing civic center and more to do with the city's image and the lack of an adequate number of hotel rooms.

Hine also noted, as the other news coverage had not, that the promise of a 1,200-room hotel, the original rationale for the new center's construction, "is no longer the sure thing it once seemed." He went on to note, "If we are going to end up with an 800-room hotel as the chief benefit of a great deal of public expense and inconvenience, it should be noted that there is one just sitting around—the Benjamin Franklin." Hine suggested that renovating the closed Ben Franklin as a convention hotel might be a more prudent path to building convention trade than constructing a costly new center.

The column also noted that the two main sites under consideration by the city would create serious aesthetic problems for the surrounding communities. While the Reading site would "forfeit the opportunity for small-scale commercial revival," the Franklin Town location, Hine claimed, "wastes other opportunities by placing a barrier between Center City and lively, still improving residential areas." Hine was most enthusiastic about a site to the west of center city, near the Amtrak railroad station, although he noted that this site had not been seriously considered by city officials and that the site's owner "has not shown the degree of organization, or the hunger for the center, that Reading and Franklin Town have." The column concluded with a cautionary note, "The right decision may be not to snatch up either of the offers but rather to ruminate on whether the convention center will perform as advertised, and whether the city can afford to place it on either of the vying sites."

A month later, the Reading site was selected as the location of the new center, in part because only Reading was able to get a hotel company, the Hyatt Corporation, to sign an agreement to manage a 1,200-room hotel near the site. After the Reading site had been selected, Hine wrote another column expressing concern over the selection, titled, "Will success spoil Reading train shed?"[11] In the column, Hine noted the unfortunate irony that his own columns had been instrumental in changing public perception of the Reading train shed from "a blight to a magnet," when he feared the use of the site might mar the aesthetic value of the shed. Hine wrote, "the Reading proposal could threaten the city's amenities even as it seems to exploit them . . . Huge projects such as convention centers have a way of assuming imperatives of their own and crushing everything around them."

He went on to describe how the design of the new center would detract from the shed's potential glory. "The convention center proposal severely threatens the simple majesty of the space itself." Hine added, "Early studies show the construction inside obscuring the spring of the arch and compromising the sense of enclosed openness that make the shed such a thrilling space." Hine also discussed how other parts of the construction of the mammoth center—such as the necessity for the exhibition hall to bridge four blocks of street—might create a highly unpleasant environment for the city's residents.

> The simple fact is that streets that have been bridged over are unpleasant to walk on, and frightening, even when they are well-illuminated. The convention center will be lively only sporadically. At most hours of the day on most days of the year, these bridges will be a formidable barrier. The advocates of the Reading site have lavished thoroughly deserved praise on Philadelphia as an extraordinary city for walkers. Will they be able to prevent their project from being a formidable barrier?

Hine ended the column by noting, "I once argued that a way had to be found to make the train shed part of the city's future. But now that a plan has come forth, I, for one, am terrified."

The fact that the *Inquirer* printed such comments suggests that there was no order from the management of the paper to keep coverage of the project keyed to boosterism. Rather, it would seem that providing interesting coverage to the target audience was more important than advancing any particular proposal. Indeed, columns on art and architecture like Hine's "Surroundings" have been created in many metropolitan newspapers as an attempt to create features that appeal to an upscale, educated suburban audience. Hine's once-a-week columns allowed him the time to reflect more critically on the city's claims about the proposed convention center than daily news reporters writing on deadline.

However, while Hine's consideration of the merits of the Convention Center proposal were far more balanced than the news coverage or editorials that appeared in the *Inquirer,* his expertise in architectural criticism led to a predominant focus on the aesthetic aspects of the project. Although his first column delved into commentary on the realism of the hopes for a 1,200-room hotel, he quickly confined his comments to the architectural and aesthetic aspects of the center. The question of whether the project made sense, from an economic perspective, was not his domain.

Moreover, the ability of two subtly constructed columns on a features page to counter the overwhelmingly positive headlines and news stories that had appeared in other parts of the paper for months appears to have been minimal. Hine's column, in general, seemed to have its greatest impact in calling for the preservation of buildings that he considered to be of historic and aesthetic value. His ability to influence the public on the merits of a major development proposal, however, was not as powerful. While Hine had suggested that the best location for a mammoth convention center would be the site to the furthest west of center city or that the Franklin Town site might have less disruption on the city, his recommendations were ignored.

The Emergence of Opposition

When organized opposition to the new proposed convention center did emerge, it was not from a general taxpayers' group claiming that the project's benefits did not justify its costs, but rather from the small businesses which would be forced to locate from the vicinity of the Reading Terminal, the site selected for the new Convention Center. One hundred and fifty-two businesses with 1,609 employees and 37 residences were going to have to be relocated from the site.

On October 2, 1983, the *Inquirer* ran a story in its Sunday Real Estate section headlined, "They resist moving for a new center,"[12] which described the objections of some of the companies that needed to be relocated for the new center. Many of the businessmen worried that the kind of networks that were crucial to their small businesses (many in the garment trade) would be disrupted by a move and that the city would not put together an adequate relocation plan. Workers expressed fear that their trips to work would be changed and extended. While the positive views of the president of the Reading Co., Steven Park, on the benefits of the center are expressed in the fourth paragraph of the story, clearly the article was weighted toward the plight of the small businessmen. The reporter juxtaposes their position with that of the Reading president:

> printer Frank Busillo bellies up to a tray of lead linotype slugs and talks of making his stand against Philadelphia's proposed new convention center . . . 'I'm going to get me a couple of .44s and sit at the back of the shop with a cowboy hat on and wait for 'em' vows the 30-year-old journeyman printer.
>
> A few blocks away, Steven G. Park, Reading Co. vice president, sits in his eighth floor suite at the Reading Terminal Headhouse and recites the litany of economic benefits that are expected to flow from construction of the mammoth, $401 million convention center and nearby 1200-room Hyatt Hotel.

After three paragraphs of Park's position, the reporter writes, "Despite the sweet sound of Park's song in a city that has lost thousands of jobs and related tax revenues over the last decade, it's not playing too well down on the street . . ." and spends the rest of the lengthy article reporting the comments of those unhappy with the prospects of relocation.

Later that month, the businessowners formed an organized group to oppose the center, which the *Inquirer* announced in a story headlined, "Business owners organize to fight Reading convention center project."[13] The story described the formation of a group called "Businesspeople Against the Reading Center" (BARC), which claimed that it supported a convention center "because of the revenues" but opposed the location of the center because it would force their relocation. The fact that the *Inquirer* sympathetically and prominently covered the arguments of the opponents to the center again suggests that the newspaper was not presenting only one side of the issue or that the publisher was exerting censorship over negative articles.[14] Moreover, even though the newspaper was editorially supportive of the project, in the news pages editors ran a story that portrayed the center in a more negative light.

The same factors which explain the *Inquirer*'s early positive coverage could now be seen to encourage coverage of the opposition. The account of how small businesses were being threatened made an interesting story that continued to keep the Convention Center a lively issue for the regional audience. At the same time, sources played a role in influencing the coverage. The organizers of BARC, a young entrepreneur and an architect, were eager and articulate and relatively sophisticated in the techniques necessary to gain media attention. Once this kind of organized opposition to the center formed, the newspaper was willing to cover their arguments. It should be noted, however, that this opposition remained focused on the issue of location only, not on the broader questions of whether the center was needed or whether the benefits of the project justified the costs.

The *Daily News*'s coverage of BARC was somewhat more extensive. The paper detailed BARC's formation in an article headlined, "Reading Center Proposal 'Railroaded,' Some Say"[15] and a few months later covered the front page of its business section with a story headlined, "The Convention Center: Getting Untracked?"[16] While the story gave prominent play to the criticisms of BARC, interview comments by BARC's president such as "A concrete block the size of Veterans Stadium would be dropped in our neighborhood" were featured high in the story, while criticism of the city's cost and benefit data was relegated to the twenty-second paragraph, after the story had jumped to another page.

A month later, the *Daily News* again devoted the front page of its business section to two articles related to BARC, one covering the arguments against the center offered by a prominent Philadelphia businessman who had become BARC chairman[17] and one detailing the numbers of businesses that would be forced to relocate for the center.[18] The tenor of this coverage could again be linked to the newspaper's target audience: sympathetic stories detailing the plight of small businesses which would appeal to a largely middle- and working-class audience.

The impact of the news coverage of BARC's opposition to the center in both newspapers was not to stop the Convention Center plan, but rather to encourage the city to develop a better relocation plan and to designate a planner in the city's Redevelopment Authority to handle the relocation of the businesses. Some observers claimed that news coverage of BARC had an additional effect on the project: raising the amount of compensation businesses received in order to relocate and thereby increasing the overall cost of the project.

Investigative Reporting and the Center: The Search for Scandal

As the proposal for a new convention center made its slow way through the public approval process, it encountered another source of negative publicity. In the spring of 1985, reporter Juan Gonzalez of the *Daily News* began to investigate city property records related to the Convention Center site. Prior to Gonzalez's efforts, the *Daily News* had assigned coverage of the Convention Center project to the business section of the newspaper. However, Gonzalez, a city news reporter, actively sought the beat. "Anywhere there's a half-billion dollars being spent, somebody's going to be getting part of the action for themselves," Gonzalez explained in an interview. "My sense told me this was going to be a long running project with a lot of money involved and there were bound to be a lot of good stories coming from it—news stories, not business stories. Then I just started looking."[19]

As a result of Gonzalez's month-long investigation of city property records, the *Daily News* uncovered stories which suggested conflict of interest and private benefit from land acquisition around the center site. For two straight days, the *Daily News* covered the front page of its tabloid newspaper with headlines suggesting impropriety related to the Convention Center project. On April 4, 1985, the newspaper's front-page headline read, "Land Deal Conflict? Convention Center Advisers Suspended," while the next day, the front-page headline read, "City Probes Land Deal, Convention Center Site Targeted."

The first story reported that two members of a consulting firm hired by the city to prepare financial projections for funding the Convention Center had invested in land on which the center was to be built. As a result of the newspaper's discoveries, the city had suspended the consulting firm's contract in order to "evaluat[e] their various relationships," according to the city commerce director.[20] The second story suggested that there had been attempts by real estate speculators to drive up land prices before the city condemned and acquired five blocks for the Convention Center. The main story and a side bar detailed the transactions that had taken place by certain real estate owners in the vicinity of the center site. It suggested that some property owners were engaging in a process called "churning," or turning over the properties unnecessarily to drive up their values.[21]

The two stories were also covered by the *Inquirer*, although with markedly different play. The day after the *Daily News* broke the story about the consultants, the *Inquirer* ran a story on the first page of its metro section with a small headline reading, "City consultant suspended in possible conflict."[22] Similarly, the *Inquirer* followed the *Daily News* land deals story with an article in its Saturday edition with the small headline, "Deals at site of new center monitored."[23] In contrast to the *Daily News* coverage, the *Inquirer*'s stories were less prominently played and the headlines less suggestive of scandal concerning the center.

Why did the news coverage of the two papers differ, particularly when both newspapers share the same publisher who was publicly in favor of the Convention Center? Some observers suggested that the editors of the *Inquirer* might have been more sensitive to the interests of the publisher. "The editors at the *Inquirer* know McKeel's position without being told and they usually exercise more self-restraint because of that," one outside observer noted. Insiders in the two newspapers offered another explanation, however, describing the staffs of the two newspapers as fiercely competitive despite joint ownership. The *Inquirer*, it was suggested, was never eager to play up an investigative revelation by the other newspaper because of professional jealousy. Following the *Daily News'* articles too closely would have been an admission of their own slack investigations, it was suggested. "As a reporter, the last thing you want to do is follow someone," one journalist remarked.

Still another explanation comes from the direction of the differences in the two newspapers' target audiences. The *Daily News*, a middle- and working-class newspaper with a largely city and commuter audience, faces a constant need to find dramatic stories and headlines to attract people picking up the paper on the newsstand each day. Like other tabloid newspapers, it thrives on stories which report the misdoings of public officials or the profiting by wealthy private individuals on city-funded projects. While the suggestion of scandal surrounding the Convention Center was just the kind of story that could appeal to the *Daily News* audience, the same angle may have been deemed less important to the *Inquirer*'s more affluent and educated suburban audience.

Despite the differences in coverage, it is important to note that when a reporter was allowed release time to engage in investigative reporting on the Convention Center, the target was the search for scandal. Rather than examining whether the project represented a misallocation of city and state funds, the *Daily News* reporter investigated whether any individuals were making undue profits from the city project. Gonzalez noted that at one point the city editor asked him to write an in-depth analysis of the Convention Center and that he responded with a 38-inch story examining issues such as the costs and benefits of the project. In the editing process, however, the story was cut to eighteen inches by higher editors, apparently because it was not compelling enough to warrant that much space.[24] In other words, even when knowledgeable and critical reporters try to write stories focusing on the need for public development projects, they may be stopped by editors concerned with simple audience appeal. In contrast, release time and prominent play are awarded to stories which uncover scandal and impropriety.

A week after Gonzalez's articles ran in the *Daily News*, Pennsylvania Governor Richard Thornburgh's administration announced that it would withhold the state's $185 million share of the center's costs unless there was public bidding to select a developer and public ownership of the center.[25] Some observers claimed that the move to push for public ownership was a response to the *Daily News* investigations. "If I were governor and I were committing $185 million to a project like the Center, I'd want to have the people of Philadelphia love me for it, maybe have it named for me—and I'd want to be real sure it wasn't tainted if anything went wrong. The best way to make sure there wasn't any private scandal would be to make the whole project public," was the observation of one official.[26] However, by making the project public, the tax benefits intended to be realized by the original public-private partnership were lost. In effect, the investigations into possible land speculation around the center, while doing little to limit the gains to the property owners, may have simply served to raise the cost of the project.

Some officials also questioned the value of investigating the land deals surrounding the center, claiming that the process of buying low, selling high, and taking a risk that the Reading site would be selected for the Convention Center was perfectly legal. "You don't build a convention center with boy scouts latching thatches together," said the official directing the project for the city.[27] "Someone experienced in real estate would see those articles and say it happens everyday, it's shrewd business, but someone in Kensington [a lower-middle-class neighborhood in the city] will say 'What the hell—they're ripping off my tax dollars.'" And while searching for such scandal, it was suggested, the project got further delayed, leading to further escalations in cost.

Meanwhile, on May 8, 1985, a one-column article appeared in the business section of the Saturday *Inquirer* with the headline, "Reading plan is changed," and the subhead, "Convention hotel may be smaller," which suggested that the size of the convention center's hotel was more likely to be 600 or 900 rooms.[28] A hotel industry analyst was quoted as saying, "It always appeared to us that it would be difficult for Philadelphia to support a 1,200-room hotel . . . That's an extremely large hotel. There are two convention seasons—spring and fall. How do you fill those rooms during the rest of the year?" The original rationale for building a new convention center—to generate a 1,200-room hotel—had been lost, but the *Inquirer* marked the change with little fanfare and the *Daily News* did not cover the change at all.

The Debate Over Costs and Benefits

While stories about the rising costs of the center continued to appear over the years, in 1986 an unusual set of articles appeared which directly discussed the estimates of the project's benefits. On April 2 of that year, an article appeared in the *Daily News* headlined, "Convention Center's a Loser, New Analysis Says,"[29] which described a study carried out by the city council's technical staff. The study, as reported by the newspaper's city council beat reporter, estimated that the center would produce a maximum of 4,350 permanent jobs, as opposed to the administration's estimate of 9,960 jobs. The analysis also found that rather than producing $2.1 billion in tax revenues, the center would lead to the city's losing $23 million. The council's analyst claimed that the city's estimate of benefits was highly exaggerated as a result of two mistaken assumptions. First, the administration had chosen a job multiplier of 3 (that is, for every one job directly produced by the center, the administration estimated that three indirect jobs would be created). The new study argued that a more realistic employment multiplier for a project of this type would be 1.4.

Second, the analyst's study found that the administration's estimates had allowed for inflation in worker's salaries and wage tax receipts without discounting the value of future tax receipts. In other words, the city's cost and benefit estimates represented a comparison of the present costs of the center with a nondiscounted or inflated estimate of future tax benefits. More realistic comparisons could be made between the inflated future tax benefits, on the one hand, and the cost plus the interest on the money that the city would be investing in the center on the other hand. That is, just as future tax receipts were being inflated, the cost of the center should also, reflecting the returns the city would earn should it have simply allowed that money to gain interest over the period.

The *Inquirer* did not report the story of the city council's technical staff report. However, a week later, the paper did run a story with a banner headline across the top of its business section headlined, "New study backs up city on convention center's effects."[30] The story reported that a new study, which had been commissioned from Professor Edward B. Shils of the Wharton School of the University of Pennsylvania the previous December by the Philadelphia Convention and Visitors Bureau, supported the previous estimates by the city administration of the project's economic impacts. The article described the estimates of employment and income to the city and regional economy and then presented comments from the president of the Philadelphia Industrial Development Corporation (the chief lobbyist for the project), the professor who had authored the report, and the president of the Convention and Visitors Bureau. No mention was made of the city council technical staff's report released a week earlier, which had questioned the multiplier and failure to discount future income.

The study was also covered by the *Daily News,* on the same day as the *Inquirer*'s story, on the first page of the paper's business section.[31] Similar to the *Inquirer*'s story, the *News'* account recited the litany of economic benefits described by the new study and concluded with quotes by the same sources as the *Inquirer*'s story. Again, no mention was made of the conflicting estimates produced by the city council's technical staff the previous week, which had been reported in the news section of the *Daily News.*

One more voice in the debate over the estimates of costs and benefits was raised several months later. A small one-column story on the business page of the *Inquirer,* the article was titled, "Benefits of center questioned" and, in smaller type, "Fewer conventions and jobs foreseen."[32] This article reported the results done by another professor, William Grigsby of the City and Regional Planning Department at the University of Pennsylvania, which predicted that the new center would generate only 3,200 permanent jobs, rather than the 10,000 predicted by the city's studies. The new study claimed that the city administration's job estimate had overstated both the number of conventions the center would attract and the amount of money delegates would spend on hotels, food, and entertainment.

The author of this new report is quoted as saying, "I am not suggesting that the notion of a new convention center should be abandoned . . . My study, however, raises several questions that should be investigated." His statement was followed by one from the executive director of the agency administering the project for the city, "I think it's time to get beyond the second-guessing and academic exercises and get on with building the project." At the end of the article, after the jump to another page, the reporter referred to the other study that had questioned the city's estimates: "Grigsby's study was the second this year to raise questions about whether projections for the center were overly optimistic. Earlier this year, Marc Breslow, a research analyst for City Council, said in a memorandum to Council President Joseph Coleman that the convention center would produce fewer than half the nearly 10,000 jobs predicted by the Goode administration and never generate enough taxes to offset its cost."

This coverage of the conflicting studies raises several questions. Why were two studies questioning the basic benefit estimates of a project that represented the city's largest single expenditure given relatively short shrift in the city's two newspapers? Why was news coverage of the Shils' study of the positive impacts of the center given far more prominence than the study released a few months later by another Penn professor disputing the findings? And why did neither newspaper carry out its own independent investigation into the employment and tax impacts to attempt to reconcile the estimates?

While it could be that subtle pressures from the publisher, particularly at the *Inquirer,* played a small role in the coverage, other factors are likely to have been more important. In particular, the fact that the city council technical study was never publicly released at a press conference, as the Shils' study was, undoubtedly had a bearing on media coverage. Marc Breslow, the author of the council study, had simply prepared a memorandum summarizing his results for the president of city council. But the council president, perhaps reluctant to alienate the powerful business and labor interests pushing for the project, never released the study. Therefore neither the author of the first report nor the elected official for whom it was done was an eager media source.

In comparing coverage of the Grigsby and Shils studies, it is clear that sources must not simply be eager to transmit their information to the media, but they must package their messages in a certain way to gain prominent media attention. While the Shils report was released at a press conference where top city officials and the author stated unconditionally that the project should be pursued, the Grigsby study was disseminated by a press release issued by the University of Pennsylvania in which the author was much more conditional in his evaluation of the center.[33] Grigsby's message that the center required more study was simply not framed in as strong symbolic terms as Shils' stance and therefore did not receive as prominent press coverage.

A second factor which explains the coverage concerns fragmented beat structures. The fact that the Breslow study was covered (or ignored) by city council beat reporters, while the Shils study was covered by business reporters, suggests why the two studies were never reconciled. When the *Inquirer* business reporter covered the press conference where the city administration released the Shils report, he may have simply been unaware of the existence of the Breslow report. Similarly, the business reporter who covered the Shils study for the *News* may not have remembered a story covered by the city council reporter in his own paper the week before. As a result of fragmented beat structures, where the coverage of events related to a major development project is assigned to reporters on many different beats, some reporters are not aware of stories about the project that other reporters on their paper or other papers have covered previously.

As to why neither newspaper carried out its own investigation and coverage of the conflicting estimates in an attempt to reconcile the disparities, the answer lies with a combination of journalists' professional fear of numbers and their need for the "sexiness quotient." A story about disparate multipliers and the failure to discount future tax estimates would be both beyond the technical expertise of most reporters and not terribly exciting to them or their editors. While, in retrospect, one of the *Inquirer*'s editors felt that such an article would have been important and useful, in the daily rush of breaking news, the story was not given much importance. He added, "It's a tricky story to write and make interesting. Most newspaper editors and reporters want to make something interesting."[34]

Local Television News

Philadelphia's two major newspapers were not alone in providing residents of city and suburbs with news coverage of the new center. Local television news also reported on the issue.[35] Although the first announcement that the city planned to build a new convention center received great play in the *Inquirer,* it was barely mentioned on local television news. A spokeswoman for WCAU–TV, the local CBS affiliate, said the station did not cover the story at all,[36] while KYW–TV, the NBC affiliate, reported the story as a 20-second voice-over on the noon news and dropped the story from its evening lineup.[37] As a journalist at one station said in an interview, "It's hard for local television to cover development stories because all you get is officials standing at podiums talking."

As consideration of the proposal advanced, local television news stations did cover the center more extensively. In March 1983, KYW–TV covered a press conference at which the city's commerce director described the three sites being considered for the center. In the one-minute voice-over sound report, the anchor concluded with the statement that "the cost of the proposed four-square-block complex ranges between 182 and 256 million dollars but the center is expected to bring in 128 million dollars a year and also bring with it 9,100 jobs."[38] Like the newspapers, this report relied on the estimates of costs and benefits provided by project supporters. However, in the brief time allotted to the television story, the anchor mistakenly left the impression that the center would generate benefits for the city indefinitely, rather than over the restricted life of the center.

A few months later, KYW ran another piece (introduced by the anchor with the statement that "it would be a complex that would bring more jobs and money to the city") concerning the "unveiling" of plans by the two developers competing for the project. After a description of each plan and sound-bites from competing developers, the reporter concluded his report with, "One thing that the Reading Plan will accomplish is to get rid of the blight in the shadow of City Hall—the area bounded by 11th Street, 13th, Race and Arch. This is a hot-bed of street crime and homosexual activity and City Hall has wanted to get rid of it for a long time . . . That could be a point in favor of the Reading plan."[39] Such pieces took for granted that the center was needed and suggested the Reading site would help "clean up" the city.

The selection of the Reading Terminal as the site for the new center in September was covered in a one-minute-forty-five-second story that ran on KYW's six o'clock news. The reporter announced, "After many, many weeks of hearings and discussions, the Site Selection Committee has chosen the Reading Company plan and the site on which I'm standing for a new convention center in Philadelphia. It was rumored for a long time and now it's official. The Reading Company plan, of course, is the one whose boundaries are 11th to 13th Street and Race to Arch, and according to the chairman of the Selection Committee, the big job ahead will be relocating businesses." A sound bite from a city official was presented, after which the reporter concluded, "So for the moment, the Reading Company plan has the nod over the Franklin Town plan, but down the road there will be hearings and more approvals necessary because the mayor, the city council, and the state legislature must all approve the plan."[40] While this report was fairly balanced, in the limited time available it gave only the barest details of the plan, providing the viewer with little information with which to evaluate the wisdom of the proposal.

An editorial that ran on the same station on October 10, 1983, provided more information to viewers, but its views came from the uncritical standpoint of local booster. The editorial was a response to a viewer letter which asked why there was a need to spend so much money on a new convention center. The station manager, Pat Pollillo, responded in his editorial:

> It's a good question and I think there's a good answer. A new
> center would create thousands of new jobs. I don't have to tell
> you how many jobs Philadelphia's lost lately. The Frankford Ar-
> senal, the *Bulletin,* Jack Frost Sugar. You know one industry
> that's bringing jobs here is tourism. All of Philadelphia's historic
> landmarks like Christ Church here attract thousands of tourists
> who spend millions of dollars. And new hotels have opened in
> the city which provide more jobs. But Philadelphia still ranks be-
> hind nine other big cities in big conventions and the main reason
> is that our convention hall is too old. We really do need a new
> one. So the city plans to build a new one right here in the back of
> the old Reading shed on Market Street. It'll be massive but it's
> worth it because it's an investment in the city's future.[41]

Not only did this editorial accept unquestioningly that the new center was "worth it" because of the jobs it would provide, but it reinforced a sense that the new center was needed because the Civic Center was "too old." The actual rationale—the need for an adequate number of hotel rooms—was too complicated to get across on local television news.

Although the BARC group formed in the fall of 1983 and was covered then by both newspapers, KYW did not cover the group's activities until the following year, when a public forum was held to present the opponents' views. In a three-minute live report aired on the 5:00 P.M. news, the reporter noted that the "massive project" will "take over most of the area between the Reading Terminal and Race Street." The reporter than characterized the "two" sides. The "advocates" are described as saying the current convention hall is "out-of-date compared to the centers other cities have built and to be competitive we need a new one." In describing BARC, the reporter notes that "the big public reasons for their opposition is the size of it and the cost of it." However, little time is devoted to the question of cost, the report focusing rather on the issue of the relocation of businesses.[42] Therefore, while the story presented an alternative view of the Convention Center's merits, again, the issue of whether the project was needed was passed over.

When, a few years later the debate over the costs and benefits of the project emerged, the television station, like the newspapers, covered the results of the city-sponsored Shils study with little question. In its story about the press conference, KYW's anchor read, "There is new information tonight that the proposed Philadelphia Convention Center would be a major financial boost to this area. At a news conference today in center city, Wharton professor Ed Shils released a new economic impact study. He says the center would bring millions of much-needed dollars to this city. [Shils speaking:] 'I'm not concerned with that. I'm concerned that it's time we saved our state economy and our city economy. Our growth rate is the forty-seventh lowest of any state in the United States.' Shils says the center would bring $381 million dollars to the city economy in the first year that it's opened. The entire region will benefit, with $582 million in the first year. And he says a new convention center would create 10,500 new jobs." This story was then followed by a considerably longer (one minute, fifty seconds) package by the station's political reporter which investigated the political pressure from black officials for a strong affirmative action plan for the project.[43]

In summary, local television news's coverage of the Convention Center was marked by a number of weaknesses. First, the project was not accorded the length or depth it received from the newspapers. Over the years, television news tended to cover the center only when press conferences were called, when a legislative body voted on the issue, or when a rally, protest, or meeting was called either in favor of or in opposition to the new center. This paucity of coverage can be explained by both the relatively dry nature of the story and the limited visuals, with stations using and reusing the aerial shot of the center's site and footage of the model. Second, local television provided even less information to the audience concerning whether or not the center was needed. Although eager to cover the controversy surrounding the center—whether the arguments of BARC, the political battles between city and suburban legislators, the fights over affirmative-action hiring—they were equally eager to relay without question the city's estimates of costs and benefits. Of particular importance was the fact that in their editorial and in lead-ins to stories, the station under study emphasized the notion that the new center would provide vast economic benefits for the city and left its audience with the general impression of the project's need.

The Specialized Media: Alternative Voices?

Other more specialized local media also covered the proposal for a new Convention Center. In April of 1984, *Philadelphia* magazine offered its first assessment of the center, over a year after the city's announcement of its plans and selection of a site.[44] The article was called "Center of the Storm," with the tagline, "The fight over the proposed gigantic $380 million convention center is just beginning. The outcome could go a long way toward putting to rest forever the Old Philadelphia Attitude." As this lead-in suggests, the article focused less on whether the project made sense for the city and region than on the political struggles to gain its approval and on the relation of the project to the "old Philadelphia attitude" that projects should be studied forever. As the concluding paragraph of the first section states,

> And yet, while almost no one thinks building a convention center is a bad idea—in theory—it is still possible that the center will never be built or that two years of research and study will be ignored or repeated. Why? Why can't we just *build* the damn thing? The answers lie in the tortuous, unpredictable, highly complex, politically charged process that a great city must employ to make such a decision. The answers are particularly poignant in a city that seems to insist on fighting itself at every step, a city where it is said that nothing is ever accepted until it becomes a tradition.

The rest of the article was an in-depth examination of the behind-the-scenes considerations that went into the decision to build a convention center and the selection of the Reading site. Information that had not appeared in the two newspapers shed new light on the issue of site selection and particularly on the question of whether a 1,200-room hotel had ever been feasible. The writer suggested that the developer of what might have been the best site—west of center

214

city—withdrew from bidding because he believed that Philadelphia could not support such a large hotel.

Despite the fact that the article contained new information that cast a somewhat negative light on the design and location of the Convention Center, as proposed, it did not address the question of whether the project made sense. By focusing on personalities and on the city's image, the article conformed to the formula familiar in city magazines, reducing its impact on the policy process. As the reporter himself noted, he doubted if many people outside those described in the article read the story all the way through.[45] Moreover, the magazine's reputation of slanting articles toward the sexy and sensational aspects of an issue had diminished its credibility by the 1980s. While its readers may have trusted its every word on the best restaurants in the city, they tended to be more skeptical of its political news coverage.

Another, far more critical appraisal of the Convention Center project came from an article written in the Philadelphia *City Paper,* a small weekly newspaper whose circulation at that time was generally limited to center city Philadelphia neighborhoods. In 1985, freelance writer Noel Weyrich wrote an article for the *City Paper,* called "The $441 M Boondoggle," with the subhead, "A tiny group of unelected city officials found the wrong people to build the wrong convention center in the wrong spot. Then they wanted us to pay for it, give it away, and spend $600 million to rent it for 30 years. They almost did it, and they still may."[46]

Weyrich's article was highly critical of the city's decision to build a large convention center on the Reading site. It referred back to the original consultant's study and pointed out how the study itself had found that by simply building a long-planned West Philadelphia stop on the airport High-Speed line, the existing Civic Center would have been able to attract a sizable number of additional conventions. He also emphasized that although the Reading site had been chosen because of its ability to secure a commitment for a 1,200-room hotel, that commitment had disappeared. He claimed that the project was a costly effort that would never yield the returns city officials had promised. And he criticized the city's newspapers for their "repeated calls for the center to be built without delay."

While the *City Paper*'s article on the center clearly presented an alternative view of the proposal and an argument that the costs of the project outweighed the benefits, it is arguable that such an article had much impact. First, newspapers like the *City Paper* have a limited circulation, usually confined to young center-city professionals who read the paper more for its club listings and advertisements than for its political commentary. Its news articles tend to have a limited legitimacy with readers, as opposed to those appearing in the major newspapers in the city. As the author himself later said in an interview, "A story half as strong [as his] from the *Inquirer,* or an editorial from either the *Inquirer* or the *Daily News* would have had much more impact."[47] Second, the article was written two years after the project was proposed, long after most people had gained the general impression from the other newspapers that the city needed a new convention center. And as consideration of the Convention Center proposal continued through the 1980s, newspapers like the *City Paper* were putting an increasing emphasis on arts and entertainment coverage, rather than on social and economic issues.

Analysis of the Convention Center Coverage

While focusing on only a few key junctures in the Convention Center proposal's approval process, this case study does suggest how the local news media tend to cover and influence crucial phases in a major new development project. In this case, two highly respected newspapers and other news media in one of the nation's largest media markets, were found to give inadequate initial consideration to the question of whether a new center was needed and whether the site selected was the best location for such a center. Coverage of the negatives of the center tended to focus on the issue of relocation and on the private speculation efforts of developers near the site. In contrast, the question of whether the city had correctly estimated the costs and benefits of the project was virtually dismissed, even in the unusual case where competing studies were made available to dispute the city's figures.

The case is instructive in pointing out that even first-rate journalists who provide incisive coverage of other national and local issues tend to falter when it comes to the coverage of complex regional development proposals as a result of a number of factors.

The economic interests of the media: the symbolic appeal of city issues to the suburban audience. It was argued by critics that the publisher of the city's two newspapers, an active lobbyist for this project in the state legislature, influenced the coverage. However, the fact that both newspapers shared the same publisher, while the tenor of the news coverage differed, suggests that other economic interests may have been stronger that the publisher's personal preferences. In particular, different kinds of themes concerning the convention center appealed to the different audiences of the two newspapers. For the *Inquirer,* the need for a new convention center served as a useful symbolic issue linking city and suburban audiences; in particular, it represented a city-based but arguably regional problem with an upbeat solution. For the *Daily News,* while initial coverage of the center was similarly upbeat, stories about scandal and impropriety in the use of public funds and the plight of the small business-man held greater appeal to a middle- and working-class audience.

The role of sources: eager public officials and the lack of initial opposition. The coverage was also influenced by the fact that the only sources who made themselves available at the beginning of the center proposal process were the public officials and business leaders who wanted to see the center approved. Before organized opposition to the Reading site had formed, there was no eager source providing reporters with more critical evaluations of the city's plans. As one journalist who covered the story noted, "Nobody was saying the things Gray Smith [an opponent of the center] was saying at the time the proposal was made." In the absence of organized opposition, the journalists who covered the story did not attempt to present or seek out an alternative to the city's claims for the new development proposal.

The editorial editor of the *Daily News,* which changed its editorial stance on the project midway through the approval stage, was asked why his newspaper was not more critical of the project early on. "They fooled me," the editor, Richard Aregood, answered frankly. "They made it an issue of civic need. We were too unsophisticated about our sources. For a moment I was sleeping." He suggested that he changed his position on the center after the long strike that closed down the *Inquirer* and *Daily News* in 1985. "I had forty-six days to think," he said, adding that during that time he spoke to many sources with more negative evaluations of the project.[48]

Even when opposition to a project emerges, often long after the initial an-nouncement, as in this case, reporters tend to give more prominent coverage to the claims of city officials—and their estimates of costs and benefits—because city officials are considered more reliable, authoritative sources. Critics of big public development projects are often regarded as cranks, far less credible and legitimate than city officials and private businessmen.

Journalists' technical limitations and the "fear of numbers." Although journalists are trained to be critical, particularly when covering the pronouncements of public officials, their critical faculties seem to stop short in the face of the kinds of numbers that are presented when new, glamorous capital projects are announced. Moreover, even if they were inclined to investigate city claims for costs and benefits, their lack of technical background would prevent them from evaluating the claims themselves. As one reporter said, "It was difficult for journalists to cover—the questions were technical—no reporter should be expected to understand it." When another reporter who had covered the center was asked whether he personally thought the project was needed or whether there might have been a better use of the public funds, he fell back upon the journalistic reliance on attribution by saying, "Philadelphia officials feel very much that they need the center."

The failure to meet the "sexiness quotient." The question of whether the project made economic sense, while a crucial policy question for residents of the city and region investing millions of public dollars, was not deemed interesting enough to attract audiences. As one critic of the project described it, "It's a scandalous misuse of the taxpayers' dollars but not a scandal as defined in newspaper terms." One journalist from the *Daily News,* when pressed on why the *News* was not more critical of the economic claims of the project early on, responded, "It's hardly one of the more exciting issues of our time." This thought was echoed by another reporter who had written about the project who commented, "It's a difficult issue to get excited about. People don't live and die with this issue." Instead, other "sexier" themes were adopted in the coverage—from the importance of a new center for the image of the city to the plight of the little guy being relocated from his business, to the scandal surrounding a land speculator.

The fragmented beat structure. A complicated issue like a proposal to construct a new convention center is often divided among many different beats at a newspaper, each with their own angles and sources. The fact that many stories were considered "business" stories, and that business stories are traditionally not covered from an adversarial bent, may have affected the tenor of the coverage. Conversely, some political stories may have suffered from the reporter's not having had the experience of covering the project before. As one editor noted, "Sometimes newspapers fail when covering things in a fragmented way."[49]

The recognition that different sections of the same paper cover development issues differently was reflected in the comments of one official involved in the Convention Center project who was asked to evaluate the press coverage. "You tell me what section of the *Inquirer* and I'll tell you how good the coverage was. The editorials were good, excellent, supportive. If it ever comes to one of our crunch points, the editorials will even be more helpful. The business section was very supportive. When you get into the day-to-day reporting in the state and local sections, you're getting into what sells newspapers, you're getting into the more flamboyant, less substantive aspects. The metro section goes on a quest for finding controversy at the lint level, capturing all the loony tunes in the state capital."

In summary, the case of Philadelphia's new convention center has pointed out some of the weaknesses of news coverage of major urban development projects. It is not meant to suggest that all newspaper reporting of local issues is inadequate or that the local news media never succeed in revealing important policy problems or in engaging in investigative reporting concerning the wisdom of public proposals. Rather, it suggests that in one particular type of important policy coverage they often stumble: the coverage of major development projects, involving the commitment of millions of dollars of public funding, where the estimation of costs and benefits is somewhat technical and the coverage is typically divided among a number of beats. As one reporter noted in reflecting on the newspaper coverage of the Convention Center, "This is the kind of issue newspapers are typically lousy at." While other local media existed to provide alternative views on the project, none attempted or succeeded in informing the residents of the region as a whole on the wisdom of this proposal.

Conclusions
and a Look to the Future

Over the course of this study, we have seen how the metropolitan news media define and cover local issues and how local news coverage may influence the direction of urban policy and the outcome of issues. The economic interests of media firms, the professional values of local journalists, and the strategies of local officials as sources have all been shown to influence the way the local news media cover the news of their cities and regions. As a result of these factors, many imbalances come to be incorporated into the coverage of local policy issues, particularly when those issues concern major development projects.

This chapter summarizes the major conclusions of the book and makes some recommendations on how both local journalists and public officials may improve the kind of information the media presents to the public concerning major development policies. Also, some of the new forms of local media on the horizon will be briefly surveyed in regards to the impacts they may have on the competitive nature of the metropolitan news media. Finally, we will consider the future shape of local identity in metropolitan areas and the challenges that continue to be posed to the local media in their attempts to draw together the regionwide audience.

The Metropolitan News Media and the Coverage of Urban Policy

While any number of theories have been proposed to explain the nature of news coverage, from the simple "sensationalism" argument to the need to protect the interests of advertisers or the pet projects of publishers and station managers, we have seen how a more complex web of factors comes to influence the coverage of local policy issues. These factors were grouped into three broad categories—economic, professional, and source-related—and each one plays a role in determining how local news comes to be covered. The factors may be summarized as follows.

The Economic Imperative

The suburbanization of the metropolitan area and the decentralization of residences, employment centers, and retail areas have created a fundamental change in the nature of local news markets. As the target market of both national as well as local advertisers has shifted from city to suburbs, the metropolitan news media have had to become more concerned with producing a news product capable of attracting the suburban audience.

The task of finding local news of interest to the entire regional population has become increasingly difficult, given the proliferation of the small, independent political jurisdictions that characterize most suburban areas. The metropolitan news media have been faced with the dilemma of how to overcome the fragmentation of local identity that has occurred with suburbanization in order to find news and major issues of common interest to their diverse and dispersed audiences. Their answer has been, in part, to maintain a focus on the affairs of the central city, because the city is the only source of symbolism strong enough to bind the regional audience. In addition, the local media have at times exaggerated the importance of downtown-oriented developments and other regional projects because of their symbolic capital in attracting the suburban audience.

Professional Values of the Local Journalist

The personal and professional values of the typical local journalist play a key role in local news coverage and in reinforcing the notion that the central city continues to occupy the most important political, economic, and social position in the region. The accessibility of city officials with skilled press arms, the physical proximity of the city to newspaper offices, and preferences for the kind of traditional conflict and scandal-laden news produced by the city government all lead to a bias in favor of city news—and a city-oriented perspective on regional news—by the local journalist.

The accessibility of information from city government and the reliance of journalists on city officials as sources often leads to positive coverage of city development projects and to a greater emphasis on the city's public redevelopment efforts than on the more widespread private suburban development. In addition, personal values often contribute to a willingness to believe official promises and to ignore questions of the relocation of residences and businesses or alternative uses of public funds. As upper-middle-class professionals who often live as well as work in the heart of city downtowns, reporters are often eager to see the city made more glamorous and cosmopolitan.

The reliance on official sources of information and the reluctance of reporters to question quantitative estimates of costs and benefits often arises because of local journalists' "fear of numbers," which prevents them from delving into official estimates of costs and benefits. The tools of the reporter's trade are rooted in the interview and the exchange of verbal information, not the analysis of the kinds of quantitative data crucial to the scrutiny of the uses of public funds.

The "sexiness qotient," or need to come up with stories and angles on stories that stimulate audience interest, often leads to a built-in bias in the coverage of new development projects. Because of the professional desire to gain prominent play for a story, a reporter is more likely to emphasize the need for a new project than to focus on the reasons why the status quo is preferable. Combined with their own technical limitations, the sexiness quotient leads journalists to de-emphasize the coverage of the costs and benefits of the project and devote more space to the symbolic aspects. While the sexiness quotient works to create positive initial news coverage of development proposals, the "boredom factor" discourages investigations later in the approval process, when the project has lost the interest of the "new."

While newspapers carry on a continuous series of investigations, the "Pulitzer-Prize mode" suggests a narrow professional definition of public scandal. In particular, local journalistic investigations tend to be focused on the illegal or immoral activities of public officials rather than on the efficacy or wisdom of the proposals and plans of those officials. Fragmented beat structures also weaken coverage of urban development. Because the coverage of projects is sliced up among several beats, often a reporter covering one stage of a project is unfamiliar with previous stages and the claims and rationales of local officials that came earlier. Moreover, reporters on different beats take divergent angles on stories, some concentrating on the political repercussions of projects, others on the potential stimulus to the regional economy, and none may have as their objective evaluating the overall wisdom of the project.

The Role of Local Officials as Sources

While many studies of national newsmaking have suggested that public officials routinely manipulate news coverage, at the local level such manipulation is much more limited, because of the great variation in the media skills of both appointed and elected officials. While some local officials are very adept at gaining positive coverage, many more have little or no understanding of how to influence the media. Many officials unwittingly adopt media "styles" which fail to achieve, or even work counter to, their policy objectives.

Some local officials fail to gain positive media coverage for themselves or their initiatives because they do not understand how to create suitable information for the media and, as a result, become "paranoid media avoiders" or "naive professionals." Still others, such as the "dancing marionettes," or the "colorful quotables," or the "liars" receive substantial coverage but not the kind that ultimately helps them achieve their policy objectives. A successful strategy is only forged by those officials who understand how to meet the needs of the local media without pandering to them and who do so in a way which makes the official appear to be an active and effective leader.

The success or failure of a local public official in media relations has broader implications than the official's own political or professional career path since it also influences the kinds of policies and proposals that get enacted. Some local officials may receive negative coverage for sound policy proposals because of their incompetence or naivete in dealing with reporters. In other cases, savvy officials who understand how to deal with the media may gain positive coverage for costly initiatives that will benefit only a narrow segment of the public. In addition, when officials with mediocre media skills are transformed into public villains, news coverage may divert attention from the real causes of social and economic problems and the need for solutions.

The Other Local Media: Alternative Voices?

Local television news, although watched by millions of people, is hardly an effective alternative to metropolitan newspapers in the investigation of the merits of major urban development proposals. The emphasis on local news anchors and the "cult of personality," the constraints of time and format, the limited number of television news reporters and the lack of beat assignments, the need for effective video and sound bites, and the premium placed on emotional content and drama all weaken the informational content of local television news. Government news, in general, tends to be downplayed by local newscasts, and when policy stories are covered, the sexiest and most emotional angles are taken. In addition, the need to humanize government plans and proposals often leads to emphasis on conflict and to the coverage of demonstrations in opposition to policies, no matter how small.

While the more specialized local news media play many important functions for their audiences and may influence voting behavior and the direction of policy, they do not serve as alternative voices on general development issues in the metropolitan area. Where city magazines and alternative weeklies once focused on such serious social and political issues, challenging the viewpoint of metropolitan newspapers, by 1990 most had turned their attention to lifestyle and consumer issues. The specialized press has remained focused on those political and social issues related to their own communities, but they have not challenged the metropolitan newspaper's news and editorial coverage of urban and regional issues. In general, none of the smaller local media may be said to provide a consistent alternative voice to the metropolitan newspaper's coverage of the kind of major development issues that involve the expenditure of millions of dollars in public funds.

In part, the flaws in metropolitan news coverage of major development plans could be reduced by a recognition among local journalists of the importance of the questions involved in such plans. News organizations need to allocate the resources and time required to allow at least some reporters to become proficient in the skills necessary to evaluate the costs and benefits of such projects. Although large-scale development proposals represent convenient sources of news with regionwide appeal, journalists need to more deliberately separate symbolic considerations from the coverage of economic, social, and environmental costs and benefits. The same investigative resources that are brought to bear on improprieties in the public or private sector could produce much more incisive coverage of the pros and cons of new development plans, despite their glamour and audience appeal.

Equal responsibility for improving the coverage of policy issues, however, lies with local governmental officials and other local sources, who often do not understand how to interact with the local media in order to get important points across and create informed public debates. Local public officials must begin to recognize the importance of the communication function in the governance process and allocate more of their own and their staff's time to maintaining accessibility with reporters and providing the media, and ultimately the public, with the kind of information that creates constituencies for change. While dealing with the media may seem dangerous to some officials and a waste of valuable time to others, the communication of policy information to the public via the local news media must come to be viewed as an essential part of the local governance process.

The Future Direction of Local News Coverage

In looking to the future, it is likely that a number of developments, particularly changes in technology, may alter the landscape of the local news media and the way local news is covered. In particular, the proliferation of local cable news programs and the emergence of videotex and audiotex systems for transmitting news and advertising may be expected to change the nature of local news and further alter the economic fortunes of the metropolitan newspaper and the regional television station.

Local Cable News

The first arena in which local news should change in the future is in the major expansion that is likely to take place in the production of local news by cable television. For several years, community access channels have enabled local governments or community groups to broadcast meetings to limited geographic areas. In many states, cable companies receive franchises from local communities and are required by local governments to set aside at least one channel for local community use. As a result of such set-asides, many local governments are broadcasting their council meetings via local cable television networks, such as in White Plains, New York, where the local council has begun to broadcast its meetings on the White Plains government-access cable station Channel 35.[1]

White Plains is just one of several Westchester and Putnam County communities in New York which broadcast local government meetings.[2] In addition, in these communities the local access cable channel is also used often by mayors and other local officials to discuss government policies with their constituencies. In some cities, the community access channels are allowing citizens groups to produce programs about the issues facing city neighborhoods. In Boston, for example, the Boston Neighborhood Network produces a daily news program that focuses on neighborhood news.[3]

The prospect for increased use of government access channels to broadcast such meetings suggests an increased potential for participation by local citizens in the affairs of their local governments. Local officials in areas with such access channels claim that the broadcasts have renewed citizen interest in the affairs of local government and have improved people's understanding of local issues. In addition, increased availability of cable-access channels suggests that in the future there may be less reliance on the local news media to serve as the mediating force between the actions of public officials and their constituents, as citizens can watch for themselves the speeches by their elected officials.

While community access channels are likely to have some impact on the way elected officials communicate to their constituencies and the way local policies are made, the major change should be the emergence of increasing numbers of suburban cable news programs. By the beginning of the 1980s such news operations had begun to make their appearance on the local news landscape. For some cable companies, the provision of local news has been merely an attempt to satisfy the governmental units that award them franchises—similar to the local broadcast stations of the 1960s which produced news simply to satisfy the FCC requirements for public affairs programming. Many suburban cable companies produce little more than a scrolled screen of local news headlines, similar to a teletext system, with headlines borrowed from wire services or local newspapers.

But in some areas of the country suburban cable news is becoming a more sophisticated and lucrative product, particularly well suited to carrying local advertisements to a targeted local market, similar to suburban newspapers. In addition to serving isolated towns that are too small to be served by a broadcast television station, local cable news operations have begun to spring up in the suburbs of major metropolitan areas, in part because of the regional television stations' failure to devote much coverage to news outside of their cities. For example, News 12 serving Nassau and Suffolk Counties on Long Island in 1988 began the first 24-hour regional news broadcast in the nation.[4] As one cable television executive commented concerning the success of News 12,

> You have to ask yourself, in the case of New York, when was the last time you saw information about Long Island, Connecticut or New Jersey schools—or any of the things that really affect people's pocketbooks, how their children are brought up, the way people live? There's no way that even the most responsible over-the-air broadcaster can deal with that. It just doesn't work when you're hitting an ADI as large as any of the top 10 or 20 markets. You can't go into detail about the things that really affect people's lives directly. That's where the experience on Long Island has been successful.[5]

The advantage of this suburban cable television news is what has been called its "hyperlocalism"—the coverage of the small-scale events of suburban life that were once the province of only community newspapers. For example,

News Center 13 in New Bedford, a daily 30-minute newscast produced by Greater Fall River Cable TV and Whaling City Cable TV, features a sports segment each night which covers high school sports in detail. Rather than report the sports news of a professional team in a somewhat distant urban center, News Center 13 on a typical night began its newscast with a piece about the New Bedford Whaler's women's high school softball team. It then followed with a detailed report from a crew reporting from a local school-board meeting.[6]

The availability of such suburban cable news programs should increase in the future as many cable companies explore the potential for such programs throughout the country. For example, in 1989 NBC Cable created a new position of senior vice president for regional news to conduct market research into what areas are ripe for local cable news. The company is setting out to follow the example of the successful News 12 Long Island, "finding a subsection of a metropolis that gets too little local news from the primary TV-news outlets, but is large enough to support operation through subscriber fees and ad revenue."[7]

Such explorations pose threats to regional broadcast television news stations, much in the same way that suburban newspapers have threatened metropolitan newspapers with their highly localized news. As a result, in some areas of the country local broadcast television news stations are exploring opportunities to get into the suburban cable news business themselves. For example, the vice president and general manager of San Francisco's station KGO is investigating the possibility of using the station's resources to provide news for residents of suburban Contra Costa County. In addition to posing threats to regional broadcast news shows, suburban cable news may also challenge the monopolies of suburban newspapers for the provision of local news. Moreover, as they begin to serve as another source of news and information and the occupation of scarce leisure time, these stations may add additional incentives for many suburban residents to drop their subscriptions to metropolitan newspapers.

Videotex and Audiotex: Implications for Local News

Two other technological changes that are likely to have implications for the metropolitan news media in the future are the introduction of videotex and audiotex systems. Videotex has been defined as "systems for the widespread dissemination of textual and graphic information by wholly electronic means, for display on low-cost terminals . . . under the selective control of the recipient and using control procedures easily understood by untrained users."[8] The earliest American videotex systems were started by newspaper chains, Times Mirror's "Gateway" and Knight Ridder's "Viewtron," both created in the early 1980s. In describing why Knight-Ridder began Viewtron, which offered a database of news, advertising, and "transactional services" such as home banking, company executive James Batten wrote, we "first got into this field for defensive reasons. We were concerned about the possible impact of new electronic technologies on newspapers."[9] Both Gateway and Viewtron failed, however, in part because of the high prices of the systems (the terminal needed for interaction with the systems cost as much as $1,000 and connect time with the system was high) as well as confusing user interfaces.

While CompuServe, a videotex system with approximately 500,000 subscribers that accesses information via a personal computer and a modem, has been in existence since 1979, a major innovation in the videotex technology came in October 1988 with the introduction in seven U.S. cities of the Prodigy system, developed by IBM and Sears. The advantages of Prodigy, over the earlier Viewtron and Gateway systems, were that it ran on a personal computer, as opposed to tying up a television, that it delivered information rapidly, since it was connected to a regionally located minicomputer, and, most important, that it offered flat-rate pricing rather than a per-minute charge. And unlike most videotex systems, Prodigy used advertisements to offset costs of the system not covered by subscribers' fees.

Prodigy has offered its subscribers national news, business news, weather, sports, and *Consumer Reports* excerpts, but this news has been described as modeled after *USA Today,* or as one observer put it, "you'd have to call Prodigy a capsule of a newspaper that already is a summary." Unlike older videotex systems, the only local information that is available is weather. As Prodigy's manager of public relations commented, "There's not alot of value that we can add to the newspaper. We're not doing local movie listings. As far as local news, that's something that could be done but we have to consider the cost factor and whether there is added value there."[10]

But while Prodigy may not be competitive with local newspapers for the delivery of local news, it may provide stronger competition as an advertising medium because of its customized targeting of messages. Ads appear in Prodigy as "teasers," which appear at the bottom of every page, with advertisements individualized for each user. If the user wants to learn more about the advertisement, there is a special "look" option, which brings up a full page advertisement onto the screen; an "action" option allows the user to buy the product.

Companies using the system pay Prodigy between $20,000 and $80,000 up front to have their products displayed, but also pay each time an advertisement is viewed or leads to a sale, as well as giving a percentage fee for each product sold using the service.[11] Because of such customized advertising, Prodigy may become a very effective threat to metropolitan newspapers' advertising bases.

The other technological innovation that poses a threat to the newspaper's advertising base is audiotex, which enables a user to dial a telephone number and receive or transmit information using the key pad on the touchtone telephone as an input terminal.[12] The simplest audiotex applications were begun by telephone companies providing weather and time information. However, audiotex services expanded greatly in 1982, when an FCC ruling allowed independent information service providers access to information provided over the telephone. In the past few years, a new type of audiotex system has emerged which provides callers with information and advertising at no charge from any touchtone telephone. The cost of providing the service is completely absorbed by the advertisements that precede and follow the requested information.

One of the largest suppliers of audiotex information is Donnelly Directory's Talking Yellow Pages, which provides two basic kinds of information. First, information ranging from current weather forecasts to the latest Dow Jones report can be accessed. The information, which is purchased from outside vendors including the Dow Jones Voice Information Network, is preceded and concluded with advertisements and users have the option of being connected with a representative to find out more about the product or service that is being advertised. While the service does claim to offer national and community news, its "World News Report" provides only basic summaries of national and international news, and its community news, including high school, college, and community events, is minimal. The other type of information available from the Talking Yellow Pages are messages from companies who include an access number along with their yellow page listing, with messages changed throughout the year to advertise specials, extended store hours, etc. Such advertising could provide a strong form of competition to metropolitan newspaper's retail and classified advertising.

Another perhaps more threatening challenge to metropolitan newspapers has come from the changes in restrictions on telephone companies from competing with newspapers in generating the information used in both videotex and audiotex services. In 1982, when courts ordered the breakup of the Bell System, restrictions were placed on the information-generating functions of both AT&T

and the seven regional Bell operating companies. The "Baby Bells" were allowed to passively transmit data, but permanently prevented from entering the content-generating side of the business. At the same time, AT&T was barred from transmitting and generating electronic services for seven years.[13]

However, these restrictions have since been changed. On March 7, 1988, Judge Harold Greene allowed the regional phone companies to offer electronic "gateways" for others' information, providing a service that enabled a computer user to call a single local number to access a variety of data bases. Then, in August of 1989, the bans stopping AT&T from entering the information services industry were allowed to expire, allowing the company to compete directly with providers of electronic information in creating computerized information services that are delivered over the telephone.[14] At the same time, a bill was being prepared by United States Representatives Al Swift and Thomas Tauke to allow the "Baby Bells" to enter into the information services and manufacturing activities.[15] This bill was being actively fought by newspaper publishers because of the threat such competition provides in the domain of generating information. Before these restrictions were lifted, local publishers, although moving cautiously, enjoyed the unchallenged position of providing electronic versions of their information bases.[16]

The emergence of effective videotex and audiotex services such as Prodigy and the Talking Yellow Pages, respectively, and the potential entrance of the telephone companies into the information-generating business, could pose major threats to metropolitan newspapers as both purveyors of news and vehicles for national and local advertising. While such services were hardly competitive for the provision of news—particularly local news—at the outset of the 1990s, their threat lay in part in their provision of customized advertising that is sensitive to information updating. The increasing trend toward at-home shopping in general, using catalogs in addition to electronic means, keeps people from using their metropolitan newspaper to find out about products. In addition, the threat of the new electronic information services is in their use of leisure time that people may have previously spent reading the newspaper. These services continue the trend for people to turn toward sources of "news you can use" and away from the metropolitan newspaper.

The Metropolitan Media and the Future of Local Identity

The new technologies of videotex and audiotex and the emergence of community and suburban cable television news may be said to repre-

230

sent steps in the further decentralization of information sources. Increasingly, not simply traditional news but other kinds of data and advertising messages are being tailored to more individual needs and tastes. Moreover, users of a Prodigy System or the Talking Yellow Pages may find that they are less interested in and have less time for consuming "news" and prefer to access data that has more immediate impact on their lives. They may no longer scan pages of newspaper for the small number of ads that interest them but rather will turn to more specialized advertising forms, which will be tailored to their specific demographic characteristics and interests.

With increasingly localized cable television news, there may similarly be less interest in the metropolitanwide newspapers and regional broadcast television stations. The demand for news directly relevant to people's lives—the decisions of a local zoning board meeting, the scores of the high school soccer team—will be more readily available than ever before and as a result will further decrease the demand for regionwide news. To the extent that the metropolitan news media follow these trends—newspapers continuing to offer zoned editions, broadcast television stations attempting to produce news for suburban cable systems—the decentralization and fragmentation of both news and advertising information will be further encouraged.

However, these trends do not necessarily spell the disappearance of a common sense of regionwide identity among citydwellers and suburbanites alike. To the contrary, it appears that even as metropolitan residents exhibit an increasing hunger for highly localized news with direct relevance to their everyday lives, they still maintain a need for a broader sense of identity tied to city and region. While it has been the central argument of this book that the metropolitan news media work to create just such a sense of identity out of their own commercial self-interest, it is quite possible that in doing so they are responding to a genuine need in their audience. Despite the bonds they form to their own townships and jurisdictions, suburbanites seem to exhibit a continuing need for a geographically based sense of belonging that is linked to the larger unit of city and region.

The need for a sense of "common ground" and shared symbols in urbanized societies was recognized in the early twentieth century by sociologist Emile Durkheim. Durkheim argued that the anomie and disintegration produced by large, industrialized societies required that people regain a sense of membership in their communities. He argued for the need for new "intermediate associations," that is, communities that were smaller than the political entity of the state, which he considered too large to give people a true sense of belonging, and yet larger than the village or community, which he viewed as too parochial. While Durkheim suggested that such "intermediate associations" might be based on occupation, the need for the sense of identity may have come to be fulfilled by the emotional ties to a city-based sense of regional identity. The city, at least in its more symbolic locales, has become the kind of "sacred ground" that Durkheim viewed as providing societies with a necessary form of communal bond, providing meanings that go beyond the pragmatic or utilitarian.[17]

Such ties seem tenaciously in evidence in the way suburbanites, although lessening their actual interactions with their central cities, still continue to identify themselves to outsiders by reference to those cities. When asked where they are from, the resident of Englewood Cliffs, New Jersey, replies "New York," just as the person who makes Orange County, California, her home answers, "Los Angeles," and both seem to continue to maintain an interest in the affairs of those cities' governments. Similarly, suburban residents seem to exhibit a need to stay symbolically connected to regional institutions, whether sports teams, or orchestras, or natural resources, and to have the opportunity to react emotionally to the local heroes and villains connected with them. As the metropolitan media continue to search for news and issues that reinforce that sense of regional identity, they will likely be responding to a strong and continuing sense of need for those kind of symbols by the members of their audience.

The local media's continued efforts to create a sense of regionwide identity may serve other, more pragmatic, purposes, as well. The metropolitan news media may provide the unique function of developing the constituencies necessary to push for policies which address serious regional issues, such as the control of environmental pollutants, or the preservation of resources, or improvements in the transportation network. At the same time, there may be dangers as well lying in the media's identity-setting behavior, as this book has attempted to show. While in every metropolitan area in the country, many crucial regional issues require attention, the need for local symbols may lead the media to examine the more glamorous projects or plans, not the most important issues. Moreover, the omnipresent interest in the symbolic importance of new projects—their impacts on improving the "image of the city" or helping the city compete with other areas of the country—may divert attention from the crucial comparison of costs and benefits that is essential for the efficient allocation of public resources.

Similarly, the continued use of the central city as the "sacred common ground" with which to create a social bond among the suburban population has both its good and bad sides. While it may be very important for the future of American society that suburban residents not forget the social and economic problems of central cities, news coverage which suggests that the suburbs could not survive without their cities may be counterproductive. Suburbs can and do survive without cities, and it is their very sense of economic, political, and geographical independence that leads many suburban residents to view the political wranglings and tragic inner-city happenings as merely a Byzantine form of entertainment. In other words, the continued news focus on the plight of the central city may simply encourage the suburbanite to further dissociate himself from the city.

In addition, the use of costly city development projects as a symbolic communal glue for the regional audience, rather than benefiting the city, may divert important resources from less glamorous but more vital uses. Instead of distorting the importance of downtown convention centers and sports complexes, local news coverage needs to stress the importance of more substantive issues such as inner-city education efforts and the need for improved health care systems. If the metropolitan news media can convey the magnitude and roots of the economic and social problems that remain concentrated in central cities, they may serve a crucial social function, far more important than uncovering governmental scandal. While the local media can never succeed in reversing the trends that led to suburbanization, they may be instrumental in creating and maintaining the kind of public consciousness that is necessary for long-lasting solutions to fundamental urban—and ultimately societal—problems.

The ability of the metropolitan news media to remind their suburban audience of the plight of the urban poor and the struggles of central cities is nowhere clearer than in the writing of Joe Stroud, editorial page editor of the *Detroit Free Press* since 1969. Stroud came to the *Free Press* from the South shortly after the riots that devastated Detroit and caused many middle-class residents to flee to the suburbs. But despite that exodus and the growing need of the *Free Press* to appeal to the suburban audience, Stroud for years wrote a column which was unfailingly devoted to chroniclng the hopeful signs that emerged in the city's rubble. With headlines like "Renaissance Center Is Only a Start," "There's Still Hope for the Old Town," "The city brightens in the summer sun," and "A city learns to like itself better," Stroud's column in the 1970s focused on the more positive events that were occurring in the city of Detroit. In an interview in 1984, Stroud freely admitted that his columns had not led to the whole-sale revitalization of Detroit, or the return of suburbanites to city living, or the disappearance of racial animosity. But he stressed the importance of his having served to help "ameliorate" some of the schisms between city and suburbanite. "In the 1970s it was so important that there be one voice of hope in Detroit, and I wanted to play that role," Stroud commented.[18]

In the years ahead, the metropolitan news media will face a difficult chal-lenge in their continuing efforts to bridge the chasm between city and suburb. They will need to continue to appeal to a suburban audience with localized news while at the same time working to mold a unified sense of regional iden-tity. They will need to provide a balance between reporting on those alarming social, economic, and political problems now plaguing cities and offering cov-erage of the more upbeat, entertaining, and "sexy" topics that attract audiences and ultimately advertisers. They need to understand and work to meet the local news preferences of their target audiences without sacrificing the sense of social consciousness that has always encouraged the reporting of important issues au-diences would at times sooner ignore. The response of the metropolitan news media to this challenge will determine not simply their own future survival but much about the future of their cities and regions as well.

Notes

Chapter One

1. For example, see Alfred M. Lee, *The Daily Newspaper in America* (New York: Macmillan, 1937); Sidney Kobre, *The Yellow Press and Gilded Age Journalism* (Tallahassee: Florida State University, 1964); and Frank Luther Mott, *American Journalism* (New York: Macmillan, 1962).

2. Michael Schudson, *Discovering the News: A Social History of American Newspapers* (New York: Basic Books, 1978), 15.

3. As Pred notes, "Given the role of overseas trade in the national economy and the consequent concern with foreign markets, shipping and politics, the perpetual prominence of European items in the press of the Federal era is understandable" (Allan R. Pred, *Urban Growth and the Circulation of Information* [Cambridge, MA: Harvard University Press, 1973], 22).

4. Sam Bass Warner, *The Private City: Philadelphia in Three Periods of Its Growth* (Philadelphia: University of Pennsylvania Press, 1968), 19–21. This point is also made by Bruce Owen in *Economics and the Freedom of Expression: Media Structure and the First Amendment* (Cambridge, MA: Ballinger, 1975), 40.

5. Pred, *Urban Growth and the Circulation of Information,* 18.

6. Schudson, *Discovering the News,* 19–22.

7. David Ward, *Cities and Immigrants* (New York: Oxford University Press, 1971), 53.

8. George Juergans, *Joseph Pulitzer and His World* (Princeton, NJ: Princeton University Press, 1966), 135.

9. Warner, *The Private City,* 61–62; and David Paul Nord, *Newspapers and New Politics: Midwestern Municipal Reform 1890–1900* (Ann Arbor, MI: UMI Research Press, 1981), 22.

10. Both Juergans (see note 8) and Schudson (see note 2) discuss these innovations extensively.

11. Juergans, *Joseph Pulitzer,* 46–47.

12. Ibid., 118–31.

13. The way in which the general tone of the newspaper was broadened in an attempt to increase circulation is discussed in Owen, *Economics and the Freedom of Expression,* 47.

14. Nord makes the case that newspapers created, for the first time, a sense of attachment to city in chapter 3 of *Newspapers and New Politics,* 21–35.

15. Ibid., 27.

16. Juergans views Joseph Pulitzer as the original muckraker, using his newspaper to spotlight the social injustices of the day. He writes, "There is nothing prior to 1883 to

match [the *World*'s] crusades on behalf of immigrants, workingmen, tenement dwellers, middle income taxpayers and so on. This was militant journalism of a new intensity, not concerned solely with Star Route frauds and Tweed rings . . . but also with conditions that bore down directly upon thousands of anonymous men and women in their daily life" (Juergans, *Joseph Pulitzer,* xii).

17. W. A. Swanberg, *Citizen Hearst* (New York: Scribner's, 1961), 56–58.

18. William Lutz, *The News of Detroit: How a Newspaper and a City Grew Together* (Boston: Little, Brown and Co., 1973).

19. Schudson, *Discovering the News,* 102.

20. Robert Park, "The Natural History of the Newspaper," in *The City,* 4th ed., edited by R. Park, E. W. Burgess, and R. D. McKenzie (Chicago: University of Chicago Press, 1967), 81.

21. Richard Hofstadter, *The Age of Reform: From Bryan to FDR* (New York: Random House, 1955), 188.

22. The relation between communication and urban governments in the late nineteenth century is described in Seymour Mandelbaum, *Boss Tweed's New York* (New York: Wiley, 1965) and Charles N. Glaab and A. Theodore Brown, *A History of Urban America,* 2d ed. (New York: Macmillan, 1976).

23. Owen, *Economics and the Freedom of Expression,* 63–65.

24. "Money Income and Poverty Status of Families and Persons in the United States," *Current Population Reports,* series P-60, no. 154 (Washington, D.C.: U.S. Bureau of the Census, 1985).

25. This data is drawn from John R. Meyer and José Gómez-Ibáñez, *Autos, Transit and Cities* (Cambridge, MA: Harvard University Press, 1981), 29–30, and from the *1980 Census of Population, Journey to Work: Characteristics of the Population* (Washington, D.C.: U.S. Bureau of the Census, 1982).

26. For a discussion of metropolitan fragmentation and the trend toward suburban political independence, see Kevin R. Cox, *Conflict, Power and Politics in the City: A Geographic View* (New York: McGraw-Hill, 1973), 27–69.

27. Benjamin Compaine, *The Newspaper Industry in the 1980's: An Assessment of Economics and Technology* (White Plains, NY: Knowledge Industries Publications, 1980), 58.

28. Compaine, *The Newspaper Industry,* 64.

29. Anthony Smith, *Goodbye Gutenberg: The Newspaper Revolution of the 1980's* (New York: Oxford University Press, 1981), 64.

30. Compaine, *The Newspaper Industry,* 72.

31. Ibid., 77.

32. The competition to newspapers for the blue-collar audience posed by television was pointed out in an interview with newspaper analyst John Morton, September 12, 1989.

33. This data is derived from *Editor and Publisher International Yearbook,* 1940 and 1989 (New York: Editor and Publisher Co.). The metropolitan newspapers included the *Philadelphia Bulletin,* the *Inquirer* and the *Daily News.* The suburban newspapers in-

cluded were: the *Pottstown Mercury, Delaware County Times, Coatesville Record, Doylestown Intelligencer, Lansdale Record, Bucks County Courier Times, Norristown Herald, Phoenixville Phoenix, West Chester Daily Local News, Burlington County Times, Woodbury-Gloucester County Times,* and the *Courier Post.*

34. Philadelphia is a useful example because newspaper penetration data is collected by county and the county of Philadelphia is identical to the city. It should be noted, however, that Philadelphia is a market with particularly strong suburban newspaper competition.

35. It should be noted that these penetration figures are for entire counties, whereas many advertisers are concerned with penetrations of markets that are smaller than counties. It may also be true that some retailers might prefer a smaller penetration of more affluent readers to a larger penetration of less upscale readers.

36. Leo Bogart, *Press and Public: Who Reads What, When, Where, and Why in American Newspapers,* 2d ed. (Hillsdale, NJ: Lawrence Erlbaum, 1989), 54–55.

37. Benjamin Compaine, *Who Owns the Media: Concentration of Ownership in the Mass Communication Industry,* 2d ed. (White Plains, NY: Knowledge Industry Publications, 1979), 57.

38. This information is drawn from *Editor and Publisher International Yearbook* (New York: Editor and Publisher Co.), 1940 and 1989.

39. For more on the difficulties experienced by afternoon newspapers in big cities, see Bogart, *Press and Public,* 2d. ed., 20–23.

40. Christopher H. Sterling and Timothy R. Haight, *The Mass Media: Aspen Institute Guide to Communication Industry Trends* (New York: Praeger, 1978) 25–26.

41. Bogart, *Press and Public,* 2d ed., 30.

42. Robert Park, "Newspaper Circulation and Metropolitan Regions," in *The Metropolitan Community,* edited by R. D. McKenzie (New York: Russell and Russell, 1933), 98–110.

43. James N. Rosse, "Economic Limits of Press Responsibility, A Discussion Paper," *Studies in Industry Economics,* #56 (Stanford: Department of Economics, Stanford University, 1975).

44. Interview with James Houck, managing editor, *Baltimore Sun,* October 10, 1989.

45. Chapter 5 will examine these alternative voices in more detail, focusing particularly on the extent to which they provide alternative perspectives to the metropolitan newspapers on policy issues.

Chapter Two

1. See for example, Alex S. Jones, "Issue for Editors' Meeting: News vs. Profits," *New York Times,* April 12, 1989, C–24; Jones, "Knight-Ridder Tries to Balance Profits and News," *New York Times,* August 7, 1989, D–1; and Jonathan Kwitny, "The High Cost of Profits," *Washington Journalism Review* 12, no. 5 (June 1990):19 + .

2. This chapter will deal primarily, although not exclusively, with the local print media. Economic influences specific to local television news content will be discussed in chapter 4.

3. See, for example, John O'Connor, "Blending Fact with Fiction," *New York Times,* Sunday, May 21, 1989, B–27.

4. Herbert Gans makes the point that the media often ignore societal trends in favor of isolated instances, which come to be exaggerated in the news. As he puts it, "whereas sociologists summarize from recurring patterns or random samples, journalists gravitate toward what sociologists term deviant cases" (Gans, *Deciding What's News: A Study of CBS Evening News, NBC Nightly News, Newsweek, and Time* [New York: Vintage Books, 1980], 92).

5. Ibid., 91–92.

6. Sidney Schanberg, "Cajun Flies and Westway," *New York Times,* July 27, 1985, 23.

7. Donna St. George, "Baby's fatal fall is probed," *Philadelphia Inquirer,* February 25, 1990, B–1.

8. Interview with Donna St. George, March 22, 1990.

9. Interview with Eugene Roberts, Jr., March 24, 1987.

10. See chapter 4 for more on how the need to increase ratings affects television news decisions.

11. The *Daily News* was criticized by African-American groups for this news decision and it, in part, led to a boycott of the newspaper by those groups in April 1990.

12. Interview with Zachary Stalberg, *Philadelphia Daily News,* March 29, 1990.

13. Benjamin Bagdikian, *The Media Monopoly* (Boston: Beacon Press, 1983).

14. Ibid., 154–55.

15. Ibid., 170–75.

16. Ibid., 168.

17. Interview with Eugene Roberts, Jr., March 24, 1987.

18. For example, see Elizabeth M. Whelan et al., "An Analysis of Coverage of Tobacco Hazards in Women's Magazine's," *Journal of Public Health Policy* 2 (March 1981):28–35.

19. Anthony Smith, *Goodbye Gutenberg: The Newspaper Revolution of the 1980's* (New York: Oxford University Press, 1980), 55.

20. Harvey Molotch, "The City as Growth Machine: Toward a Political Economy of Place," *American Journal of Sociology* 82, no. 2 (September 1976): 316.

21. David Jones, "The Press and the Growth Establishment," in *Mass Media and the Environment: Water Resources, Land Use and Atomic Energy in California,* edited by David M. Rubin and David P. Sachs (New York: Praeger, 1973), 191–247.

22. Ibid., 191.

23. Edward C. Banfield and James Q. Wilson, *City Politics* (Cambridge, MA: Harvard University Press and MIT Press, 1963), 321.

24. Sean Devereux, "Boosters in the Newsroom: The Jacksonville Case," *Columbia Journalism Review* 14 (January–February 1976):38–47.

25. Molotch, "The City as Growth Machine," 316.

26. Banfield and Wilson, *City Politics,* 315.

27. Edward Banfield, *Political Influence* (New York: Free Press, 1961), 231.

28. Ibid., 95.

29. Robert Gottlieb and Irene Wolt, *Thinking Big: The Story of the* Los Angeles Times, *Its Publishers, and Their Influence on Southern California* (New York: G. P. Putnam Sons, 1977), 530.

30. Ibid., 533.

31. Harold Kaplan, *Urban Renewal Politics: Slum Clearance in Newark* (New York: Columbia University Press, 1963), 80.

32. Carl Abbott, *The New Urban America: Growth and Politics in Sunbelt Cities* (Chapel Hill: University of North Carolina Press, 1981), 154–55.

33. Ibid., 165.

34. Chester Hartman et al., *Yerba Buena: Land Grab and Community Resistance in San Francisco* (San Francisco, CA: Glide Publications, 1974), 68.

35. Michael N. Danielson and Jameson W. Doig, *New York: The Politics of Urban Development* (Berkeley: University of California Press, 1982), 145.

36. See Gottlieb and Wolt, *Thinking Big,* and David Halberstam, *The Powers That Be* (New York: Alfred Knopf, 1979).

37. Edward Hayes, *Power Structure and Urban Policy: Who Rules Oakland?* (New York: McGraw Hill, 1972).

38. See John Cooney, *The Annenbergs* (New York: Simon and Schuster, 1982).

39. Banfield, *Political Influence.*

40. Richard Hebert, *Highways to Nowhere: The Politics of City Transportation* (Indianapolis: Bobbs-Merrill, 1972), 123.

41. David Altheide, *Creating Reality: How TV News Distorts Events* (Beverly Hills: Sage, 1976), 16.

42. Bagdikian, *The Media Monopoly,* 41–42.

43. Ibid., 3.

44. Kim W. Heron, "Bad news overplayed, Young says," *Detroit Free Press,* February 27, 1984, 1.

45. Interview with James Houck, managing editor, *Baltimore Sun,* October 10, 1989.

46. This discussion of zoning is drawn in part from Smith, *Goodbye Gutenberg,* 143–57.

47. Ibid., 151.

48. Interview with Lionel Linder, editor, the *Detroit News,* May 16, 1984.

49. Smith, *Goodbye Gutenberg,* 145.

50. Sunday, January 14, 1990.

51. Interview with James King, editor, *Seattle Times,* January 10, 1984.

52. Interview with Lionel Linder, *Detroit News,* May 16, 1984.

53. Interview with Eugene Roberts, Jr., March 24, 1987.

54. The individual reporter's central-city bias will be examined in more detail in the next chapter.

55. American Society for Newspaper Editors, *Newspaper Credibility: Building Reader Trust* (Minneapolis, April 1985), 24.

56. See chapter 4 for more on local television news.

Chapter Three

1. For a description of the efficiency principles underlying hierarchical systems, see Phyllis C. Kaniss, *Evolutionary Change in Hierarchical Systems* (Ithaca, NY: Regional Science Dissertation and Monograph Series 9, Program in Urban and Regional Studies, Cornell University, January 1981).

2. For a description of changing ownership structure in newspapers, see Benjamin Compaine, *Who Owns the Media?: Concentration of Ownership in the Mass Communications Industry,* 2d ed. (White Plains, NY: Knowledge Industry Publications, 1982), 27–82.

3. Gaye Tuchman, *Making News: A Study in the Construction of Reality* (New York: Free Press, 1978), 104.

4. Tuchman, *Making News,* 209. The journalist's need for such standard operating procedures is also examined in detail in Gaye Tuchman, "Making News By Doing Work: Routinizing the Unexpected," *American Journal of Sociology* 79 (July 1974):110–31 and Mark Fishman, *Manufacturing the News* (Austin: University of Texas Press, 1988).

5. Herbert Gans, *Deciding What's News: A Study of CBS Evening News, NBC Nightly News, Newsweek and Time* (New York: Vintage Books, 1980), 81–93.

6. Ibid., 78–145.

7. Gary Cohn, "For City, the Stakes in Keeping Cigna Are High," *Philadelphia Inquirer,* August 20, 1987, A–1.

8. Leon Sigal, "Sources Make the News," in *Reading the News,* edited by Robert Karl Manoff and Michael Schudson (New York: Pantheon, 1986), 16.

9. This memo was presented in an interview with Mindy Cameron, city editor, the *Seattle Times,* January 13, 1984.

10. Herbert Gans, *The Urban Villagers* (New York: The Free Press, 1962), 172.

11. Paul Taylor, "Gene Roberts, Down-home Editor of the *Philadelphia Inquirer,*" *Washington Journalism Review* 5 (April 1983):36–41.

12. For a discussion of the use of multipliers in regional economic analysis, see Walter Isard et al., *Methods of Regional Analysis: An Introduction to Regional Science* (Cambridge, MA: MIT Press, 1960), 182–231.

13. Harold Kaplan, *Urban Renewal Politics: Slum Clearance in Newark* (New York: Columbia University Press, 1963), 32.

14. Interview with Tom Livingston, managing editor, *Philadelphia Daily News,* November 5, 1987.

15. Fishman, *Manufacturing the News,* 92–94.

16. Robert Caro, *The Power Broker: Robert Moses and the Fall of New York* (New York: Vintage Books, Random House, 1974), 557.

17. Sandra McDonough, "Navy Fleet Could Provide 15,000 Jobs," *Seattle Times,* January 11, 1984, A–1.

18. Sandra McDonough, "State Overestimated Local Tax Gains from Proposed Navy Base," *Seattle Times,* January 19, 1984, A–1.

19. Sandra McDonough, "Poll Shows Support for Navy Fleet Here," *Seattle Times,* January 13, 1984, A–1.

20. See Gans on the process through which a reporter must sell his editor on a story idea. *Deciding What's News,* 90–93.

21. Fishman, *Manufacturing the News,* 76.

22. Martin Meyerson and Edward C. Banfield, *Politics, Planning and the Public Interest: The Case of Public Housing in Chicago* (Glencoe, IL: Free Press, 1964), 215.

23. Carlin Romano, "The Grisly Truth About Bare Facts," in *Reading the News,* edited by Robert Karl Manoff and Michael Schudson (New York: Pantheon Books, 1986), 52.

24. Romano, "The Grisly Truth About Bare Facts," 53.

25. For example, see Christopher Hepp, "Meter Running High for Parking Authority Director's Calls from City Car," *Philadelphia Daily News,* July 29, 1985, 5.

26. Irving Kristol, "The Underdeveloped Profession," *Public Interest* 6 (Winter 1967):47.

27. Fishman, *Manufacturing the News,* 139.

28. Craig R. McCoy, Glen Macnow, and Bob Ford, "New Jersey Sweetens Offer on Arena for Sixers, Flyers," *Philadelphia Inquirer,* January 31, 1990, A–1.

29. Robert Zausner and Marc Duvoisin, "Pa. Refuses to Raise Ante for Teams," *Philadelphia Inquirer,* February 1, 1990, A–1.

30. Bob Ford and Craig McCoy, "Sixers' Owner Threatens to Seek His Own Deal On a New Sports Arena," *Philadelphia Inquirer,* February 3, 1990, A–1.

31. Craig McCoy, "A Critical Decision on Bid to Teams Confronts Florio," *Philadelphia Inquirer,* February 13, 1990, B–1.

32. Dan Meyers and Craig R. McCoy, "Port Panel Split as Pa. Vows to Spoil Teams' Move," *Philadelphia Inquirer,* March 22, 1990, A–1.

33. Larry Eichel and Andrew Cassel, "When Sports Teams Have Moved, Economic Growth Hasn't Followed," *Philadelphia Inquirer,* April 5, 1990, A–1.

Chapter Four

1. For a detailed discussion of the extent to which people use television news as their main source of information, see John P. Robinson and Mark R. Levy, *The Main Source: Learning from Television News* (Beverly Hills, CA: Sage, 1986).

2. For example, a study carried out for the American Society of Newspaper Editors found that, when asked the question, "If you had to choose one source for local news, which source would you choose?" 50 percent of a national sample chose television as compared with 36 percent who chose newspapers. Similarly, while 58 percent of respondents chose television as the most reliable source of local and state news, only 31 percent selected newspapers. American Society of Newspaper Editors, *Newspaper Credibility: Building Reader Trust* (Minneapolis: MORI Research, Inc., April 1985), 42–43.

3. It should be noted that there is a great variety among the 212 local television news markets in the United States. (For an analysis of the nature of these differences, see Raymond L. Carroll, "Content Values in Television News Programs in Small and Large Markets," *Journalism Quarterly* 62 [Winter 1985]:877–82.) This chapter attempts to generalize across local television markets and identify common characteristics.

4. It is beyond the scope of the book to examine the effects of local television news

on audiences. For studies of how local television news about public affairs is processed by audiences, see Lee B. Becker and Charles Whitney, "Effects of Mass Media Dependencies: Audience Assessment of Government," *Communication Research* 7 (January 1980):96–120, and Peter Clarke and Eric Fredin, "Newspapers, Television, and Political Reasoning," *Public Opinion Quarterly* 42 (Summer 1978):143–60.

5. Maury Green, *Television News: Anatomy and Process* (Belmont, CA: Wadsworth, 1969), 3.

6. Av Westin, *Newswatch: How TV Decides the News* (New York: Simon and Schuster, 1982), 207–8.

7. Gwenda Bair, *Almost Golden: Jessica Savitch and the Selling of Television News* (New York: Simon and Schuster, 1988), 112.

8. For a description of recent experiments with early morning local news in New York City, see Max J. Robins, "Local News Reveille," *Channels* 9 (June 1989):78.

9. *Broadcasting/Cable Yearbook* (Washington, D.C.: Broadcasting Publications, Inc., 1989), C–142.

10. It should be noted, however, that more central-city residents tend to be television news viewers than metropolitan newspaper readers.

11. "Local TV News: The Emphasis Is on Content," *Broadcasting 99* (December 1, 1980):44–50.

12. H. F. Water, "TV News: The Rapid Rise of Home-rule: Local Newscasts Are Stealing the Networks' Beat," *Newsweek* 112 (October 17, 1988):94.

13. See, for example, Westin, *Newswatch,* 210–14, and Edwin Diamond, *The Tin Kazoo: Television, Politics, and the News* (Cambridge, MA: MIT Press, 1975), 87–109.

14. Westin, *Newswatch,* 208.

15. For example, see Herschell Shosteck, "Factors Influencing the Appeal of TV News Personalities," *Journal of Broadcasting* 18 (Winter 1973/74):63–71.

16. Donald Horton and R. Richard Wohl, "Mass Communication as Para-Social Interaction," *Psychiatry* 19 (1956):215–29.

17. Mark R. Levy, "Watching TV News as Para-Social Interaction," *Journal of Broadcasting* 23 (Winter 1979):69–80.

18. Interview with Jim Gardner, anchor, WPVI–TV, April 2, 1987.

19. For example, see Westin, *Newswatch,* 212–15.

20. Ben Yagoda, "When Leibner Calls, the Networks Listen: The reason: He speaks for the Biggest Names in TV News," *New York Times Magazine,* June 18, 1989, 50.

21. Interview with Gardner, April 2, 1987.

22. Carol Towarnicky, "Soapy Messages from the Media," *Philadelphia Daily News,* January 18, 1988, 42.

23. Conrad Smith, "News Critics, Newsworkers and Local Television News," *Journalism Quarterly* 65 (Summer 1988):341–46.

24. Edward J. Epstein, *News from Nowhere: Television and the News* (New York: Random House, 1973), 135–38.

25. Abby Van Pelt, "This Is Abby Van Pelt, Signing Off. For Good," *Philadelphia Magazine,* April, 1984, 117–21.

26. Westin, *Newswatch,* 217.

27. Westin discusses the example of television reporters' mispronunciation of Houston Street in New York City, which outsiders pronounce like the city in Texas but which is actually pronounced like "Houseton" (*Newswatch*, 218).

28. Altheide's study of local television news suggested that more than half of local television news stories were obtained from press releases and related announcements, while the rest were taken from police and fire checks (David Altheide, *Creating Reality: How Television News Distorts Events* [Beverly Hills, CA: Sage, 1976], 61–95). Fishman has shown how local television news stations rely heavily on the print media for their definition of what is newsworthy in a locality. His research suggests that in policy-related matters, local newspapers set the agenda for news coverage, which local television stations then pick up (Mark Fishman, "Crime Waves as Ideology," *Social Problems* 25 [June 1978]:531–43).

29. Dan Berkowitz, "TV News Sources and News Channels: A Study in Agenda Building," *Journalism Quarterly* 64, no. 2 (Summer–Autumn 1987):508–13.

30. See, for example, Edwin Diamond, *Sign Off: The Last Days of Television* (Cambridge, MA: MIT Press, 1982).

31. Interview with Jim Gardner, anchor, WPVI–TV, April 2, 1987. Such story placement is particularly common in highly competitive television markets. For example, media critics in Denver describe the cutthroat competition that gave rise to one local television station's attempts to raise its ratings by giving prominent play to dramatic video. "Often their first few stories are highly visual things that don't necessarily mean much as news—car wrecks or ghetto killings, for example . . . I've seen them do that on nights when there were major news stories. The world is falling apart and KMGH is broadcasting live from a domestic disturbance in the poor part of town" (Ben Daviss, "Man the Minicams, Rev Up the Choppers," *TV Guide*, November 6–12, 1982, 34–38).

32. Interview with Jim Gardner, April 2, 1987.

33. Michael Arlen, *The View from Highway One* (New York: Farrar-Strauss, 1976), 37–38.

34. Joseph Blake, "Confronting Grief on the Air," *Philadelphia Daily News*, June 10, 1986, 57.

35. Bob Teague, "To Get a Story, 'I Flimflammed a Dead Man's Mother,'" *TV Guide*, April 3–9, 1982, 4–10.

36. Teague, "To Get a Story," 10.

37. "Local TV News: The Emphasis Is on Content" and "Local TV Journalism," *Broadcasting*, July 27, 1981, 39.

38. Water, "TV News: The Rapid Rise of Home-rule," 94.

39. Michael Schudson, "Deadlines, Datelines, and History," in *Reading the News*, edited by Michael Schudson and Robert Karl Manoff (New York: Pantheon, 1986), 81–82.

40. The period examined included February 5–9 and March 19–23, 1990. The weeks were selected in order to include one week in "sweeps" month (February), as well as one week in a non-sweeps month (March). The analysis is based on the 6:00 P.M. and 11:00 P.M. broadcasts of KYW–TV, WCAU–TV and WPVI–TV. On March 23, WCAU–TV did not air a late night news program because of basketball tournament coverage.

41. "Newstime" refers to the amount of time devoted to news (as opposed to weather, sports, or commercials) in the local broadcast. The figures, therefore, measure the percentage of the total time allocated to news in the newscasts that each category represented. The figures do not refer to the percentage of the total thirty-minute broadcast.

42. It should be noted that crimes allegedly committed by those in government and the corruption trials of officials were categorized as "government" stories rather than as "occurrences."

43. KYW–TV, February 6, 1990, 6:00 P.M. broadcast.

44. Ibid.

45. It should be noted that all local news stations increase their coverage of international news at 11:00 (included in the table as "world event"), but this increase does not reduce the importance of the finding that local governmental news is de-emphasized from 6:00 to 11:00 P.M.

46. The shortening in time of stories, in part, reflects the fact that the newshole at 11:00 is typically reduced, generally from an average of twelve minutes to an average of eight minutes, to increase time for sports coverage.

47. WPVI–TV, February 5, 1990, 11:00 P.M. broadcast.

48. KYW–TV, February 5, 1990, 11:00 P.M. broadcast.

49. WCAU–TV, February 5, 1990, 11:00 P.M. broadcast.

50. WCAU–TV, February 12, 1990, 11:00 P.M. broadcast.

51. KYW–TV, February 12, 1990, 11:00 P.M. broadcast.

52. Interview with Tia O'Brien, political reporter, KYW–TV, April 2, 1985. When local news stations cover government, they are also more likely to focus on the more entertaining or ceremonial stories than the substantive policy issues. For example, one media critic monitoring New York City's local news for a two-week period in 1982 noted that all three local stations gave far greater prominence to Thomas Kean's inaugural festivities as Governor of New Jersey than to Governor Hugh Carey's budget message on the same day. While one of the stations was seen to do a competent job on the New York governor's budget message, the critic noted that the story was ranked fifteenth on the six o'clock news and, therefore, considered less important than four separate fires and two air crashes. See Tony Schwartz, "What's Wrong with Local TV News?" *New York Times,* February 21, 1982, B–1.

53. WPVI–TV, February 13, 1990, 11:00 P.M. broadcast.

54. Bill Miller, "The safety of subways is debated," *Philadelphia Inquirer,* February 14, 1990, B–2.

55. Edie Goldenberg's exhaustive study of how private interest groups attempt to use the media to reach their objectives was written before the practice of using local television news became widespread. It is interesting to compare the tactics used by the groups in her study, largely to obtain newspaper coverage of their activities, to the television-savvy strategy adopted by many protest groups two decades later. See Edie Goldenberg, *Making the Papers: The Access of Resource-Poor Groups to the Metropolitan Press* (Lexington: Lexington Books, Heath and Company, 1975).

56. WPVI–TV, March 14, 1990, 6:00 P.M. broadcast. The tax-hike package led the

broadcast at two minutes fifteen seconds, while the Rocky statue package was the eighth story at one minute and fifty-five seconds.

57. WPVI–TV, March 15, 1990, 6:00 P.M. broadcast.

58. *Philadelphia Daily News,* March 16, 1990, 1–2.

59. WCAU–TV, February 6, 1990, 6:00 and 11:00 P.M. broadcasts.

60. Robert Zausner, "A Budget That May Not Stack Up to Its Billing," *Philadelphia Inquirer,* February 7, 1990, A–8.

61. WPVI–TV, February 6, 1990, 6:00 and 11:00 P.M. broadcasts.

62. Zausner, "A Budget That May Not Stack Up."

63. KYW–TV, February 7, 1990, 11:00 P.M. broadcast.

64. WPVI–TV, February 6, 1990, 6:00 P.M. broadcast.

65. Zausner, "A Budget That May Not Stack Up."

66. As Danielson and Doig observed in noting the lack of effective coverage of regional issues by local television news in their study of urban development in New York: "At best . . . [local] television provides sporadic coverage of the region, its development, and its problems. Local news broadcasts devote most of their time to New York City, where the largest single bloc of the region's viewers live. And this coverage—which tends to feature crime, drugs, racial conflict, commercial sex, corruption, official incompetence and fiscal plight—serves to reinforce suburban fears of the city, rather than bolster feelings of regional togetherness. Outside New York City, disasters, crime, and other sensational events are more likely to get attention on the local television news than problems such as regional transportation or water supply . . ." (Michael Danielson and Jameson W. Doig, *New York: The Politics of Urban Development* [Berkeley: University of California Press, 1982], 145).

67. KYW–TV, February 12, 1990, 11:00 P.M. broadcast.

68. WCAU–TV, February 7, 1990, 11:00 P.M. broadcast.

69. KYW–TV, February 6, 1990, 6:00 P.M. broadcast.

70. WCAU–TV, February 5, 1990, 6:00 P.M. broadcast.

71. February 8, 1990, 11:00 P.M. broadcast.

72. WPVI–TV, February 7 and 8, 1990, 6:00 P.M. broadcasts.

73. "Broadcast Journalists Ask Themselves Tough Questions," *Broadcasting,* September 1, 1986, 35–38.

74. "Local TV Journalism," *Broadcasting,* July 27, 1981, 42.

75. "State of the Art: Journalism," *Broadcasting,* December 3, 1984, 50.

Chapter Five

1. Ben Moon, "City Magazines, Past and Present," *Journalism Quarterly* 47 (Winter 1970):711–18.

2. Moon, "City Magazines," 712.

3. William Taft, *American Magazines for the 1980's* (New York: Hastings House, 1982), 159.

4. John Tebbel, "City Magazines: A Medium Reborn," *Saturday Review,* March 9, 1968, 102.

5. Bob Abel, "The City Slickers," *Columbia Journalism Review* 7 (Spring 1968):11.

6. Taft, *American Magazines*, 163.

7. *Philadelphia*, July 1968.

8. *Philadelphia*, April 1968.

9. *Los Angeles*, February 1968.

10. *Los Angeles*, July 1968.

11. *Philadelphia*, January 1988.

12. *Philadelphia*, February 1988.

13. *Philadelphia*, April 1988.

14. *Philadelphia*, July 1988.

15. *Philadelphia*, October 1988.

16. *Philadelphia*, November 1988.

17. *Los Angeles*, January 1988.

18. *Los Angeles*, March 1988.

19. Michael Johnson, *The New Journalism: The Underground Press, the Artists of Nonfiction, and Changes in the Establishment Media* (Lawrence, KS: University Press of Kansas, 1971), 14.

20. *Berkeley Barb*, July 3, 1980, 1.

21. David Armstrong, *A Trumpet to Arms: Alternative Media in America* (Boston: South End Press, 1981), 276.

22. Albert Scardino, " 'Alternative' Weeklies on the Rise," *New York Times*, May 25, 1989, A–35.

23. Armstrong, *A Trumpet to Arms*, 276.

24. Ibid., 277.

25. Interview with Bruce Schimmel, publisher, *City Paper*, October 26, 1989.

26. Ibid.

27. *Bay Guardian*, October 5, 1988.

28. *Boston Phoenix*, October 7–13, 1988.

29. The *Reader*, October 7, 1988.

30. The Baltimore *City Paper*, October 7–13, 1988.

31. *Dallas Observer*, October 6, 1988.

32. Interview with David Brewster, editor, Seattle *Weekly*, January 12, 1984.

33. Interview with Russ Smith, former editor of the Baltimore *City Paper*, October 27, 1988.

34. Interview with Bruce Schimmel, publisher of Philadelphia's *City Paper*, October 26, 1989.

35. Interview with David Brewster, January 12, 1984.

36. Margaret Bernstein, "Pressing On," *Black Enterprise*, June 1989, 143.

37. Sharon Murphy, *Other Voices: Black, Chicano, and American Indian Press* (Dayton, OH: Pflaum/Standard, 1974), 79–81.

38. Alex Jones, "Black Papers: Businesses with a Mission," *New York Times*, August 17, 1987, B–1.

39. Albert Scardino, "Black Papers Retain a Local Role," *New York Times*, July 24, 1989, D–1.

40. Bernstein, "Pressing On," 143.

41. *Editor and Publisher: International Yearbook, 1989* (New York: Editor and Publisher Co., 1989).

42. Interview with Paul Bennett, editor, *Philadelphia Tribune*, November 15, 1988.

43. Carolyn Martindale, *The White Press and Black America* (Westport, CT: Greenwood Press, 1986), 54.

44. Ibid.

45. Roland Wolseley, *The Black Press, U.S.A.* (Ames: Iowa State University Press, 1971), 301–3.

46. Ibid., 310–14.

47. Bernstein, "Pressing On," 143.

48. Tony Chapelle, "Black Media in Spotlight," *Crain's New York Business*, August 29, 1988, 3.

49. Bernstein, "Pressing On," 142.

50. Ibid.

51. *City Sun*, "We're for You, Dave, but Just Remember . . ." November 1–7, 1989, 1.

52. Interview with Andrew Cooper, publisher of Brooklyn's *City Sun*, November 5, 1989.

53. Sally Miller, ed., *The Ethnic Press in the United States: A Historical Analysis and Handbook* (New York: Greenwood Press, 1987), 204.

54. Joseph Berger, "At 90 Years Old, the Forward Still Crackles," *New York Times*, May 25, 1987, I–21.

55. Ibid.

56. Ibid.

57. Interview with Al Erlick, editor of Philadelphia *Jewish Exponent*, November 3, 1988.

58. Miller, *The Ethnic Press*, 221.

59. Donald Altschiller, "The Problems and Prospects of Jewish Journalism," in *The Sociology of American Jews*, edited by Jack Porter (Washington, D.C.: University Press of America, 1980), 165.

60. Gary Rosenblatt, "The Jewish de-Press," *Moment* (November 1977):46–50.

61. Interview with Al Erlick, November 3, 1988.

62. *Baltimore Jewish Times*, October 27, 1989, 35.

63. Altschiller, "The Problems and Prospects of Jewish Journalism," 162.

64. Doris Goldstein, "The Temple as Historic Landmark," *Atlanta Jewish Times*, November 3, 1989, 8.

65. Miller, *The Ethnic Press*, xvi.

66. Robert E. Park, *The Immigrant Press and Its Control* (New York: Harper and Brothers Publishers, 1922).

67. Joshua A. Fishman et al., "The Non-English and Ethnic Group Press, 1910–1960," in *Language, Loyalty in the United States: The Maintenance and Perpetuation of Non-English Mother Tongues by American Ethnic and Religious Groups*, Joshua A. Fishman et al., (The Hague: Mouton and Co, 1966).

68. Albert Scardino, "A Renaissance for Ethnic Papers," *New York Times,* August 22, 1988, D–1.

69. Ana Veciana-Suarez, *Hispanic Media, USA: A Narrative Guide to Print and Electronic News Media in the United States* (Washington, D.C.: The Media Institute, 1987).

70. Veciana-Suarez, *Hispanic Media, USA,* 36.

71. Harold Corzine, *The Gay Press* (Ann Arbor, MI: University Microfilms International, 1977), 104–5.

72. Interview with Mark Segal, publisher of the *Philadelphia Gay News,* November 3, 1988.

73. Corzine, *The Gay Press,* 200–229.

74. Carrie Woffard, "Mass. Gay Rights Bill Clears Another Hurdle," *Gay Community News,* October 29–November 4, 1989, 1.

75. Shilpa Mehta, "Officials Meet with PLGTF to Discuss Violence Issue," *Philadelphia Gay News,* November 24–30, 1989, 3.

76. *Philadelphia Gay News,* November 3–9, 1989, 24.

77. Miller's *The Ethnic Press in the United States* provides an excellent survey of the ethnic press and its functions.

78. Park, *The Immigrant Press,* 114.

79. Morris Janowitz, *The Community Press in an Urban Setting,* 2d ed. (Chicago: University of Chicago Press, 1967), 23.

80. Kenneth Byerly, *Community Journalism* (Philadelphia: Chilton, 1961), 5.

81. Janowitz, *The Community Press,* 36.

82. Ibid., 172.

83. Interview with Marie Reinhart Jones, editor of Philadelphia's *Chestnut Hill Local,* November 14, 1989.

84. *The Villadom News,* November 22, 1989.

85. David Sachsman and Warren Sloat, *The Press and the Suburbs: The Daily Newspapers of New Jersey* (New Brunswick: Center for Urban Policy Research, 1985), 5.

86. Interview with Tyree Johnson, editor of Philadelphia's *Westside Weekly,* November 21, 1989.

87. Alex Jones, "The Weekly Newspaper Becomes a Hot Property," *New York Times,* May 15, 1989, D–6.

88. James Duncan, Jr., *American Radio: Spring 1989 Report* (Indianapolis: Duncan's American Radio, Inc., August 1989). Data is compiled in Duncan's reports for the 175 rated markets in the country.

89. These comments come from George A. Burns, a media consultant, quoted in George Swisshelm, "All-news Stations: Are They Dispensing in Smaller Doses?" *Television/Radio Age* (October 31, 1988):45.

90. Swisshelm, "All-news Stations," 47.

91. See, for example, Joseph Turow, "Talk Show Radio as Interpersonal Communication," *Journal of Broadcasting* 18 (Spring 1974):171–79, and Robert K. Avery and Donald G. Ellis, "Talk Radio as Interpersonal Phenomenon," in *Inter/Media: Interpersonal Communication in a Media World,* edited by Gary Gumpert and Robert Cathcart (New York: Oxford University Press, 1979), 108–15.

92. For example, see John Crittenden, "Democratic Functions of the Open Mike Radio Forum," *Public Opinion Quarterly* 35 (Summer 1971):200–210.

93. See Murray B. Levin, *Talk Radio and the American Dream* (Lexington, MA: Lexington Books, 1987).

94. For example, see Jane Bick's book review of *Talk radio and the American dream* in *Journal of Broadcasting and Electronic Media* 32 (Winter 1988):121–22.

95. Richard Zoglin, "Bugle Boys of the Airwaves," *Time,* May 15, 1989, 88–89.

96. Ibid., 89.

97. "Urban Contemporary FM Stations Pulling More Ad Dollars," *Television/Radio Age* 32 (February 18, 1985):B–8–B–14.

98. See, for example, Ronald Smothers, "Station Offers Perspective of Black New Yorkers," *New York Times,* July 3, 1987, B–2.

Chapter Six

1. Robert Caro, *The Power Broker: Robert Moses and the Fall of New York* (New York: Vintage Books, Random House, 1975).

2. Delmar Dunn, *Public Officials and the Press* (Reading, MA: Addison-Wesley, 1969), 59.

3. A fourth channel could be considered to be televised debates with opposing candidates, but these tend to be limited in scope among local government officials.

4. Bernard C. Cohen discusses this function of news in *The Press and Foreign Policy* (Princeton: Princeton University Press, 1963), 184–96.

5. Interview with Philadelphia Police Commissioner Kevin Tucker, April 3, 1986.

6. Leon Sigal, *Reporters and Officials: The Organization and Politics of Newsmaking* (Lexington, MA: D. C. Heath, 1973), 132–35.

7. Dunn, *Public Officials and the Press,* 103–4.

8. Interview with Southeastern Pennsylvania Transit Authority Board Member Patrick Swygert, April 11, 1988.

9. Sigal, *Reporters and Officials,* 135. The use of trial balloons in making policy is also discussed by Cohen, *The Press and Foreign Policy,* 202–4.

10. Sigal, *Reporters and Officials,* 140.

11. Dunn, *Public Officials and the Press,* 100.

12. Interview with Joan Specter, April 12, 1988.

13. Interview with Patrick Swygert, April 11, 1988.

14. Interview with Philadelphia District Attorney Ed Rendell, April 19, 1984.

15. Wallace S. Sayre and Herbert Kaufman, *Governing New York City: Politics in the Metropolis* (New York: Russell Sage Foundation, 1960), 257.

16. Interview with Craig Schelter, November 10, 1982.

17. Sigal, *Reporters and Officials,* 144.

18. Interview with Leslie Schism, *Philadelphia Daily News,* March 31, 1988.

19. Edie Goldenberg, *Making the Papers: The Access of Resource-Poor Groups to the Metropolitan Press* (Lexington, MA: Lexington Books, D. C. Heath and Co., 1975), 17–32.

20. Interview with Ed Rendell, April 19, 1984.

21. Interview with State Representative Charles Nahill, April 12, 1990.

22. Herbert Gans uses this term in *Deciding What's News: A Study of CBS Evening News, NBC Nightly News, Newsweek, and Time* (New York: Vintage Books, Random House, 1980), 9.

23. For example, see the *Philadelphia Inquirer*'s Sunday magazine article on the issue by Mark Bowden ("Who's Sorry Now, William Stead Back in San Francisco, or You Stuck in Philadelphia?" February 28, 1988).

24. For example, see Gans, *Deciding What's News,* 116.

25. These "styles" are impressionistic findings based on observations of news coverage and interviews with local officials and journalists.

26. Interview with Leslie Schism, *Philadelphia Daily News,* March 31, 1988.

27. Interview with Bob Warner, *Philadelphia Daily News* reporter, March 16, 1988.

28. Interview with Christopher Hepp, *Philadelphia Inquirer* reporter, March 24, 1988.

29. Interview with Philadelphia Police Commissioner Willie Williams, April 19, 1990.

30. The importance of neutralizing criticism was pointed out by Fred Stein, director of Philadelphia's "We the People" celebration, in an interview on December 1, 1987.

31. Interview with Willie Williams, April 19, 1990.

32. Caro, *The Power Broker,* 983.

33. Interview with Randy Baker and Carol Boudreaux, Houston Metropolitan Transit Authority, March 15, 1984.

34. Interview with Ed Rendell, April 19, 1984.

35. Michael N. Danielson and Jameson W. Doig, *New York: The Politics of Urban Development* (Berkeley: University of California Press), 334.

36. Interview with Philadelphia Police Commissioner Kevin Tucker, April 3, 1986.

37. Dunn, *Public Officials and the Press,* 117.

38. James Lardner, "A Reporter At Large: Painting the Elephant," *The New Yorker,* June 25, 1984.

39. See chapter 3 for a discussion of the way local journalists report study results that draws on the Seattle example.

40. Gil Bailey, "Dicks, Gorton, and Evans Urge Enthusiastic Welcome for the Navy," *Seattle Post-Intelligencer,* December 21, 1983, A–1.

41. Darrell Glover, "Back Navy or Lose Base to California, Spellman Warns," *Seattle Post-Intelligencer,* January 7, 1984, C–1.

42. Gil Bailey, "Dicks, Gorton and Evans urge enthusiastic welcome for Navy," *Seattle Post-Intelligencer,* December 21, 1983, A–1.

43. Sandra McDonough, "Wright Criticizes Royer for Failing to Encourage Navy," *Seattle Times,* January 7, 1984, A–6.

44. *Seattle Post-Intelligencer,* January 10, 1984, A–3.

45. Caro, *The Power Broker,* 984–1004.

46. Interview with Representative Charles Nahill, April 12, 1990.

Chapter Seven

1. The chapter examines only the first four years of the attempts to gain approval for the Center, highlighting certain key stages in the project's approval: the initial city proposal, the emergence of opposition to the proposal, the investigation into alleged improprieties in the project, and the debate that occurred in 1986 over the project's costs and benefits. To examine all news coverage of this complex issue for the six years of the approval process is beyond the scope of the chapter.

2. George Wilson, "Convention Center Is a Must for Area," *Philadelphia Inquirer,* July 16, 1982, A–11.

3. Jan Schaffer, "Exhibiting a Need for Convention Space," *Philadelphia Inquirer,* September 26, 1982, F–1.

4. Jan Schaffer, "Big Civic Center Is a Must, Study Says," *Philadelphia Inquirer,* January 12, 1983, A–1.

5. Jan Schaffer, "City Pushes Convention Center Plan," *Philadelphia Inquirer,* January 14, 1983, A–1.

6. Jan Schaffer, "With Center, City Hopes to Fix Image," *Philadelphia Inquirer,* January 23, 1983, G–1.

7. "A New Convention Center: Do It Now and Do It Right," *Philadelphia Inquirer,* January 17, 1983, A–10.

8. Bob Warner, "Panel Has Sites Set on Convention Center," *Philadelphia Daily News,* January 14, 1983, 4.

9. "A New Convention Center," *Philadelphia Daily News,* September 16, 1983, 93.

10. Thomas Hine, "Perfect Site Still Eluding the Planners," *Philadelphia Inquirer,* August 14, 1983, H–14.

11. Thomas Hine, "Will Success Spoil Reading Train Shed?" *Philadelphia Inquirer,* September 18, 1983, K–14.

12. Huntly Collins, "They resist moving for a new center," *Philadelphia Inquirer,* October 22, 1983, H–1.

13. Huntly Collins, "Business owners organize to fight Reading convention-center project," *Philadelphia Inquirer,* October 28, 1983, B–3.

14. It should be noted, however, that members of BARC continually criticized the *Inquirer*'s coverage of their group's activities and of the project as a whole.

15. Kitty Caparella, "Reading Center Proposal 'Railroaded,' Some Say, *Philadelphia Daily News,* October 26, 1983, 12.

16. Charles Robb, "The Convention Center: Getting Untracked?" *Philadelphia Daily News,* February 6, 1984, 21–22.

17. Charles Robb, "He's a Defector on Reading Site," *Philadelphia Daily News,* March 28, 1984, 27.

18. Charles Robb, "Who's Who of the Threatened," *Philadelphia Daily News,* March 28, 1984, 27.

19. Interview with Juan Gonzalez, March 25, 1986.

20. Juan Gonzalez, "'Conflict'?: City Suspends Consultants," *Philadelphia Daily News,* April 4, 1985, 3.

21. Juan Gonzalez, "City Probing Acquisitions at Center Site," *Philadelphia Daily News,* April 5, 1985, 3.

22. Vernon Loeb and Russell Cooke, "City Consultant Suspended in Possible Conflict," *Philadelphia Inquirer,* April 5, 1985, B–1.

23. Vernon Loeb and Russell Cooke, "Deals at Site of New Center Monitored," *Philadelphia Inquirer,* April 6, 1985, B–3.

24. Interview with Juan Gonzalez, March 25, 1986.

25. Juan Gonzalez, "State Ties Strings to $185M Center Aid," *Philadelphia Daily News,* April 12, 1985, 3.

26. Interview with Craig Schelter, executive director of Philadelphia Industrial Development Corporation, April 16, 1985.

27. Ibid.

28. Gregory Byrnes, "Reading Plan Is Changed," *Philadelphia Inquirer,* May 8, 1985, D–1.

29. Howard Schneider, "Convention Center's a Loser, New Analysis Says," *Philadelphia Daily News,* April 2, 1986, 7.

30. Ron Wolf, "New Study Backs Up City on Convention Center's Effects," *Philadelphia Inquirer,* April 11, 1986, C–18.

31. Gary Thompson, "New Study Centers on $6B Boost," *Philadelphia Daily News,* April 11, 1986, 117.

32. Gary Cohn, "Benefits of Center Questioned," *Philadelphia Inquirer,* December 1, 1986, D–1.

33. "PennNews: Proposed Convention Center Not All It Is Cracked Up to Be, Says Penn Report," press release, University of Pennsylvania, November, 1986.

34. Interview with Craig Stock, business editor, *Philadelphia Inquirer,* April 15, 1987.

35. To get a sense of how local television news covered the proposal, an examination was made of the logbooks of one local station, KYW–TV, the NBC affiliate in Philadelphia, and of the station's story tapes. Interviews with staff at KYW and the other stations were also conducted.

36. Interview with Joann Wilder, WCAU–TV, February 14, 1990.

37. KYW–TV, January 14, 1983, noon broadcast.

38. KYW–TV, March 4, 1983, 6:00 P.M. broadcast.

39. KYW–TV, July 28, 1983, 11:00 P.M. broadcast.

40. KYW–TV, September 15, 1983, 6:00 P.M. broadcast.

41. KYW–TV, October 10, 1983, 6:00 P.M. broadcast.

42. KYW–TV, May 2, 1984, 5:00 P.M. broadcast.

43. KYW–TV, April 10, 1986, 6:00 P.M. broadcast.

44. Loren Feldman, "Center of the Storm," *Philadelphia,* April, 1984.

45. Interview with Loren Feldman, April 4, 1985.

46. Noel Weyrich, "The $441 M Boondoggle," *City Paper,* June 21–July 5, 1985, 3.

47. Interview with Noel Weyrich, April 13, 1986.

48. Interview with Richard Aregood, March 25, 1987.

49. Interview with Craig Stock, April 15, 1987. Stock later noted that sometimes

governments fail for precisely the same reason: fragmentation and overlap of responsibility.

Conclusions and a Look to the Future

1. "Westchester Journal: Prime Time," *New York Times,* March 20, 1988, sec. 20, 3.

2. "Cable TV Renews Interest in Local Government," *New York Times,* April 9, 1989, sec. 22, 39.

3. National Federation of Local Cable Programmers, *Community Television Review* 11, No. 4 (Washington, D.C.: September/October 1988), 2.

4. *New York Times,* September 5, 1988, I–30.

5. Chuck Reece, "The Home Town Report," *Channels,* September 1989, 57–62.

6. Ibid., 57.

7. Ibid., 60.

8. Kevin Wilson, *Technologies of Control: The New Interactive Media for the Home* (Madison, WI: University of Wisconsin Press, 1988), 15.

9. James K. Batten, "The First Months of Viewtron and What the Future Holds," in *Electronic Publishing Plus,* edited by Martin Greenberger (White Plains, NY: Knowledge Industries, 1985), 158.

10. Michael Antonoff, "The Prodigy Promise," *Personal Computing,* May 1989, 69.

11. Subrata N. Chakravarty and Evan McGlinn, "This Thing Has to Change People's Habits," *Forbes,* June 26, 1989, 122.

12. Haines Gaffer, "Audiotex: An Overview," in *Videotex '86* (New York: Online International, Inc., USA, 1986).

13. Calvin Sims, "Judge Will Allow AT&T to Publish Electronic Data," *New York Times,* July 29, 1989, A–1.

14. Ibid.

15. John Burgess, "Drive to Relax Restrictions on 'Baby Bells' Gains Strength," *Washington Post,* October 13, 1989, D–1.

16. Joe Sharkey, "Newspaper Publishers Debate Pros, Cons of Allying with Phone Firms," *Wall Street Journal,* April 26, 1989, B–6.

17. This brief summary of Durkheim's ideas is drawn from Robert Nisbet, *The Sociology of Emile Durkheim* (New York: Oxford University Press, 1974).

18. Interview with Joe Stroud, editorial page editor, *Detroit Free Press,* May 15, 1984.

Index

Abbott, Carl, 55
Advertisers: demand for suburban audience, 28, 31, 35–36, 44; influence on editorial content, 50–52, 66; in the Penny Papers, 15; shift from newspapers to television, 29–30
Afternoon newspapers, 35–36
Allentown Call, 33
Alternative newspapers. *See* Urban news-weeklies
Altheide, David, 57
Altschiller, Donald, 148
Amsterdam News, 44, 142, 144
Anchors. *See* Television news, local: and role of anchors
Annapolis Capital, 44
Annenberg, Walter, 56
Architectural critics, 93–94, 199–202
Aregood, Richard, 218
Arizona Informant, 144
Arizona Republic, 137
Armstrong, David, 137–38
Atlanta, 24–27, 56–57, 149
Atlanta Constitution, 60
Atlanta Jewish Times, 149
Audience considerations, 85–88, 96, 210, 218; importance of suburban, 4, 59–70
Audience fragmentation, nineteenth century, 19
Audience targeting, 46, 59, 72, 205
Audiotex, 227, 229–30; Donnelly Directory's Talking Yellow Pages, 229, 231; Dow Jones Voice Information Network, 229
Avatar, 136

Bacon, Edmund, 1
Bagdikian, Benjamin, 50, 57
Baltimore, 24–27, 100
Baltimore City Paper, 140
Baltimore Jewish Times, 148
Baltimore Sun, 44, 57, 58, 59

Banfield, Edward, 53, 54, 87–88
Batten, James, 228
Bay Guardian, 139
Beats: cultivating sources on, 165; fragmentation of in metropolitan newspapers, 5, 91–95, 210, 218–19, 222; in local television news, 106; regional institutions as, 64–65; suburban, 77
Bellevue Journal-American, 155
Bennett, James Gordon, 15
Berkeley Barb, 136
Berkowitz, Dan, 107
Black-oriented radio and television, 143, 158–59
Black press, 10, 44, 141–45
Bogart, Leo, 36
Boosterism, 3, 7, 10, 52–53, 58; in city magazines, 133–34; in nineteenth-century newspapers, 19–20; in Philadelphia convention center coverage, 196, 201, 212
Boston, 24, 26–27, 35, 36, 78, 148–49
Boston Globe, 65
Boston Phoenix, 137, 139
Breslow, Marc, 209
Brewster, David, 139–40
Bucks County Courier Times, 32, 33
Buffalo, 100
Burlington County Times, 33
Bush, George, 47, 148
Business coverage, 91, 166, 204, 219
Byerly, Kenneth, 153–54

Cable television news, local, 225–27; Boston Neighborhood Network, 225; Channel 13, New Bedford, 226; Channel 35, White Plains, New York, 225; News 12 Long Island, 226, 227
Camden, New Jersey, 96–100
Camden Courier Post, 32, 33
Caro, Robert, 82, 160, 180
Casey, Robert, 117, 124–25, 128, 129

Chain ownership of newspapers, 72, 155
Chandler family, 56
Chestnut Hill Local, 154
Chicago: black newspapers in, 142; news-
    paper coverage of development issues, 54–
    56, 87; suburbanization of, 24–27
Chicago Herald Tribune, 35
Chicago Reader, 139
Chicago Sun-Times, 55, 87–88
Chicago Tribune, 20, 37, 40, 54, 60–62
Cincinnati, 26
Cities, nineteenth-century, 3
Cities, symbolic importance of, 65–68, 77–
    78
City magazines, 7, 10, 43, 44, 69, 133–35
City myopia, 4, 5, 74–78, 99–100, 126
City papers. *See* Urban newsweeklies
Cleveland, 24, 26, 35, 66, 100
Coatesville Record, 34
Colorful quotables, 173–74, 223
Commercial newsletters, 14
Commercial pressures on local news, 10, 46–
    70
Community access channels, 225–26
Community newspapers, 7, 11, 153–56, 167,
    176
Consultants, as news sources, 84–85, 182,
    191–93, 195–96
Consumer news, 3, 111
Corporate ownership of newspapers, 46, 58
Costs and benefits of development projects,
    coverage, 5, 7, 10; architecture critic's ig-
    noring of, 94; journalists' acceptance of of-
    ficial estimates of, 79, 80–84, 182; in Phila-
    delphia's convention center, 190, 192,
    194–95, 203, 207–10, 215, 224
Crime coverage, 15, 58, 76, 78, 154
Crusades, newspaper, 3, 21

Dallas, 26, 27, 35
Dallas Observer, 139
Dana, Charles, 15
Dancing marionette, 7, 172–73
Danielson, Michael N., 56, 180, 223
Day, Benjamin, 15
Delaware County Times, 34
Demographics, and local news markets, 3, 9
Denver, 2, 5, 27

Denver Post, 37, 41
Department stores, 3, 17–18, 23, 54, 55
Detroit, 4, 9; demographic shifts, 24–27;
    metropolitan newspaper competition, 35;
    news coverage in, 58, 66, 67, 233–34
Detroit Free Press, 58, 233–34
Detroit News, 20, 62
Detroit Times, 35
Devereux, Sean, 53
Diario Las Americas, 150
Doig, Jameson W., 56, 180, 223
Downtown bias in the local media, 54–56
Doylestown Intelligencer, 33
Dunn, Delmar, 160, 162, 181
Durkheim, Emile, 231–32
Dwyer, Budd, 48–49

Editorials, 94–95, 177, 181, 190, 219
Editors, role of, 72–75, 77–78, 85–86
Ethnic newspapers. *See* Specialized press

Fear of numbers, 5, 80–84, 96, 210, 218
Federal Communications Commission (FCC),
    102, 229
Field, Marshall, Jr., 55, 56
Fishman, Mark, 82, 86–87, 90–91
Florio, James, 96–97, 120, 122, 177
Freedom's Journal, 141

Gans, Herbert, 47, 73–74, 78
Gardner, Jim, 101, 105, 109
Gay Community News, 151
Gay press, 10, 150–52
Ginsberg, Douglas, 47
Gloucester County Times, 32, 33
Goode, Wilson, 1, 168
Gottlieb, Robert, 55
Greeley, Horace, 15
Green, Bill, 188, 189
Grigsby, William, 208–10
Growth, local, interest of media in. *See*
    Boosterism
Guardian Angels, 121

Hart, Gary, 47
Hartford Courant, 60
Hartman, Chester, 55–56
Health coverage, 107, 111, 119

Index

Hearst, William Randolph, 20, 21
Hebert, Richard, 56
Hine, Thomas, 199–202
Hispanic media, 10, 150
Hofstadter, Richard, 21
Horse-race theme, in development news coverage, 5, 87, 96, 183
Horton, R. Richard, 104
Houston, 2, 9; demographic shifts in, 24–27; news coverage of, 65, 66; newspaper competition in, 35
Houston Chronicle, 37, 42, 180
Houston Metropolitan Transit Agency, 65
Houston Post, 58, 180
Houston Press, 35

Il Diario, 149
Il Progresso, 149
Image of the city, in news coverage, 5
Immigrant press, 149–50
Immigrants, and newspapers, 16, 18, 20
Investigative reporting, 72, 88–91, 184, 204–7, 222
Irish Echo, 149

Jacksonville Times-Union, 53
Janowitz, Morris, 154
Jewish Advocate, 148
Jewish Exponent, 146–47
Jewish press, 10, 145–49
Johnson, Michael, 136
Jones, David, 52
Journalists, local, personal and professional values, 5, 10, 71–100, 221–22

Kansas City, 24, 35
Kaplan, Harold, 55
KGO, San Francisco, 227
KING, Seattle, 158
KIRO, Seattle, 157
Knight-Ridder, 51, 190, 196, 228
Knowland, Joseph, 56
Korea Herald, 149
Kristol, Irving, 90
KRLD, Dallas-Fort Worth, 157
KYW-TV, 115–19, 127, 129, 211–14

Lansdale Reporter, 34
Leaking news, 164–65, 176–77, 185
Levy, Mark R., 104
Local economy, links to media, 2, 30, 52–53
Local identity, 2, 3, 4, 11, 59, 75, 221; in the nineteenth century, 19–22; television's effects on, 29
Local news, defining in metropolitan media, 4, 64–70
Local television news. *See* Television news, local
Long Island Newsday, 43, 63
Los Angeles, 24, 26, 27, 35, 55, 56
Los Angeles Free Press, 136
Los Angeles magazine, 135
Los Angeles Times, 55, 57, 60, 65
Lying to the media, 174, 223

McCormick, Colonel, 56
McKeel, Sam, 196
Mandela, Nelson, 49
Mayors, coverage of, 11, 167–68, 173
Media events, 74, 107, 124, 178, 181, 186
Metropolitan Transit Agency, New York, 181
Metropolitan Transit Authority, Houston, 180
Meyerson, Martin, 87–88
Miami, 2
Miami Herald, 150
Miami Times, 144
Middletown Times Herald, 43
Milwaukee, 26
Minneapolis, 26
Molotch, Harvey, 52, 54
Moses, Robert, 82, 160, 180, 184
Multipliers, coverage of, 81–82, 90

Naive professional, 7, 171–72, 207, 223
National news, 2, 3, 8, 9
Newark News, 55
Newark Star Ledger, 43
Newspapers: competition with other media, 43; in the nineteenth century, 13–22
Newspapers, metropolitan: advertiser pressures on, 50–53; competition from suburban cable, 227; competition from suburban newspapers, 31–34; competition from television and radio, 29–31; competition from videotex and audiotex, 227–30; effects of

Newspapers, metropolitan (*continued*)
suburbanization on, 22–29; focus on central city, 54–56, 64–70; market structure,
13, 36–45; organizational structure, 71–74;
response to suburbanization, 59–70, 72
Newspapers, suburban, 7, 9, 11, 153, 155–
56; appeal to advertisers, 31–32; competition from suburban cable TV, 226; as competition to metropolitan newspapers, 31–
34, 36, 43, 44, 63; use of by local officials,
167
New York, 134
New York City, black newspapers in, 142;
foreign-language newspapers in, 142;
nineteenth-century newspaper structure in,
16–18, 22; public transit use in, 27; structure of newspaper competition in, 35–37;
urban development coverage in, 56, 82,
180–82, 184–85
New York City Sun, 145
New York Daily News, 37, 38, 43, 63
New Yorker, 133–34
New York Port Authority, 180
New York Times, 9, 43, 47, 56, 63, 65
New York World, 18–20
Nord, David Paul, 20
Norfolk, Virginia, 55
Norristown Times Herald, 34

Oakland, California, 56
One-newspaper cities, 7, 35, 103, 159

Paine, Tom, 13
Paranoid media-avoider, 7, 170–71, 223
Park, Robert, 21, 36, 152
Penny Papers, 14–16
Personalizing policy issues, 168–69, 187
Philadelphia, 9, 56; Cigna relocation coverage in, 74–75; Flyers-Sixers move coverage, 96–100; fragmentation of suburban
governments in, 66; height-limitation, coverage of, 1, 4; newspaper competition in,
31, 32, 35; in the nineteenth century, 16,
17; post-war demographic shifts, 23–26;
transit coverage in, 89, 121, 124, 168; use
of public transit in, 27
Philadelphia Bulletin, 32–35, 62

Philadelphia City Paper, 137, 139, 140, 215–
16
Philadelphia Convention Center, 11, 188–
219; architectural critic's views of, 199–
204; background of the proposal for, 188–
90; cost and benefit considerations of, 207–
10; initial coverage of, 190–99; search for
scandal in, 204–7; specialized media coverage of, 214–16; television news coverage
of, 210–14
Philadelphia Daily News, 1, 51; competition
with other newspapers, 35; need to attract
audiences, 49; news coverage of, 89, 124,
142, 190–209
Philadelphia Gay News, 151–52
Philadelphia Inquirer, 1; advertiser pressure
on, 51; competition from other newspapers, 32–35; market of, 37, 40; news
coverage of, 65–66, 74–75, 96–100, 121,
124–26, 190–209
Philadelphia Magazine, 134–35, 214–15
Philadelphia Tribune, 142, 143
Phoenix Gazette, 137
Phoenix New Times, 137
Phoenixville Phoenix, 34
Pingree, Hazan, 20
Polish Daily News, 149
Political jurisdictions, fragmentation of, 3, 4,
28, 60, 118, 128
Pottstown Mercury, 34
Power Broker, The, 82, 160
Press conferences, 74, 79, 80; in Philadelphia's convention center coverage, 210; re-
porting of by local television news, 107;
use of by local officials, 163, 170, 176,
182, 183
Private interest groups, as sources, 122, 165–
66
Protests and demonstrations, coverage of, 6,
119–22, 223
Public officials, use of local media, 6, 11,
143, 153, 160–87, 222–24
Publishers, metropolitan newspapers: influence on editorial content, 52, 56–58, 66;
organizational role of, 72, 75; role in Philadelphia's Convention Center coverage,
196, 205, 209, 216
Pulitzer, Joseph, 18–19

Index

Radio, 11, 29, 43, 69, 156–59

Ratings. *See* Television news, local, importance of ratings

Ravitch, Richard, 181

Regional economy, ties to local media, 2

Regional identity, importance of to local media, 10, 167, 184, 230–34

Regional institutions, coverage of, 64–65

Relocation and displacement coverage, 78,
81, 97–99

Retailing, and newspapers, 3, 17–18, 23, 27,
32

Ribbon cutter, 172

Rizzo, Frank, 62, 101, 109, 117, 128, 168,
188

Roberts, Eugene L., Jr., 48, 51, 79, 190

Romano, Carlin, 88–89

Rosse, James, 43

Rouse, Willard, 1

Royer, Charles, 83, 183

Sachsman, David, 155

St. Louis, 24, 26, 27, 35

St. Louis American, 144

St. Louis Republic, 20

San Diego, 25

San Francisco, 27, 36, 55–56, 66, 151–52,
227

San Francisco Chronicle, 55–56

San Francisco Examiner, 20, 55–56

San Jose Mercury, 52

Schanberg, Sidney, 47–48, 57

Schelter, Craig, 164

Schudson, Michael, 15, 20–21, 112

Scripps, E. W., 20

Seattle, 9, 24, 27, 77; naval home-port coverage in, 83–84, 140, 183–84

Seattle Times, 65, 66, 77, 83, 184

Seattle Weekly, 137, 139–40

Seed, 136

Sensationalism, 10, 25–27, 46–50

Sexiness quotient, 85–88, 96, 210, 218

Shils, Edward B., 208–10

Shoppers, 32, 43

Sigal, Leon, 76, 162–63, 165

Sinclair, Upton, 13

Sing Tao Daily News, 150

Sloat, Warren, 155

Smith, Conrad, 105

Sound bites. *See* Television news, local: the
importance of video and sound bites

Sources, in local television news, 106–7,
124–26; in Philadelphia's Convention Center coverage, 198–99, 203, 209–10, 217;
reporters' reliance on, 74, 75, 79, 82, 84,
140

Southeastern Pennsylvania Transit Authority
(SEPTA), 89, 121, 124, 168

Specialized press, 141–53

Spellman, John, 83, 184

Sports coverage, 19, 64, 66, 96–100

Stalberg, Zachary, 49

Steffens, Lincoln, 13, 88

Stroud, Joe, 233–34

Suburbanization, 3, 9, 22–29, 221; effect on
metropolitan newspapers, 3, 28–29

Suburban news coverage, 60–63, 126–29; of
development, 67–68, 76–77, 79, 155

Suburban newspapers. *See* Newspapers, suburban

Swift-Tauke bill, 230

Symbolic issues, importance in attracting regional audience, 4, 184, 221, 232–33

Talk-radio, 44, 157–58

Tarbell, Ida, 13

Teague, Bob, 110–11

Telephone companies, supply of electronic information, 229–30

Television news, local, 5–7, 10, 49, 68–69,
101–32; advertisers, 103; competition between stations, 103, 112; competition from
suburban cable, 227; coverage of Philadelphia's proposed convention center, 210–14,
223; government and policy coverage,
113–30; importance of ratings, 102–3,
109–12; importance of video and sound
bites, 6, 107–8, 117, 120–22, 129, 177;
importance to local officials, 166–67; market structure, 103–4; role of anchors, 104–
5; role of news director, 105, 108, 110,
120; role of owners, 57; satellite newsgathering, 6, 103–4, 130–31; sweeps month
coverage, 102, 129–30; use of, by local officials, 171, 172, 176, 177, 186

Television news, network, 6, 102, 105, 118, 130–31
Television viewing, as competition to newspapers, 9, 29–31, 35, 43
Times-Mirror, 57, 228
Transportation and newspaper use, 3, 35; in the nineteenth century, 17, 19, 23; in the post-war era, 27, 54, 55
Transportation coverage, 4; in Chicago, 55; in Houston, 65, 180; in New York, 181; in Philadelphia, 123–24, 168, 180
Tuchman, Gaye, 73
Tucker, Kevin, 181

"Umbrella" structure of competition, 9, 35–45
Underground press, 135–36
Union leaders, 164, 166, 174, 185
Urban development and newspapers, 13–45
Urban development coverage, 52, 67–68, 78–100, 174, 179–85
Urban newsweeklies, 7, 10, 135–41, 224
Urban reform, newspapers' role in, 22
Urban Renewal Program, coverage of, 55–56, 78, 90, 98

Videotex, 227–29
Villadom News, 155
Village Voice, 44

Vineland Times Journal, 33
Virginia Ledger, 55
Virginian Pilot, 55

Washington, D.C., 27
Washington Post, 9, 44
WCAU-TV, 115–16, 118, 119, 127, 130
West Chester Local, 34
Westchester Rockland group, 32
Westside Weekly, 155
Westway project, New York City, 48, 57
WHAT, Philadelphia, 158
White Plains Reporter Dispatch, 63
Williams, Willie, 121, 177
Wilson, James Q., 53, 54
WINS, New York, 157
Winston-Salem Chronicle, 144
WLIB, New York, 158
WNBC-TV, 110
Wohl, R. Richard, 104
Wolt, Irene, 55
WPVI-TV, 101, 115, 116, 118, 119, 127, 130
WRKO, Boston, 158

Young, Coleman, 58, 66, 168

Zoning, 3, 60–63, 231